THE
FORTUNATE HEIRS
OF FREEDOM

DANIEL J. MCINERNEY

THE FORTUNATE HEIRS OF FREE=DOM: ABOLITION & REPUBLICAN THOUGHT

UNIVERSITY OF NEBRASKA PRESS

LINCOLN & LONDON

Acknowledgments
for the use of previously
published material are
included on page x.

The paper in this
book meets the minimum
requirements of
American National Stan-
dard for Informa-
tion Sciences – Permanence
of Paper for
Printed Library Materials,
ANSI Z39.48-1984

Library of Congress Cata-
loging in Publication Data
McInerney, Daniel John,
1951-
The fortunate heirs of freedom: abolition and Re-
publican thought / Daniel
J. McInerney.
p. cm. Includes bibliogra-
phical references and index.
ISBN 0-8032-3172-5
1. Slavery – United States –
Anti-slavery movements.
2. Abolitionists – United
States – Political activity.
3. Republicanism – United
States – History – 19th
century. I. Title.
E449.M474 1994
973'.0496–dc20
93-37454
CIP

IN MEMORY OF MY PARENTS

Susan & Frank McInerney

CONTENTS

ACKNOWLEDGMENTS

THE KIND ACTS and generous assistance of many people helped make this book possible.

At Purdue University, the project began as a dissertation under the direction of Lester H. Cohen. The depth of his thinking, the clarity of his writing, and the warmth of his friendship continue to influence me. I hope that something of his critical skill rubbed off on the pages that follow.

At Utah State University, Clyde A. Milner II offered considerable time and effort to assist me with the revisions and submission of the manuscript. I am very grateful both for his advice and his concern. R. Edward Glatfelter, head of the History Department, has continuously demonstrated his commitment to faculty needs and interests. In particular, he led me along the paths of grantsmanship, found money somewhere for travel, and allowed me to step back from teaching for one quarter in order to complete the manuscript. Carolyn Fullmer, our departmental secretary, guided me through the mysteries of chips, disks, printers, and peripherals, endured my frantic reactions to error messages and lost data, and, in general made the whole "word" process understandable. The members of the Edge, David R. Lewis, Frances B. Titchener, and Mark L. Damen, let me interrupt their work with questions about my own, solved more problems than they can possibly imagine, and knew when it was time to chuck it all and head to The Owl for a brew and burger. I am very fortunate that the people who are my colleagues are also my dear friends.

James Brewer Stewart and John R. McKivigan generously shared their time and insight to review the manuscript and to show where it might lead.

Support for this project came from the Purdue Research Foundation, through a David Ross Fellowship, and Utah State University, through a University Faculty Research Grant. Both programs provided much needed and much appreciated assistance.

Acknowledgments

A version of Chapter 3 first appeared as "'A Faith for Freedom': The Political Gospel of Abolition," in *The Journal of the Early Republic* 11 (Fall 1991): 371–93; reprinted by permission of the Society for Historians of the Early American Republic. Portions of Chapter 5 first appeared as "'A State of Commerce': Market Power and Slave Power in Abolitionist Political Economy," in *Civil War History* 37 (June 1991): 101–19; reprinted by permission of Kent State University Press. I thank both journals for granting permission to reprint this material.

Finally, my wife, Irene, while pursuing her own studies and career, offered unfailing patience and constant reassurance as I worked through this project. I am grateful that she kept me on track with professional responsibilities – and also kept me in touch with the world outside archives, carrels, and conferences. Re, so many thanks, so much love.

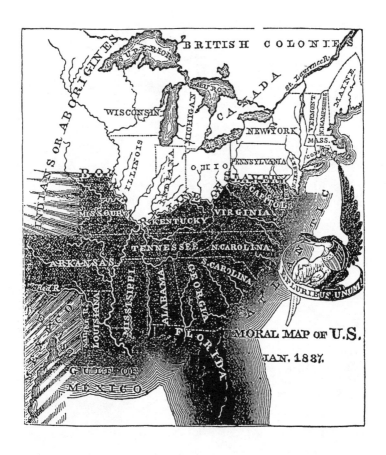

2. Moral Map of U.S. representing slavery as "a dark spot on the face of the nation" (Lafayette). January 1837. Frontispiece from "The Legion of Liberty! and Force of Truth, Containing the Thoughts, Words, and Deeds, of Some Prominent Apostles, Champions, and Martyrs." Second edition. New York: American Anti-Slavery Society, 1843.

1. "The Land of Liberty. Recommended to the consideration of 'Brother Jonathan.'" *Punch* 13 (1848), p. 215.

INTRODUCTION

In this hopeless state of things, a few individuals, deeply impressed with the great and increasing evil of slavery, have thought it their duty to unite their efforts to undeceive the public mind, to rouse the fortunate heirs of freedom to a sense of their own obligation to extend and secure the blessings they possess. – *New-England Anti-Slavery Convention, 1834*[1]

FROM THE 1830S TO THE 1860S, American abolitionists raised a variety of arguments to explain their opposition to slavery. They condemned the chattel system as immoral in its cruelty and inhumanity, sinful in its reduction of people to property, divisive in its consequences for politics, and backward in its economic relations. Abolitionists tied these varied concerns together through a distinctive and coherent habit of mind that they brought to their examination of slavery. Reformers drew the language, logic, and legitimacy of their cause from the familiar principles and resonant vocabulary of republican thought. Across lines of race, gender, region, class, and faction, abolitionists understood their reform effort in the same basic terms: as part of an ongoing struggle between the forces of power and liberty in which vigilant citizens battled tyranny, corruption, and conspiracy, defending the independence and virtue upon which their fragile experiment in republican government depended.

Attention to the abolitionists' republican perspective helps clarify the focus of their reform efforts. The abolitionists' concern lay not just with the slavery of a race, not only with slavery in the South, not simply with slavery in general, but more precisely with the problem of slavery in a republic. The reformers' beliefs, goals, and fears reflected their deep commitment to republican principles. The question of slavery in a republic gave their movement a sense of special urgency because of the chattel system's ominous threats to liberty. And the abolitionists' republican focus shaped their sense of identity, as "heirs" of the Revolution presumably set apart from other Americans and other reform efforts.

The "abolitionists" I discuss in this book repudiated the colonization of emancipated blacks, opposed the mere containment of slavery, rejected plans to compensate slaveholders, and refused to compromise on the necessity of ending the chattel system. They chose to attack slavery head-on, in areas where it was already established, and not merely in the territories where it might develop. They were committed to immediate emancipation and equality. Though advocates did not pursue these goals in a precise and uniform manner, they generally believed that the nation could not end slavery gradually or through continual postponement, and they held that liberation required some kind of commitment to the civil and legal rights of African Americans. This definition of abolitionism includes individuals such as Harriet Beecher Stowe and Henry David Thoreau, who remained aloof from formal abolitionist organizations. The definition excludes others such as John Quincy Adams and Abraham Lincoln, who expressed concern over slavery but did not subscribe to the program of immediatism.

Beginning in the 1830s, American abolitionists agitated vigorously for immediate emancipation and equality. As they pursued these goals, advocates purposely set themselves apart from earlier antislavery campaigns that had focused on the slave trade, the fate of slaveholders, or programs of colonization and compensation. Previous reform efforts had endorsed gradual manumission and refrained from castigating masters as criminals or the institution of slavery as a sin. Abolition organizations of the 1830s challenged these positions.

The year 1831 stands as a major turning point in the movement's history. It marked the founding of William Lloyd Garrison's influential newspaper, the *Liberator,* which denounced earlier reform measures, refined the abolitionist appeal, and offered a common center for the cause. It was also the year of slave revolts in British Jamaica and the Nat Turner insurrection in Southampton County,

Virginia. Southern whites tended to interpret the Turner revolt as a sign that any movement to dismantle slavery – however moderate its plans – was an intolerable and dangerous invitation to social chaos. Virginia legislative debates on gradual emancipation, which opened soon after the Turner incident and ultimately resulted in the defeat of reform proposals, marked the beginning of the end for organized antislavery efforts in the South. Campaigns before 1831 attracted support across the nation; abolition after this time was strictly a Northern affair. In terms of goals, tactics, and sectional support, the post-1831 movement stands as a distinct unit of study.[2]

This book offers an ideological approach to the subject of abolitionism. I focus on the way reformers expressed the problem of slavery, exploring the shared patterns of thought that suffused the movement over time. I address the conscious, literary performance of abolitionists, examining the care they took with language and the profound commitment they made to bespeak as well as to enact the cause of liberty. My study shows how the values and vocabulary of republican thought formed the abolitionists' dominant mode of discourse, offering a means of announcing as well as arranging their ideas about slavery.

The history of ideas provides one way of studying subjects on their own terms, examining their self-understanding, their habits of thought, and their ideological setting. Such an approach is particularly fitting when the subjects are American abolitionists who often reflected on the history of ideas as they examined the problem of chattel slavery. Reformers held that ideas were an active force in human events. Abolition essayist William Ingersoll Bowditch wrote that "the ideas of the people[,] the public sentiments of the people" defined the course of history. For pacifist and antislavery reformer Joshua Pollard Blanchard, the influence of principle and popular opinion was of particular importance in an age marked by "the forward 'march of mind.'" Abolitionists also assumed that social change was rooted in ideas. The lessons of history taught antislavery administrator Edmund Quincy that "all reforms, all revolutions, . . . have all begun in thought." Unitarian reformer Theodore Parker even outlined a "law of historical succession," which assumed that the critical events in human experience developed first in sentiments and ideas and were only later translated into action by people of courage and leadership. In addition, reformers maintained that popular discussion of America's informing ideas was in keeping with the nation's particular character. In the view of antislavery editor and politician Edward D. Barber of Vermont, there was no better place for a wide-ranging exchange on reform principles than in a society "where the people are the source of power." By relying on "'the *power of the truth*,'" Rhode Island abolitionists declared, the emancipation movement endorsed a "'proper, legitimate, Christian-like, republican mode of proceeding.'"[3]

Abolitionists also held that their principles were the very source of their strength. Former bondsman Henry Highland Garnet proclaimed that proslavery forces were no match for reformers: while slaveholders depended upon numbers, abolitionists depended upon the truth. Antislavery leader and Garrison associate Wendell Phillips shared that conviction. In an 1858 speech, he recalled the taunts of opponents who mocked the "abstractions" and "words" of abolition. Phillips responded: "They say we are full of 'isms.' Thank God, we are! Virginia raises tobacco, Ohio pork, Louisiana sugar, Pennsylvania iron; but Massachusetts exports *Ideas*."[4] Phillips, Garnet, and other abolitionists resisted the urge simply to quantify social problems and argued that, in a republican society, it's the thought that counts.

While accepting the sincerity of the abolitionists' beliefs, one can still step back from the reformers' words and question their assumptions about the operation of ideas in human experience. I do not argue, for example, that republicanism "caused" abolition, only that advocates found in republican ideology a conceptually appropriate world view that helped them make sense of their experience. Despite the reformers' own claims, they were neither the sole nor "authentic" proponents of republican principles in nineteenth-century America. A wide variety of groups, including other critics of slavery, commonly appropriated, altered, or challenged the values and vocabulary of the Revolution. Through studies of parties, laborers, educators, evangelists, slaveholders, freed people, and others, historians have established both the presence and permutation of republican thought in American life.[5] The reformers I examine were but one part of a larger world of republican discourse in nineteenth-century America. The abolitionists' habits of thought and expression commonly connected them to the society they so strongly criticized. Their readings of republican experience could, however, also prove highly unconventional, distinguishing them sharply from other groups in America. Even within their own communities of reform, abolitionists expressed both common and divergent claims about the principles of republicanism.

The highly varied and often conflicting uses of republicanism in the past have provoked skepticism about the use of republicanism in the present as a tool of historical analysis. A few points bear consideration. First, abundant evidence exists for the popular appropriation of republican thought in the nineteenth century. The language of republicanism (its vocabulary, lexicon, its jargon and terminology) permeated the rhetoric of numerous groups and shaped the identity of their adherents; we literally have their word on it. Second, the American "republican tradition" was not a single, fixed standard adopted in a rigid and systematic manner. American republicanism was a composite ideology or "synthesis" built out of strands of classical theory, civic humanism, radical whig dissent, and colonial political experience in which themes considered central by some might be read as peripheral, insignificant, or ill-conceived by others. The very breadth of its construction may have been as much a key to republicanism's appeal and endurance as any particular argument it furthered. The problem of interpretive latitude leads to a third point. The "republican" character of antebellum public discourse derived not only from the grammar of debate but also from the underlying purpose of debate: to purge republicanism of its alleged corruptions and to establish firmly the "genuine" meaning of republican principles.[6]

In this book I examine the movement broadly rather than focusing attention on a few leaders. I wish to demonstrate the republican commitments held by both prominent and obscure proponents of the cause from various backgrounds and regions. Instead of establishing the coherence of an individual's world view, I examine both the agreements and interpretive conflicts among reformers over the meaning of republicanism. The study follows a topical rather than chronological line of argument. I discuss a variety of historical, religious, political, economic, and cultural subjects, treating specific issues, such as racism, not on their own, but in relation to the republican slant that abolitionists brought to the questions.

The opening chapter reviews the central themes of republican thought and examines the general ways in which abolitionists applied a republican frame of reference to the problem of slavery. Subsequent chapters take up five concerns of reformers, exploring how the advocates' republican principles informed key issues in the abolition argument. Chapter 2 explains how the reformers' fears of slavery grew, in great part, from the whig historical context in which they placed the chattel system. Chapter 3 explores the abolitionists' religious critique of slavery, examining the components of the reformers' arguments and the links they made between faith and freedom. Chapter 4 looks at the distinctive threats to power and policy that abolitionists found in slavery and the intense debates that reformers entered to determine their proper role in America's political order. Chapter 5 discusses how reformers viewed the economic consequences of slavery and the way they envisioned the operation of a "free" market. Chapter 6 addresses the troubling connections reformers saw between slavery and American identity and the ways in which they hoped abolitionism could build a republican culture for the nation. Closing remarks summarize the consequences of the abolitionists' republican perspective, both for their own time and for a modern understanding of reform.

1

THE FINE THREAD

THOSE WHO PRESSED for immediate emancipation and racial equality recoiled at the injustice, immorality, and barbarism of bondage. Their explanations for the necessity of abolition, however, commonly focused on a more distinct and specific set of problems posed by slavery: in the eyes of reformers, the chattel system represented the terrifying inversion of all republican values. As they defined, defended, and promoted their campaign against slavery, reformers expressed the belief that the cause of abolition embodied the core concepts of republicanism.

Advocates commonly spoke of the relationship between abolition and republicanism. In 1842, a leader of New York reformers, Gerrit Smith, stated: "We deny that any but an anti-slavery man is a republican, or fit to make laws for republicans." One year later, Smith extended the argument, bemoaning political efforts "to fill our highest offices with actual republicans, or abolitionists, whilst we were filling our least ones, with pro-slavery or anti-republican men." Lydia Maria Child, a Garrisonian abolitionist and editor, appealed to the "republican good sense" of her readers when asking them to judge the status of slaves and freemen. The 1855 Radical Abolitionist Convention argued that all who called themselves "republican citizens" had, by definition, a responsibility to carry out antislavery work. And a New England Anti-Slavery Society convention reminded members that "if you are republicans, not by birth only, but from principle, then let the avenues, all the avenues of light and liberty, of truth and love, be opened wide to every soul within the nation." The convention condemned the chattel system by arguing that "the natural effects of slavery on the mind and disposition of the master and the slave" challenged the principles of "true republicanism." The rendition of a fugitive slave in Boston led Massachusetts minister John Weiss to fear that the nation would have "to settle with God for republican corruption." The oppressive nature of slavery, warned an *Anti-Slavery Record* writer, would "drag our republicanism down to a premature and dishonorable grave." A speaker at the 1855 Colored National Convention felt it unnecessary to argue that slavery disrupted the general welfare or that it formed "a contradiction of the Republican form of government .... These things contain their own proof in the very statement of them." Ernestine Rose, a Polish emigrant and reformer, explained her support of abolition by proclaiming: "All my feelings and principles are republican; I may say I am a republican by nature."[1]

Wendell Phillips captured much of his fellow reformers' sentiment in an 1855 speech marking his second decade of abolitionism. In Phillips's view, the crusade against slavery was the special test of republican principles, its own history the critical measure of republican health. Americans had discovered much from the campaign: they had "learned what antislavery means, learned what a republican government really is." The nation had also witnessed challenges to the cause of liberty in the form of mob violence and restrictions on speech, assembly, petitions, and the mail. The historical record painted a "picture, the very copy of that which Sir Robert Peel held up in the British Parliament, within a month after the [1835 Boston antiabolition] mob, as proof that republicanism could never succeed." Yet when conditions created cause for despair, some heroic reform event reminded Phillips that "however fine the thread, there *is* a thread which bridges over that dark and troubled wave, and connects us by a living nerve with the freemen of the Revolution."[2]

Drawing on the terms and assumptions of the American republican tradition, Phillips and other abolitionists insisted that slavery undermined the freedom, righteousness, order, and prosperity of all society. They believed that the chattel system embodied the frightening force of arbitrary power. Slavery acted as an expansive and conspiratorial menace that smashed all barriers to authority, infected the moral character of a people, created widespread misery, and destroyed the fragile principles of human liberty. Having tainted the institutions and virtue of the nation, the slave power sought to consolidate its gains by corrupting the very language of public discourse. Abolition would turn back the threat, preserve independence, restore the "true" meaning of traditional values, and return the nation to its "authentic" republican course.

The abolitionists' frequent republican references were part of a comprehensive pattern of attitudes and beliefs that helped reformers define the problems they addressed, the terms they used, the identity they assumed, and the courses of action they adopted. In the reformers' usage, republicanism acted as an ideology.[3]

Among the various components of this ideological system, perhaps none was more critical to abolitionism than the political language that republicanism provided. As J. G. A. Pocock has argued, a political language sets out the basic vocabulary through which discourse is conducted, a vocabulary that not only articulates thought but arranges it as well. It is the means that a group has available to express its hopes or discontents *and* the system which "constitutes" (to use Pocock's term) their conceptual world. It prescribes not only what a group says but how and why they say it, organizing the content, style, and categories of discussion. Such language reveals both the way a people talk and the way they think.[4]

A particular vocabulary can become infused with meaning. Single words or phrases connote complex sets of values, creating a kind of conceptual shorthand. Common patterns of thought manifest the prevailing assumptions of their "speakers" and the particular problems that concern them. Together, the terms selected, the issues deemed problematic, and the patterns of thought made evident all compose the "activity" of language. They indicate a process far more complex than the mere passive reflection of the world. The work of a political language involves an ongoing process of "'abstraction' from social reality."[5]

The language of republicanism in America grew out of classical theory, civic humanist thought, and radical whig traditions elaborated during the imperial crises of the late eighteenth century.[6] Republican advocates clarified colonial discontent, fueled the movement for separation from Britain, and shaped debates over the first state and national governments. Key elements of the republican argument remained constant over time and formed a recognizable core of ideas and values. Republicanism was not only a way of organizing and operating a political order but a way of thinking about power in general and about government, society, history, ethics, and religion in particular. Proponents spoke about authority, liberty, virtue, corruption, and resistance as they tried to resolve a recurring problem: the way corruptible men and women wielded the power that had to exist in any political order.

Republicanism portrayed human beings as creatures easily overtaken by base passions. In their ordinary roles, men and women all too often succumbed to the worst selfish instincts, betraying trusts, ignoring communal responsibilities, and indulging in material, social, and sexual rapacity. Those who exercised extraordinary power were even more likely to exhibit these traits. Political leaders usually twisted legitimate authority to generate more power for themselves. A predictable process was then set in motion, one likely to create a long series of abuses and usurpations in high places. Authority gradually centralized, growing irresponsible, unaccountable, and arbitrary as it distanced itself from the people. The highest officials protected themselves – and ensured the continual compounding of self-interest – by dispensing power to allies who also sought favors for particular concerns. The ruling circle continued to spin webs of deceit and intrigue, bringing the government into disrepute and the governed into subjugation. Eventually, the foundations of freedom had to collapse under the weight of corruption and despotism.

History demonstrated that one political form, the republic, was especially prone to the problems of power and lived a tragically brief existence. This most fragile political order rested on a foundation all too quickly undermined by pressures of absolutism and avarice exerted by both the rulers and the ruled. In the rhetoric of republicanism, the ever-expansive, aggressive force of tyranny waged constant battle against delicate liberty. The fair flower of freedom could not be secured without the careful oversight of citizens alert to any despotic incursions. A people who relaxed in their efforts would encounter a horrible fate: capitulation to tyranny reduced them to a state of slavery. Enslavement characterized the condition of individuals bereft of rights, victimized by arbitrary rule, and subjugated to the will of another. Bondage inevitably flowed from tyranny's triumph over liberty.[7]

Republican theory outlined three key measures to help preserve liberty. One set of safeguards was structural in nature. Citizens fixed the state on a "contractual" basis that delegated certain powers to government, specified limits to the uses of power, held governors accountable for their actions, and ensured the governed the right to resist unlawful usurpations of authority. The people also needed to construct a "balanced" government that divided power and monitored the exercise of authority.

A second base of republican security rested on the material conditions of a nation. The most reliable support for liberty came from independent landholders, individuals who did not owe service to others and who drew a living from the soil rather than from speculation or the sale of their own labor. Title to land demonstrated a stake in the community and an ability to weather the economic storms that might sink dependent workers, debtors, and paper aristocrats. The landholder's economic independence, in turn, provided assurance of unencumbered political judgment. Sturdy yeomen provided a sound defense against the domination and servility likely to arise in societies marked by landlessness and concentrated wealth.[8]

Structural and material devices proved ineffective, however, without a third, moral base of support. Republican theory argued that the political health of a people rested on the virtue they displayed. A society marked by luxury, indolence, vice, and avarice, the typical by-products of inordinate wealth and inherited power, could not rigorously defend liberty. A republican people had to be made of sterner moral stuff. Through the practice of frugality, simplicity, industry, and sobriety, they would internalize high ethical codes. Their capacity for self-restraint allowed them to withstand temptations of power and passion. Their habits of self-sacrifice encouraged concern for the good of society. Their exercises in moral self-government cultivated the corporate-mindedness that rested at the heart of a republican people's civic virtue.

In their intense, even obsessive, suspicion of power, proponents of republicanism advocated constant vigilance over authority and zealous protection of individual liberty. In pointing to the links between character and constitution, they viewed the discipline of self and concern for the commonweal as the highest civic qualities. At the heart of republican values lay an emphasis on self-possession and self-determination. Those individuals free from subservience, those who had mastered dangerous passions, those, in other words, who had assumed control over themselves were capable of exercising the unimpeded free will that could alone grant consent to government.

While republican advocates doubted they could completely master human experience, history did at least reveal to them a certain regularity of design. The republican understanding of history tended to reduce complex human events to a series of dualistic struggles. American Revolutionaries saw their cause as the latest episode in an ongoing battle between liberty and tyranny. The struggle pitted Tories against Patriots, the forces of Old World corruption and subservience against the New World's morality and freedom. One of two systems would emerge victorious in the end: a nation enslaved or made free; an order that served the few or the many; a society infected by dependence, privilege, artifice, and depravity, or one ruled through merit, moderation, and popular consent; a community burdened by accumulated abuses or liberated by the recovery of long-buried rights. The choices themselves were as clear and unambiguous as the necessity of choosing itself. In a world of such sharp polarities, neutrality held no meaning; inaction simply lent support to ascendant historical forces.[9]

The discernible order of human events also flowed from a highly personalized reading of history applied by republican theorists. Historical causation was not clouded in mystery. Seemingly haphazard actions had an understandable purpose and direction. Events took place in the world as a result of human intention. For example, Revolutionaries believed that the imperial debate over revenues did not result primarily from bewildering and impersonal market conditions beyond human control but from a carefully crafted plan by British ministers (later, ministers and King) to expand parliamentary authority, increase colonial indebtedness, and reinforce American subordination within the empire. The home country manipulated taxes, legal rights, territorial claims, colonial legislative powers, and the military in order to achieve its ends. British rulers devised nothing less than a conspiracy against liberty. The conspiratorial interpretation of history ordered events, identified the agents of tyranny, and justified resistance by compiling a series of offenses committed against the people, evidence required by whig thought to validate confrontation with authorities.[10]

Conspiracies were more easily discussed than detected, however. Those who hatched such plots were skilled in arts of deception, maliciously misrepresenting their intentions, manipulating the surface of events, and lulling observers into a false sense of security. John Adams recognized that in any effort to trace "dark intrigues and wicked machinations, and to show the rise and progress of . . . schemes for enslaving this country," certain fundamental problems of knowledge presented themselves. How could one spot a deliberately elusive scheme that blurred reality, concealed the guilty, and befuddled its victims? In his "Novanglus" essay, Adams pointed to two answers, both drawn from political experience. First, conspirators were so ambitious and greedy that they engaged in ever more blatant acts of oppression which eventually made their plans evident to all. Secondly, even as despotism advanced, there would likely remain a small remnant of citizens adept at monitoring authority, recognizing abuses of power, and safeguarding liberty.[11]

Conspiracies were hard to recognize, Adams argued, but equally difficult to expose. Those interested in revealing such plots presumably opposed both the political maneuverings and epistemological confusions worked by evil combinations. As a result, vigilant overseers had to adopt a different mode of argument. Their appeals must remain free of the artful contrivances employed by conspirators. The friends of freedom had to "penetrate arcana," embrace "principles of nature and eternal reason," and depend for their evidence on "what has been as public as records and newspapers could make it." Proofs had to rest on accessible and verifiable propositions that existed independently of their advocates' presentation. Because tyranny challenged both liberty and knowledge, the appeal to "self-evident" principles took on special importance. In republican arguments, style and substance remained closely connected.[12]

If history offered a dismal record of corruption, it also provided a stirring account of achievement in the cause of liberty. Such heroic moments inspired and also justified opposition to power. From a republican perspective, legitimate resistance to authority was a reaffirmation of ancient liberties and guarantees, designed to challenge recent perversions of political harmony. The colonial argument against Britain, for example, did not rest on the inadequacy of traditional rights but on their subversion by King and Parliament. Colonists purposely invoked English history in the cause of liberty. Furthermore, the recollection of liberties secured in the past provided an experiential ground for "natural rights," principles realized through time, formed out of tradition rather than transmundane speculation. The patriots' claims to natural rights represented an act not of novelty but of recovery.[13]

Acknowledgment of historical ties did not mean a blind reverence for the past. The study of history fashioned a tool of liberation, offering an incentive to action rather than a souvenir of collective failure. The cultivation of memory created an interplay of recapitulation and transcendence: the recovery of past experience clarified the possibilities for future change. Historical study contained the potential for overcoming historical determinism. In this way, a people's reflection on the past was as much a historic force as their armed mobilization.[14]

Despite appeals to antiquity, however, the republican cause was not served by traditional political principles and expectations. In order to protect popular freedoms, the basic structure and location of power required radical change. At issue by 1776 was not just a troublesome monarch but monarchy, not simply ministerial intrigue but concentrated and unaccountable power, not only the colonies' political and economic status but subordination itself. Presented as an exercise in the restoration of ancient rights, the Revolution's logic nevertheless undercut the possibility of maintaining the old political and social order that had established those privileges.

Yet no standard of measurement clearly indicated what to salvage. The failure to distinguish necessary preservation from reckless innovation created a source of domestic confusion: republicanism stood simultaneously as a justification of resistance and as an appeal for order. Republicans challenged authority at the same time that they established new forms of authority. The dividing line between freedom and necessity remained blurred. Republicanism raised the call for simple home rule but also held the potential for ongoing agitation; either cause could find support in its doctrines.[15]

Citizens had to defy British power, but Americans were liable to become as tyrannical over themselves as their former rulers. Patriots may have legitimated dissent directed overseas, but dissent directed at home could prove difficult to contain and complicated the task of securing stable governments. An equally strong case could be presented to coerce conformity and obedience. Republican ideology required the sacrifice of selfish concerns for the greater good of society and expected isolated protests to be silenced in the interest of cohesion and solidarity. Self-determination had a place as a national goal, but the extent of its personal applications was left vague. Resolution of these issues proved difficult since republican principles could serve to liberate or to restrain. Republicanism's watchwords, "independence" and "virtue," while parallel and compatible, were by no means identical. One cluster of ideals challenged authority while the other validated control.

Considerable uncertainty also arose over the chances of republican success. Although inclined to trust in the efficacy of human action, republican advocates did not completely shake their grim assessment of human nature. Men and women could critically assess their current state and tap the historical power contained in memory; they were able to shape the future. But individuals served private interests so readily, wielded power so irresponsibly, and maintained republican standards so tentatively that in the end, very little might change in human experience. At the very heart of republican ideology lay a profound ambivalence concerning the human prospect. History as process provided the impetus for human aspiration; history as text offered sobering reminders of human failure.

Other concerns echoed the uncertainty evident in historical judgment and formed an underlying ambiguity in republican thought. Republicanism spoke both to preservation and to transformation, to liberty and to authority, to individualism and to corporatism. Its recurring themes lent themselves to a variety of interpretations and revisions. Republicanism supplied a broadly "multivalent" political language, processively refined, responsive to a range of needs, and conducive to misunderstandings among antagonistic advocates.[16]

Many of the great questions of republican thought remained unsettled. Its ambiguities allowed diverse groups to proclaim allegiance to republican goals. To a great extent the state and national constitutional debates up to 1789 and the first party conflicts in the 1790s grew out of the ideological collisions between self-proclaimed champions of the good old republican cause. At issue were problems of representation, balance, virtue, factionalism, sovereignty, commerce, and constituent powers. The different sides in these disputes operated from premises that, while apparently alike, proved capable of strikingly diverse readings. Similar sets of confusions intensified nineteenth-century conflicts between those with slave interests and abolitionists. Adopting the same political language, the two sides continually spoke past and condemned one another. The disputes present evidence of a consensus that generated conflict through its own variant possibilities.[17]

Despite this interpretive quagmire, republican habits of thought remained constant over time. Terms such as "liberty," "tyranny," "virtue," "corruption," "conspiracy," and "slavery" continued to form part of its distinctive lexicon, expressing a particular vision of the world. Proponents spoke of recurring struggles between freedom and despotism, between the drive for independence and social cooperation and the passion for self-aggrandizement. The drama was high and ominous. Power's aggressive course had leveled previous republican orders. Revolutionaries had only failures upon which to model their new world. Republicans themselves, old and new, were best understood as "victims"; their pose was one of suspicion and vigilance. Political, economic, and moral independence might, however, enable citizens to thwart despotism. A people's self-determination, self-possession, and self-control could provide the conditions for self-mastery that would leave free choice unencumbered and hold self-interest in check.

Nineteenth-century abolitionists expressed their reform goals in the language of republicanism, explaining the character of slavery, the nature of its evil, and the stakes involved in its continuation. For reformers, slavery created a social order most likely to follow the course of tyranny mapped by republican thought: the chattel system bred habits and relations that generated moral vice, sanctioned concentrated power, and threatened the basis of liberty. The critical problems identified by republican ideology presented themselves once again in the slavery controversy. A configuration of historical forces had developed so closely paralleling those of the Revolutionary era that by 1859 an antislavery minister would describe John Brown's raid on Harper's Ferry as "the Bunker Hill of our second revolution."[18] The future of republicanism was once again at stake. The forces of subversion had altered their form but waged the same type of war that reformers traced back to ancient Greece and Rome. The confrontation with chattel slavery re-presented the elemental struggle of republican principles for survival. American abolitionists responded, in other words, not just to the general problem of slavery but to the particular issue of slavery in a republic.

Slavery in a monarchic, aristocratic, or oligarchic order was reprehensible but understandable; the chattel system complemented institutionalized tyranny. But slavery among self-proclaimed republicans was both pernicious and incomprehensible. More than an outrage, more than a crime, slavery threatened the foundations of republican life. The chattel system forced together antagonistic principles of human relations, forming a living contradiction, an embodiment of irony, and, as Garrisonian reformer David Lee Child wrote, an establishment of pure chaos.[19] Applying a republican mode of explanation, abolitionists found in America's peculiar institutional order the unnatural and fatal commingling of tyranny and liberty, opposing forces that could never achieve any form of accord, balance, or coexistence. Tyranny not only repudiated liberty but insidiously twisted and confounded it, compelling liberty to undercut itself with every effort at self-preservation. The process created ever more oppressive forms of power. In an 1838 address to New Hampshire reformers, Nathaniel P. Rogers, then an ally of Garrison, described the most glaring result of enslavement in a republican society:

> There never before were *"Liberty and Equality"* slaveholders, and never *"land of Liberty"* slaves. . . . Republicanism must leave nothing in the slave, to which its broad, boundless doctrines of Liberty might attach. It must reduce him below reach of its "self-evident truths." It must blot out his personality. He must be stripped and shorn and bereaved, till he becomes an exception to *universal* rules, which know *no exceptions*. No mastery before ours ever was obliged to do all this, and never has done it. Russian bondage, Algerine bondage, Turkish bondage, West Indian slavery, fall as far in the rear of ours, as their mastery does in its professions of Liberty and Justice. We are the only people that ever professed or had a chance to be free, and the only people that ever held genuine, unalloyed slaves. An escape from our slavery into the deepest dungeon in Algiers, would amount to deliverance and emancipation.[20]

A republican people not only erred by tolerating slavery but proceeded, as a predictable historical consequence, to create the harshest form of enslavement in the world. Here lay a fundamental reason why reformers saw the chattel system as such a critical national issue: the logic of *republican* slavery had completely enclosed the bondsman and would inevitably entrap the free.

Abolitionists depicted slavery as raw, aggressive power carrying in its wake the seeds of political, social, economic, and moral dislocation. Reviewing the cardinal principles of American slavery in 1837, evangelical reformer George Bourne noted that, first and foremost, "slaves are under the absolute power of their kidnappers, and are deemed to be chattels and personal estate." Henry C.

Wright, an associate of Garrison, expressed the same idea more than twenty years later: "Subjection to an outward, arbitrary authority is the basis of chattel slavery, and of all oppression." In slavery, wrote another reformer, one discovers the "triumph of brute force over laws – the substitution of the dictates of arbitrary will, for the restraints of righteous principle and constitutional enactments." Unaccountable, unchecked, and tyrannical power characterized a system "which concentrates in itself the whole essence and all the attributes of despotism and oppression." Slavery had to be understood, argued Garrisonian nonresistant Stephen S. Foster, as "preeminently a political institution, and slaveholding a political act."[21]

The effect of unrestrained power on slaves, masters, and freemen challenged the vital principles of republican order. For slaves, the chattel principle required complete subservience to the will of another and the denial of any claim to self-determination.[22] Made property in the eyes of the law, slaves had no personality, no individuality, no claim to other property, no entitlement to inherent rights and protections:

> The rights of personal liberty, of property, of conscience, and of the pursuit of happiness were all inherent, immutable, and eternal. They were based on the nature of our being, and were the rich endowments of our Creator. But Slavery declared the whole of them to be absolute nonentities. It annihilated the indentity [*sic*] of the very being of the slave, and made him the mere appendage of his master.[23]

The official codes of bondage left slaves ensnared in dependence and deference, prevented from participating in republican processes, and denied the protection of law, shorn of both their power and their personhood.

For masters, slavery created forms of control and command that, from the abolitionists' perspective, knew no bounds and tolerated no dissent. Slaveholders could not judiciously exercise unquestioned, concentrated authority; their power dulled them to a sense of reciprocity or accountability. The "legality" of slavery only reinforced and perpetuated these tendencies. As one reformer noted, "the possession of absolute, irresponsible power, guaranteed by law to the American slaveholder, inevitably cultivates selfishness, cruelty, and insensibility towards the slave, especially since that law affords no redress to the injured party."[24]

Reformers added that the masters' authority extended far beyond the bounds of the plantation. Its realm encompassed all of Southern society where, as Frederick Douglass argued, there was "scarcely a shadow of difference between the cringing obsequiousness of the slave to the slaveholder, and that of the poor white man who is not so fortunate as to own a slave."[25] The authority that slaveholders had so thoroughly usurped transformed the entire structure of Southern society. Theodore Parker's 1858 survey of slavery's effects examined how,

> at the South, it rears up a Privileged Class – 350,000 slaveholders – who monopolize all the education – and do not get much – who monopolize the money, respectability, and the political power. They are the masters of the bondmen whom they own, and of the "poor whites" whom they control. So in the midst of our industrial democracy there grows up a class who despise the industry which feeds and clothes them. Not a Southern State has a "Republican form of government."[26]

Masters who had monopolized power in the South also sought to extend their control over the whole nation. The slaveholders' tactics in this great scheme were apparent, reformers argued, to anyone familiar with a republican reading of experience. The South's rulers, hampered by their small numbers but emboldened by their boundless power, resorted to the method typical of all oppressors. From the earliest days of the republic they had engaged in a "slave power conspiracy" which, abolitionists argued, gradually gained control over all branches of the federal government, shaping domestic and foreign policy in the interests of the chattel system.[27] The chain of abuses committed by this cabal not only secured slavery in the South but also tyrannized the North, forming what the *Anti-Slavery Record* described as a "grand plot against our liberties and the hopes of mankind."[28] The concentrated power of masters encouraged intrigue and subterfuge, undermined political and moral order, and posed a continuous threat to liberty, operating as it had in all of human experience. Yet, Douglass insisted, the South's record still stood apart: "There is no history extant in which is furnished a more striking illustration of what a few men can do in getting possession of political power, than in the history of the American Government."[29]

Abolitionists believed that the corrosive effects of unlimited authority extended to moral behavior as well. A Southerner who had witnessed slavery, Angelina Grimké, wrote of "the awful havock [*sic*] which arbitrary power makes in human hearts." Tyranny, she argued, lowered both the political status of the oppressed and the ethical standards of the oppressor. The latter, as abolitionists insisted, was given to a life of idleness, gambling, and intemperance that bred every imaginable vice and encouraged the most heinous barbarities. Slavery's "brood of woes" generated "pride, and hate, and lust, and crime / dark revenge and cruelty."[30] Such afflictions represented far more than character flaws. The masters' moral decay made them unfit for republicanism and destructive of its principles. Slaveholding undermined the moral uprightness that abolitionists took to be necessary for such an order. As an 1840 Liberty Party convention declared, slavery,

> naturally generates indolence and imbecility, tyranny and improvidence, prodigality and profligacy, licentiousness and cruelty; the prevalence of the senses over the mind, of selfishness over public spirit, of passion over reason, of interest over duty; and therefore is utterly inconsistent with the exalted purposes of free government.[31]

In one system the South combined the twin foes of republicanism: "unbridled licentiousness and despotic control," the lust for power.[32] In doing so, it not only threatened the order of the world but also thwarted the will of God. Unitarian minister and Garrisonian reformer Samuel J. May reminded an audience that it was God "who has filled our hearts with this *Love of Liberty*." Presbyterian minister and political abolitionist Henry Highland Garnet also argued that because "the good seeds of liberty are planted" by God in all minds, "he who brings his fellow down so low, as to make him contented with a condition of slavery, commits the highest crime against God and man." And Philadelphia Unitarian William H. Furness explained that oppressors did the work of the Devil, who focused diabolical energies on the disruption of republican institutions.[33] The slave interest, by undercutting the conditions necessary for liberty and by challenging divine intention, would soon evoke the wrath of the Almighty Republican.

The chattel system posed a distinctive set of political, moral, and spiritual dangers to America's republican order. But abolitionists were also alarmed by another of slavery's threats. The reformers' reading of the past assumed that republics could not endure the unyielding pressure exerted by despotic power. Experience appeared to demonstrate that chattel slavery had, by the early nineteenth century, created the same, destructive set of circumstances that precipitated the downfall of republican experiments in ancient Greece and Rome.[34] From the abolitionists' perspective, slavery was a peculiar historical menace.

Unitarian minister Thomas Wentworth Higginson explained that the absolute power, usurpation, and political ambition of the slave system led America to retrace the downward course of previous republics. There was little to prevent a complete decline into despotism. Yet many remained complacent in the face of imminent republican collapse: "'Do not despair of the Republic,' says some one, remembering the hopeful old Roman motto. But they had to despair of that one in the end, – and why not of this one also? Why, when we are going on, step by step, as older Republics have done, should we expect to stop just as we reach the brink of Niagara.'"[35]

Americans had once avoided that precipice: Revolutionaries successfully waged their own battle against enslavement.[36] By completing the goals of that past struggle, the nation might prevent collapse in the present. But four major problems complicated the task. First, reformers charged that the nation had fallen far below the republican standards set by Revolutionary heroes. The forebears, William Lloyd Garrison said, "made clean work of it. How degenerate we have grown! How clearly they discerned liberty as a principle! – and how blind, how besotted we are." Second, the remarkable rise of the slave power in the nineteenth century presented a far greater threat than Americans faced in the late eighteenth century. As the *Emancipator* proclaimed: "This property in human beings is immeasurably more tyrannous and oppressive than that usurpation against which our fathers took arms in '76." Third, the slaveholding forces that endangered liberty had become far more shrewd and calculating than despots of old. One indication of the masters' cunning, reformers argued, was that Southern leaders sinisterly wrapped their proslavery arguments in the very language of Revolutionary republicanism.[37]

A fourth problem arose from the other three. Because of the people's complacency and the slave power's chicanery, abolitionists claimed that a sham republicanism passed for the real thing in America.[38] While reformers believed that republican principles formed a fitting explanation and forecast for events in their own time, they had to acknowledge their conceptual distance from most Americans who had absorbed too many false republican ideas from the enemies of freedom. Abolitionists thus faced a doubly difficult task: to convince a reluctant people of the danger contained in chattel slavery and, at the same time, to reawaken audiences to the language and values within which antislavery arguments were cast. Advocates sensed that their appeal was incomprehensible to those outside the cause because its "authentic" republican framework was so unfamiliar. Garrisonian abolitionist Charles C. Burleigh, commenting on the character of popular Fourth of July celebrations, discussed the difficulty of promoting antislavery sentiment among a people who either ignored or misread republican ideals:

How large a portion of the people who were engaged in those demonstrations knew what they were about? How many of them believed in the very doctrines they were unconsciously endorsing? . . . While there were multitudes who were willing to accept the doctrine that all men have a right to be free, and that "government derives its just powers from the consent of the governed," and that those governments which do not ask the consent of the governed are to that extent unjust and anti-republican, how many were there who were ready to take the next step, and adopt the necessary logical inference from these premises, which necessary logical inference the fathers, upon a thousand times less provocation, adopted? The abolitionists only asked the people of the country to carry out, on behalf of the slaves, the same principles which their revolutionary fathers carried on in their own behalf.[39]

Emancipation would occur only when the nation understood its self-proclaimed republican values. Burleigh recognized the difficulty of this historic act for a people whose sense of the past was so deficient. He and other abolitionists believed, however, that heightened tyranny – and deception – called forth heightened republican exertion. Garrison, for example, announced that he stood as "a revolutionist with Hancock, and Otis, and Warren, but upon a broader platform, with a loftier spirit, with better weapons, and for a nobler object." An American Anti-Slavery Society committee noted what this extension of the forebears' principles entailed:

> They call on us to stand our ground – they charge us
>   still to be
> Not only free from chains ourselves, but foremost to
>   make free![40]

The ideas and values held by abolitionists prompted them to "make" history. They understood their own time by identifying the nation with a long, though uneven, republican tradition; and they believed that the cultivation of such a past obligated them to reform the present.

Mindful of their programmatic and organizational debts to British antislavery efforts, abolitionists in the United States still viewed the problem of slavery in a republic as distinctive, a shameful case of American exceptionalism that set both the nation and their movement apart. For Garrison, evidence came from a European, Daniel O'Connell. The Irish reformer saw American republican slavery as unique in its extraordinary "'slave breeding,'" its vile "'aristocracy . . . of the human skin,'" its singular "'democratic aristocracy,'" its unmatched political hypocrisy, and its unequaled persecution of abolitionists. For antislavery editor Zebina Eastman, speaking to a British audience, "no parallel premises" existed between English and American abolition. The latter movement approached reform from different historical circumstances; its republican order faced a peculiar set of threats that the concentrated power of royalty and nobility more easily resisted; and its slave interests stood firmly united among themselves and diametrically opposed to the original principles of their nation. For Wendell Phillips, the contrast between abolitionism in Britain and the United States raised nothing less than the central question of republican life:

> Fellow citizens, this generation is to work out the problem whether, under republican government, we can educate such men and women; whether we can get above the temptations that corrupt the majority; that poison the foundations of national character; whether we can ride out the tempest of a great national question like this of slavery. Every man that loves self-government, that is proud of the experiment of republican institutions here, is bound to see to it that he devotes his best energies to proving in the face of the world that we can do as much, if not more than the corrupt Governments on the other side of the water. This is one of the most momentous aspects of the slave question. It is the test question of Republicanism.[41]

Phillips and other abolitionists regarded the forces shaping America as personalized, patterned, and polarized. They sensed that power was inherently dangerous and liberty fragile. They feared concentrated authority, conspiratorial combinations, and aristocratic privilege. They believed that politics contained an ever-present moral edge. The record of history and the immediate crisis of slavery fit within and, in turn, validated the republican framework of thought that guided the antislavery cause. The reformers' approach to the problem of slavery grew out of a zealous regard for republican forms and a careful application of republican standards for evaluating political and social events. The abolitionist campaign expressed characteristically republican concerns for a republican order.

2

REPUBLICAN MEMORIES

THE POLITICAL GOSPEL OF ABOLITION

EVIDENCE OF INHUMANITY, institutional decay, political intrigue, and moral decline in their own age convinced abolitionists
that the chattel system wrought uncontrolled havoc and that its
continued existence jeopardized all remaining vestiges of republican liberty. It was not just the perception of clear and *present* dangers, however, that alarmed abolitionists. The magnitude of slavery's threat became more apparent by adopting a broader
perspective on the problem: by recognizing the chattel system's
long-standing abuses, its cumulative effects on liberty, and its recurring pattern of expansion. Such historically based arguments
offered compelling proof of slavery's perils. Little wonder, reformers argued, that apologists for the chattel principle either encouraged popular inattention to the past or tried to distort the record of slavery's tyrannical course. The slavery controversy
unfolded not only in public arenas of debate but also in private re-
cesses of memory.

Abolitionists believed in the distinctive character of republican
historical reflection. Advocates offered lessons on the proper republican standards of historical argument. They commented on
the presumed strengths and likely weaknesses of a republican people's historical sense. In addition, reformers cast their own historical surveys in terms deemed appropriate to the character of a republic. Advocates drew on a whig tradition of historical analysis in
describing the dualistic struggle of liberty and tyranny, the Saxon
heritage of freedom, the recovery of first principles, and the completion of neglected republican tasks. The movement's profession
of history was to serve as a republican reveille, rousing the nation

from its recollective slumber and stirring a people in their defense of freedom.

The abolitionists' writings demonstrate their careful cultivation of the past.[1] In longer works, such as William Goodell's *Slavery and Anti-Slavery* and Theodore Dwight Weld's *American Slavery As It Is,* in a wide variety of tracts, orations, pamphlets, poems, manuals, sermons, essays, and articles, abolitionists drew on past experience to address present problems. Their arguments frequently offered chronological retrospectives of the nation's history or of slavery's course, studies buttressed by copious citations from historical figures. Reformers also expressed a keen interest in the record of their own cause, explorations which ranged from history remembered (as in Moncure Conway's 1864 reference to "Anti-Slavery's Thirty Years' War in America") to history anticipated (in the *Liberator*'s description of antislavery as a cause "rich prospectively in historical renown"). The organizational life of abolitionism offered a yearly calendar filled with memorial observances such as the Fourth of July, the anniversary of West Indian emancipation, the martyrdom of antislavery editor Elijah Lovejoy, and the renditions of fugitive slaves. The movement's regular commemoration, Frederick Douglass once remarked, "makes the present generation the proprietors of the wisdom and experience of bygone ages. It makes the good of the past, the property of the present." Wendell Phillips noted that such attentiveness was both shrewd and prudent, "warn[ing] the living that we have terrible memories, and that their sins are never to be forgotten" while also reminding abolitionists of their own need for circumspection, aware that future generations will have memories as well. In history, humanity was both judge and judged.[2]

An April 1852 speech by Theodore Parker illustrates some of the purposes of historical observance in the movement. Parker's address was itself part of a ceremony marking the first anniversary of the arrest and rendition of Thomas Sims, a fugitive slave captured in Boston. Parker fashioned his talk not just to review the particulars of the Sims case (a subject which came up in the second half of the seventy-page discourse), but also to discuss the act of recollection he and his audience performed. Parker asked, in effect, what the remembrance of the Sims "kidnapping" signified.

Parker began by recalling an honorable habit of other societies: that of customarily invoking their own past, endowing moments of triumph (as well as tragedy) with special meaning, and providing needed occasions for popular self-examination. The Sims rendition was one such event in his own nation, and Americans had historical precedent for its manner of commemoration: "Let us remember the Boston Kidnapping, as our fathers kept the memory of the Boston Massacre."[3] The forebears' practice, according to Parker, taught that tyranny should not go unnoticed lest it result in one's own enslavement. Despotic deeds in the late eighteenth century received so much notice that they sparked both immediate popular protest and recurring ceremonial demonstrations; Revolutionary Boston, Parker noted, honored the day of the massacre every year from 1771 to 1783. Quoting from John Hancock's address to the rally of 1774, Parker reminded his own audience of three suggestions appropriate for such recollective events. First, a people should bear in mind the defiance of their ancestors. Second, citizens must challenge the tyranny that prompted the commemoration. Third, the occasion called for participants to rededicate themselves to republican practices of self-sacrifice, simplicity, frugality, and civic virtue. Parker argued that for Hancock and other Revolutionaries the exercise of memory was as much an act of republican renewal and resistance as a stamp protest.[4]

Parker used the Sims anniversary as an opportunity to look back on humanity's proclivity for looking back, to recall others' recollections. He commemorated the event by remembering a republican forebear who himself commemorated an event by remembering his own republican forebears. As this intricate meta-memorial suggested, history confronted a people with past tyranny and clarified their present responsibilities. In general, the invocation of earlier experience offered a touchstone for a people's current condition. In particular, it served as a way of measuring their republican loyalties and commitment.

Reformers traced key national problems back to the uses, abuses, and construction of history. Garrison, for example, argued that Americans tolerated slavery in great part because of their historical myopia; the nation was either unwilling or unable to appreciate the cumulative consequences of the chattel system. Evidence came in the floundering efforts of his countrymen to explain their own condition, particularly in the midst of a national catastrophe such as the Panic of 1857. Garrison noted that solutions to the panic typically focused on immediate causes and minute dislocations rather than on the long-standing source of economic misery—slavery. Garrison's response to the financial panic came in an unusual form of "recovery": one that was recollective in nature, attentive to the consequences of arbitrary power rather than to the effects of investment strategies and market cycles.[5]

Such lessons were of special importance for a nation in which, as Parker once remarked, "we dream more than we remember." Americans, he argued, avoided reflection on the past and expressed hostility toward historical instruction. The nation not only deliberately failed to train the faculty of memory but purposely avoided the encounter with its stimulants – with memorabilia:

> Such is our dread of authority, that we like not old things; hence we are always a-changing. Our house must be new, and our book, and even our church. So we choose a material that soon wears out, though it often outlasts our patience. The wooden house is an apt emblem of this sign of the times. But this love of change appears not less in important matters. We think "Of old things all are over old, of new things none are new enough."

Objects that endured and provoked recollection held little value or purpose. Planned obsolescence contained a rationale that went beyond mere economics: better to use up and dispose of objects than to have them sit as reminders, as sources of remembrance.[6]

The flight from memory held a far greater threat to the state of the nation than to the condition of its material artifacts. A people neither taught nor terrified by the past could not recognize the historically demonstrated dangers of the chattel system and risked the calamitous collapse endured by earlier slave societies. A belief in national exceptionalism only compounded the problem. Parker held that Americans blithely dismissed the lessons taught by ancient systems of bondage. "We are not Athenians, men of Corinth, nor pagan Roman, thank God, but free Republicans, Christians of America," he said. "We live in the nineteenth century, and though slavery worked all that mischief then and there, we know how to make money out of it, twelve hundred millions of dollars, as Mr. Clay counts the cash."[7] The nation stubbornly refused to learn from the past and insisted that its authority was not binding on the American strand.

Parker spoke to one other issue about the state of the nation's historical mind that troubled abolitionists: their countrymen's belief that an identification with republican forms and values somehow relieved them of the burden of history. To many, a republic stood apart from the normal flow of events. It could presumably endure crises destructive to any other political order. Its citizens were thus absolved from careful historical reflection. "So is the republic presuming upon the recuperative power of its youth," declared Boston minister John Weiss as he criticized the supposedly limitless source of energy that Americans felt they held. "What is to make a republic independent of the law of God which causes misery to spring from folly? The world's history is nothing but God's commentary upon the text, 'He that sows the wind shall reap the whirlwind.'" Yet the nation dismissed such lessons in the false expectation that land abundance and material success could counteract national misdeeds. In such circumstances, Weiss claimed, a people should turn to those familiar with the past, those "who remember the sincerity of the early days of the republic," those prepared to "recall the profligate republic to the cleanliness of its youth."[8]

The roots of national crisis lay in the slow decay of what Massachusetts minister Frederick Frothingham called "the enthusiasm and memories of the Revolution." Tracing out America's decline in the nineteenth century, Frothingham urged an audience in Maine to understand that historical neglect presented a terrible threat, "involving the very existence of the Republic." But as Wendell Phillips remarked, perhaps one had to expect such slights in this society. Commenting at Faneuil Hall in 1858 on the life of Crispus

Attucks, he recognized a particular problem in the American order, noting that "the world is very forgetful – Republics are proverbially ungrateful." Their citizens' deficient consciousness of the past had been demonstrated throughout time. Ironically, it required a sensitivity to historical patterns to recognize the problem of historical insensitivity.[9]

Garrison, Parker, Weiss, Frothingham, and Phillips addressed the failure of a people – a republican people – to confront their own history and historical thinking in general. All the more reason that in a republic, reformers had to redouble efforts at cultivating and propagating historical knowledge.

Abolitionists turned their attention not only to lapses of historical consciousness but to its sorry presence as well. Advocates believed that standard sources of historical discourse and traditional occasions for historical reflection offered little more than opportunities for willful omission or skillful deception. Abolitionist and communitarian Adin Ballou noted in 1843 that the Fourth of July, so apt a moment for recollection, had degenerated into a festival of flattery that transformed celebrants into children through the "sops and sugar plumbs of demagogues." Fifteen years later, a notice in the *Liberator* kept up the attack on the holiday's "ostentatious parade, empty declamation, unmatched hypocrisy, consummate impudence, tawdry display, official gormandizing, profligate patriotism, religious cant, measureless lying, universal dissembling, and the like." Far from encountering their Revolutionary heritage, Americans carefully avoided it in ceremonies that mocked rather than affirmed republican principles. Even a monument such as that built in honor of Bunker Hill only served to ridicule "the name and pretensions and republicanism and testifie[d] to the granite obduracy of the heart of the republic."[10]

Celebrations like those at Bunker Hill not only demonstrated how history served popular impenitence but also reinforced the notion of history's past-ness, focusing on events that *had* occurred rather than tracing tasks that remained unfinished. This was the case, announced a *Liberator* editorial, in Daniel Webster's address at the 1843 dedication of the Bunker Hill memorial. The senator argued that the Revolution had offered eighteenth-century Americans an occasion for political idealism and civic service; contemporaries never had such an opportunity. By making such a statement, the *Liberator* argued, Webster betrayed the true nature of his historical sense: alive to recollection, he provided no insight into events current and to come: "What to him is the present? Nothing. What is he doing to advance the welfare of the future? Nothing. The past – the past – the past! On that he can dwell with exultation, expatiate eloquently, and flourish abundantly."[11] By narrowly focusing on the past as a series of unique and completed acts, Webster lost sight of the continuing counsel memory supplied. Safely distanced and shorn its immediacy, historical appeal could become a stirring though harmless oratorical ornament, an antiquarian trinket or museum piece, reminding audiences of steps taken, not of paths they ought to break or reopen. Webster's approach to history was purposely cautious. Those like Webster who were committed to the preservation of the established order understood all too well that their interests were best served by a "monumental" version of history – one which simply marked time. In the eyes of abolitionists, however, America's history could all too easily slip away from such carefully circumscribed uses.

Though served up for bland consumption, the nation's past was a potent mixture ready to boil up and bubble over the present. Its events and characters, especially those of the Revolution, retained a stubborn, splendid volatility. The story of the Boston Tea Party, for example, struck one antislavery minister as particularly subversive in its potential. Baptist pastor John G. Richardson of Lawrence, Massachusetts, expressed his surprise that local citizens who encouraged submission to the Fugitive Slave Law failed to see how textbook accounts of the tea incident taught children to resist unjust acts. Perhaps, Richardson suggested, school officials could not understand their own lesson books. Writing on a similar educational concern, black physician and abolitionist James McCune Smith of New York City asserted that school systems did in fact recognize these unsettling possibilities and carefully avoided their presentation. Instructors taught America's youth to remember the battles and dates of the Revolution rather than its principles. With little else to engage their minds, it was not surprising that students despised their history lessons. Smith sensed a sinister purpose behind such methods. He suggested that "a School History, sound on the principles of liberty which lay at the root, and culminated in the result of the American Revolution, would be entirely too Anti-Slavery to command *the market*."[12]

Smith's comments made explicit what other abolitionists also recognized: in nineteenth-century reconstructions of the past, the defense of slavery had become the key determinant of historical judgment. However revolutionary past events may have been, contemporaries carefully interpreted the nation's heritage in order to spare the chattel system any challenge.

In the contest for a people's historical hearts and minds, the slave power enjoyed clear success. Frederick Douglass declared that *"Slavery has bewitched us.* It has taught us to read history backwards. It has given us evil for good – darkness for light, and bitter for sweet." In this malevolent enchantment, Douglass recognized slavery's "historical" victory. The chattel system's triumph stood historical truth on its head. Rev. Philip S. Cleland, an anti-slavery organizer in Indiana, noted the same problem, arguing that "if slavery is right, the axioms set forth in [the Declaration of Independence] . . . , are glaringly false; the American Revolution was but a successful revolution; and our fathers should be regarded as a band of rebels, engaged in unlawful resistance against the lawful authority of George III. and his parliament."[13]

Wendell Phillips witnessed this inversion of historical truth during an 1837 Faneuil Hall meeting called to discuss the killing of abolitionist Elijah Lovejoy at the hands of a mob in Alton, Illinois. Phillips heard Massachusetts Attorney General James T. Austin denounce the victim and praise his attackers by invoking the memory of the Revolution. Austin insisted that Lovejoy was guilty of rash, impudent conduct; the reform appeals spread by Lovejoy's press raised fears of slave insurrections. The white community could legitimately take up their Revolutionary forebears' arguments: they merely sought self-preservation and self-defense, now directed against new, "abolition conspirators"; and they resorted to the right to form an "orderly mob," similar to that of the Tea Party, in order to secure public well-being. An outraged Phillips responded to Austin's history lesson by arguing that the Alton mob meant to deny rights rather than to resist unjust laws. Properly understood, Phillips continued, the Revolutionary patriots had not challenged "laws" but illegal acts, "not the King's prerogative, but the King's usurpation." Phillips denounced Austin's speech as a gross, insulting distortion of the truth calculated to give aid and comfort to a despicable special interest. The audience had to recognize that "to find any other account [of Patriot intentions], you must read our Revolutionary history upside down."[14]

Even when engaged in historical inquiry, then, Americans fashioned a flattering, distant, and sanitized past for themselves. Rather than acting as an irritant, memory soothed the national conscience. The most common accounts of history exonerated and justified the actions of nineteenth-century Americans, establishing the moral blamelessness of the present through a twisted reading of prior experience. The nation dealt with issues such as slavery and racism not by denying their existence but by demonstrating that in the popular construction of American history they posed no problems, broke no pledges, and presented no contradictions. Questions about the chattel system had been settled, projected, and resolved backward in time rather than confronted in the present.

Historian David Potter wrote that from the 1820 Missouri Compromise to the 1854 Kansas–Nebraska Act, political attempts to address slavery were essentially acts of spatial evasion, dealing with the chattel system where it did not exist. Similarly, in their concern with historical awareness, abolitionists recognized evasiveness of a temporal order. The past provided Americans with the ground upon which harmony and resolution would be forged. By engaging in fanciful historical speculation, the nation avoided an encounter with its existing dilemmas. Reformers added that America's recollective error (the mistake of playing *with* time) found an ominous parallel in gradualist emancipation that projected freedom into the future (the mistake of playing *for* time).[15] In this sense, the *Liberator*'s impatience with Websterian nostalgia and Parker's comments on American anticipation were two sides of the same coin: the nation deflected responsibility away from the present and onto the past and future. The true purpose of historical analysis, abolitionists argued, was to present – to make present – one's obligations. Historical reflection offered an occasion not for boast or bombast but for humiliation, reproof, and shame, not simply for retrospect but for prospects, a reminder of the need to fulfill rather than transfer duties.[16]

Abolitionists reflected on the past through a particular set of categories and assumptions. Their writings recalled the historical habits of mind common to eighteenth-century English Opposition agitators and American Revolutionaries. To a considerable extent, the abolition argument served as a renewed exercise in "whig" thinking.[17]

Whig historical interpretation developed in the midst of seventeenth-century English political conflicts. Opponents of the Crown appealed to the presumed antiquity of Parliament and the customary nature of its claims as a means of countering the royal prerogatives of Stuart monarchs. The arguments sketched out by Sir Edward Coke, Algernon Sidney, and others were taken up by eighteenth-century commonwealthmen, including Sir Robert Molesworth, Walter Moyle, Thomas Gordon, and John Trenchard, who once more wedded historical reflection to political action in their disputes with government leaders. Colonial Americans who saw similarities between their own condition and that of whig dissenters in England selectively adapted these historical arguments and eventually turned them against the powers of the home country, making whig claims an integral part of the defense of colonial rights and, later, of republican independence.[18]

Several characteristics marked the whig historical temperament cultivated in eighteenth-century America. First its proponents took an instrumentalist approach to the past, viewing historical reflection as a potentially transformative political act. By recording history one invariably made history, discerning order in a neglected, obscured, or routinized past. Secondly, whig chroniclers assumed the patterned nature of human experience. The world they envisioned was caught in a continuing struggle between those who sought to expand power and those who tried to contain it. This construction of the past reduced the bewildering multiplicity of events to a small set of common denominators. One could understand present conflicts (and their likely outcome) by drawing analogies to past experience. History in this sense provided both recast and forecast.

Whig historians assumed, thirdly, that a people could safeguard their political order by appealing to its original charters of liberty and grants of power. A review of first principles clarified where a people stood in relation to their basic commitments, identifying which groups sought to preserve (and which to subvert) traditional guarantees and privileges. By invoking these standards, citizens defined the proper limits of authority, exposed its dangerous extension, and legitimated protest against oppression. Whig historians traced the origins of these principles back to the early Saxons and their Anglo-Saxon descendants, a people whose presumed love of liberty and hatred of despotism created "an ancient political utopia."[19]

A fourth theme emphasized the need for restoration in a political order. Societies had to reacquaint themselves with their first principles because some alteration or deviation had taken place over time. The whig argument tied in with a broader Renaissance political tradition, which held that republics in particular required periodic renewal to maintain their vigor. Republics, as Machiavelli commented, "possess some goodness by means of which they gain their first reputation and their first growth. Since in the process of time that goodness is corrupted, if something does not happen that takes it back to the right position, such corruption necessarily kills that body."[20] Citizens performed that renewal not by inventing new political forms but by recollecting the republic's elemental condition. Attention focused on origins rather than novelty. The whig project did not require slavish imitation of history, however; proponents sought to recover *and* more fully realize these fundamental principles. The act of commemoration, in other words, was purposely provocative, designed to reveal deviation, break complacency, and compel action.[21]

Historian H. Trevor Colbourn has argued that the whig interpretation generally "failed to excite American interest and allegiance" by the late 1780s.[22] Abolitionists troubled by American historical neglect would have regretfully agreed with Colbourn's assessment. They recognized a need to reacquaint the nation with eighteenth-century political, social, and economic principles as well as the historical framework in which those ideas operated. Antislavery literature appealed to a particular sense of the past. Advocates believed that the whig historical perspective of Revolutionary republicans offered an important vehicle for the transmission of fundamental republican values.

Abolitionists exhibited the whiggish character of their historical appeals in a variety of ways. One example lay in references to seventeenth-century heroes of the whig cause whom reformers called upon as ideological allies in the struggle against slavery. The legacies of Vane and Sidney were of special importance to antislavery advocates. Phillips regarded Sir Harry Vane as a preeminent statesman of unequalled integrity and wisdom, whose political insight surpassed that of the founders and whose "touch consecrated the [American] continent to measureless toleration of opinion and entire equality of rights." Boston Unitarian minister James Freeman Clarke, considering the rendition of Anthony Burns in 1854, deemed it appropriate to recall the words of Algernon Sidney who was also a victim of tyranny and who understood the threats posed by unjust law. Samuel Johnson, preaching in the Free Church of Lynn, Massachusetts, found the Fugitive Slave Act particularly disgraceful because its framers came from "the good stock" of Sidney and Vane.[23]

While other groups might try to lay claim to whig heroes, abolitionists asserted that they alone adhered to the principles of these figures. In a series of four letters penned in 1837, Garrison responded to anti-abolitionist correspondence in the Boston *Courier* from a pseudonymous "Algernon Sidney."[24] Deeply offended by the efforts of this impostor to associate Sidney with anti-reform and proslavery opinion, Garrison aimed to reveal "the *true* SIDNEY" whom he identified as "the father of modern Abolitionism, . . . an immediate emancipationist, in the strictest sense." Quoting liberally from Sidney's writings, Garrison fashioned a picture of a seventeenth-century whig who spoke the same language as nineteenth-century abolitionists. Sidney addressed himself to the struggle between power and independence, enslavement and free will, dependency and resistance. Abolitionists in America literally echoed Sidney's defense of liberty: "All that has been written in favor of the rights of man, from the martyrdom of SIDNEY to the present time, is but a repetition of these grand and glorious truths."[25] By invoking the names of Sidney and Vane, Garrison and other advocates clarified their own sense of ideological identity while historically grounding the abolitionist argument.

A second example of the reformers' whiggish historical imagination was their celebration of a Saxon heritage of liberty. Advocates linked American concepts of freedom with the political experience of early Englishmen. Saxon experience provided historical demonstration of the rights that abolitionists claimed. Such references, in the reformers' view, showed that the antislavery movement did not seek to create "new" freedoms but only to recover and extend traditional rights.

In one series of lectures, abolitionist Charles Olcott of Medina, Ohio, defined slavery as a crime against common law, a body of principles "extremely republican in its structure," that was developed by ancient Germans, extended by Anglo-Saxons, and passed directly to Americans. Phillips believed that the great achievements of the American nation – which had "founded a republic on the unlimited suffrage of the millions" and "worked out the problem that man, as God created him, may be trusted with self-government" – all rested squarely on "Saxon foundations." Parker also traced freedom's specific historical roots to the distinctive character and contributions of the Saxon people. He frequently reviewed the industry, thrift, moral rectitude, education, political progress, and republican ideas that Saxons realized and bequeathed to later generations of Americans. Alert to despotism and inclined toward liberty, the Saxon character stood as a reliable force "in favor of progress and the rights of man."[26]

In Parker's appeals, however, Saxon imagery not only bolstered principles of liberty but also supported claims of racial hierarchy. He believed that Caucasians had a special capacity for progress and argued that a nation-tribe could lose its vital strength by mixing its blood with that of inferior peoples. Historian Michael Fellman maintains that a racial, tribal consciousness rested at the core of Parker's thought, providing a set of ethnological assumptions about Anglo-Saxons through which the reformer understood the importance of abolition. For Parker, the movement served as a way of saving whites from enslavement and preventing presumably inferior blacks from seeking vengeance.[27]

As Parker demonstrated, Saxon legend could provide a vehicle for racist expression. But as the works of other abolitionists reveal, Saxon references contained other possibilities, including the deliberate repudiation of racism. Black abolitionists, for example, sensed the sinister possibilities of Saxon lore and responded to such claims. Henry Highland Garnet played off racial presumptions by comparing the legendary state of ancient Anglo-Saxons to the advanced civilization of black Africa at the same moment in time. And Frederick Douglass stated that if the proud descendants of Anglo-Saxons were as superior as they claimed to be, they had nothing to fear from open and equal competition with other peoples.[28]

Abolitionists also drew on Saxon references to explain the experience of enslaved blacks in America. For Douglass, the Saxons served as a model of resistance to tyranny. In an 1847 speech that surveyed the history of "slavery and kindred crimes," Douglass recalled ancient peoples who practiced enslavement and reviewed the evils that befell them. He asked his audience to consider sympathetically a later group, the "proud Anglo-Saxons," who became "the miserable slaves, the degraded serfs, of Norman nobles." The Saxons had created – and then lost – liberty. Their experience offered lessons that Douglass deemed important for both whites and blacks: "a profitable comparison might be drawn between the condition of the colored slaves of our land, and the ancient Anglo-Saxon slaves of England."[29]

Lydia Maria Child devised such an analogy in a short story entitled "The Black Saxons." The tale, set in Revolutionary-era Charleston, involved a clandestine meeting of slaves who discussed different paths to liberation. Child framed the slaves' debates with the reflections of a slave owner, Mr. Duncan, who came to a new understanding of the chattel system by reading the history of the Norman Conquest. Duncan realized that his admiration for Saxon serfs who struggled against Norman plunderers (and his contempt for those who submitted to subjection) found a disturbing parallel in the experience of his own slaves. Infiltrating their secret meeting and overhearing their plans for freedom, Duncan could appreciate the slaves' desires by drawing on the experiences of his forebears:

> Again he recurred to Saxon history, and remembered how he had thought that troubled must be the sleep of those who rule a conquered people. A new significance seemed given to Wat Tyler's address to the insurgent laborers of *his* day; an emphatic, and most unwelcome application of his indignant question, why serfs should toil unpaid in wind and sun, that lords might sleep on down, and embroider their garments with pearl.
>
> "And these Robin Hoods, and Wat Tylers, were my Saxon ancestors," thought he. "Who shall so balance effects and causes, as to decide what portion of my present freedom sprung from their seemingly defeated efforts? Was the place I saw to-night, in such wild and fearful beauty, like the haunts of the *Saxon* Robin Hoods? Was not the spirit that gleamed forth there as brave as theirs? And who shall calculate what even such hopeless endeavors may do for the future freedom of their race?"[30]

Duncan's historical habit of mind, like that of Child's fellow reformers, clarified confusions about the present by appealing to analogies drawn from the Saxon past. The Saxon experience that shaped Duncan's understanding spoke of a drive for liberty that cut across racial and temporal lines, linking the slaves' struggle with that of an earlier oppressed community. In the contest between power and liberty, what ultimately mattered was not the type of blood flowing in one's veins but the love of freedom held in one's heart. On that count, the slave's predicament corresponded to that of subjugated Saxons.

Phillips expressed similar ideas in an 1861 address on Toussaint L'Ouverture, calling on Saxon references to explain the Haitian hero's life and commitments. Phillips admitted in opening remarks that his audience might be surprised to hear him draw connections between black and Saxon experience:

I am about to compare and weigh races; indeed, I am engaged to-night in what you will think the absurd effort to convince you that the negro race, instead of being that object of pity or contempt which we usually consider it, is entitled, judged by the facts of history, to a place close by the side of the Saxon. . . . I attempt the Quixotic effort to convince you that the negro blood, instead of standing at the bottom of the list, is entitled, if judged either by its great men or its masses, either by its courage, its purpose, or its endurance, to a place as near ours as any other blood known in history.[31]

Phillips called upon Saxon legend in order to repudiate the claim that only certain races were predisposed toward liberty. He added that those who made such assertions ought to beware of the pitfalls of their own argument. The "blue-eyed Saxon, proud of your race" had to acknowledge that none of his or her own lineage in the nineteenth century could claim the honors bestowed on Toussaint. In addition, Toussaint's black brothers and sisters had accomplished what supposedly liberty-loving Saxon "slaves" had never even attempted: a rebellion against their masters. Phillips invoked the Saxon legend to clarify the experience of slaves; by the conclusion of the talk, he showed that blacks had *exceeded* the achievements of white America's ancestors.[32]

Black as well as white abolitionists appropriated Saxon legend; they raised it as an example of resistance to tyranny that transcended racial divisions; and, for some, the intentionally ironic use of Saxonism held a mirror up to those who tried to use the lore for racist purposes. In brief, the recollection of Saxon myth did not invariably signify a belief in racial hierarchy. In their traditional whig understanding, many abolitionists could (and did) turn the legend to advance arguments for racial equality, however awkwardly such appeals may fall on modern ears.

A third example of the abolitionists' whig thought may be found in their terminology for the key forces in history. Advocates saw the controversy over slavery as a nineteenth-century, American re-enactment of the ongoing contest between "whigs" and "tories." The abolitionists, James Brown wrote from upstate New York, struggled "for that pearl of great price, which the whigs of '76, in the day which tried men's souls, sold all that they had to purchase." Their reform movement sought to realize fully the principles of the Declaration, "the *magna charta* of our liberties." So-called Democrats and Whigs in nineteenth-century American politics comprised a comparatively sad lot of petty politicians, deserving neither the title nor the standing of their "illustrious progenitors." It was better, argued other reformers, to call these pretenders "tories," a name more befitting their record. The *Liberator,* for example, charged that Daniel Webster did not simply oppose abolitionism but viewed the reform movement in the same way Tories viewed the Revolution. The citizens of Boston, by allowing the rendition of fugitive slave Thomas Sims, confirmed suspicions held by Theodore Parker: "I knew Boston was a Tory town; the character of upstart Tories." Garrisonian reformer William C. Nell wrote that those who denigrated the black contribution to the Revolution proved themselves to be the tories of the present day. Frederick Douglass described Rufus Choate's denunciation of antislavery as "just such a speech as any old Tory might have made against the Whigs in 1776."[33]

Douglass believed that the likenesses he and others drew were not figurative but literal. The "tories" he confronted on the slavery question were part of a familiar group that "had lived before, and will, probably, ever have a place on this planet; and their course, in respect to any great change (no matter how great the good to be attained, or the wrong to be redressed by it), may be calculated with as much precision as can be the course of the stars." Though their names varied over the centuries, their goals and methods remained constant. "Tory" was simply the contemporary term for those late eighteenth-century individuals who, in the struggle against oppression, objected to any change – except, Douglass added, the monetary kind.[34]

Edward Coit Rogers, a Massachusetts reformer active in both abolitionism and spiritualism, extended some of these historical assumptions in his 1855 work *Letters on Slavery, Addressed to the Pro-Slavery Men of America . . .* Rogers believed that a "pro-slavery school" appeared regularly over the course of history and acted in predictable ways. Their schemes resulted in despotism, cor-

43

ruption, and civil strife. Fortunately, their tyranny often aroused an opposition that sought to defend liberty and virtue. Southern slaveholders were merely the latest incarnation of the dishonorable proslavery tradition, adhering to the same sets of values (and generating the same sets of problems) that had appeared throughout the ages. The pattern of proslavery activity appeared so frequently in history that it should have been apparent to all, but Rogers believed that his countrymen did not detect the threat.

> Strange that in the nineteenth century, when every man has the history of the world before his eyes, and a thousand travelers in the orient tell the same melancholy tale of the ruins of ancient nations, destroyed by despotism, and whose desolations forewarn America of the deadly effects of slavery – strange, in view of this, that there should be a party in this new world so corrupt, so base, as to plunge the people into that terrible contest so often and so fatally repeated in the old world![35]

Rogers saw events in his own world as the replay of a strikingly familiar struggle: the proslavery advocates of America were nothing less than a native version of England's tories, the long-standing proslavery school that gained control under the Stuarts and saw their program enacted by the likes of Sir Robert Filmer and assorted doctors of divinity. Rogers drew a one-to-one correspondence between the tories of England and America: "There was Dr. Laud, who answers to your Dr. Lord. And then there was Dr. Sibthorp, who sits well beside your Dr. South-side-view. And then there was Dr. Manwarring, who is answered by Dr. Manstealer."[36]

Rogers argued that English tories and American slaveholders were linked not only by sentiment but by personnel as well. He described how large numbers of tories fled late seventeenth-century England, settled in Southern colonies, and established the region's distinguishing institutions and characteristics. Fortunately, in the eighteenth-century, tories both in England and America confronted opponents. These whig forces summoned the ideals of Sidney and other "friends of freedom" against the agents of aristocracy, oligarchy, and absolutism.[37]

Rogers made sense of the slavery controversy by appropriating some of the basic components of whig historical thought, such as its labels for heroes and villains, its assumptions about causation, and its descriptions of the human condition. He assumed that the past not only had a design but one of a distinctive order, with the chattel system placed at the center of a continuous struggle that would decide the fate of republican liberty. It was to this form of argument that other abolitionists would regularly appeal in their treatments of the past, allowing, as they saw it, for a valid, coherent, and inclusive explanation of historical events.

In Parker's view, the nation was divided between two parties: freedom, serving progress and the popular welfare; and slavery, "tending to Despotism, which must diminish progress, lessen welfare, and end in the ruin of people." Such a picture was not drawn too starkly; Parker insisted that "all things are double." William Goodell, an orthodox Congregationalist from New York, echoed these sentiments, asserting that the course of American history had been shaped by "the opposite tendencies of freedom and slavery." Slavery, enjoying ascendancy since the late eighteenth century, steadily sought to eradicate freedom. "With this simple key," Goodell observed, "the historian may unlock the otherwise inexplicable labyrinths of American politics, for the last sixty years." German immigrant and New England Anti-Slavery Society member Charles Follen placed American history in the same context. Behind apparent fluctuations in power and position ran an incessant struggle between two hostile forces: "The internal history of every nation, every republic in particular, consists in the workings, the successful or unsuccessful conflicts, of the principles of Liberty and of Oppression."[38] A basic dualism was at work in human affairs, and its central conflict involved the disposition of power. It was in this context that the nation had to understand the chattel system.

Despite their assumptions about the duality of history, advocates did not believe that all forms of liberty or all systems of oppression were the same. The fate of republican liberty bore special significance for reformers. And the problem of republican slavery was far more menacing in their eyes than any other system of tyranny. Abolitionists tried to convince the public of history's patterned nature without flattening the record of the past. Douglass spoke to this issue during an 1845–1847 tour of Europe. Asked why he came to the continent to talk about American slavery when Europeans faced their own forms of oppression, Douglass insisted on the distinct character of the chattel system. He denounced all kinds of oppression, appreciated the multitude of miseries suffered by different peoples, and condemned the tyrants who ruled over them. But he set American slavery apart. The generic use of the term "slavery" diminished the bondsman's unparalleled anguish: "It must be regarded as one man holding property in another, subjected to the destroying of all the higher qualities of his nature, deprived of his own body, his own soul." The degradation of black men and women was not just the latest form of oppression but a complete denial of conscience, choice, and personhood – of humanity itself.[39]

The distinctiveness of slavery required certain modifications in whig historical argument. Douglass described Patrick Henry as a patriot who "excited other *white* slaves to rebellion." Some black abolitionists defined the key problem in their society as the contest pitting liberty and equality against slavery and *caste*. Others pointed to earlier struggles between freedom and despotism to prove that the world's republicans would not support American abolition unless blacks demonstrated *agitational* self-reliance. Black reformers sensed their participation in a long-standing, dualistic conflict; they argued that the multiplicity of historical experience fit into a discernible pattern of events; but they also maintained a particularist focus on the slaves' condition often slighted by their white counterparts.[40]

Douglass's comments on Patrick Henry, as well as the reflections of fellow advocates on Saxons and tories, testified to a fourth whig element in abolitionist historical thought. Reformers not only conceived of their cause in terms of whiggism's general historical patterns; they also saw precise historical parallels between the antislavery cause and previous struggles for human rights. Proponents waged what Rev. Samuel Johnson called "a new war for Liberty on the old battlefields."[41]

The parallels spanned recorded time. Abolitionists believed that

American bondage recalled the despotic power that regularly surfaced in the ancient world. Slavery's injustice in Egypt, Greece, and Rome created widespread poverty, ignorance, inequality, and barbarism, conditions sure to emerge, if not already present, in America. Ancient history demonstrated that the march of absolute power inevitably jeopardized the rights, prosperity, and character of the enslaved and free alike. Reformers also drew more precise parallels to the degeneracy of earlier societies. The political system of the South had taken on the character of parties in the Grecian republic, dominated by the interests of slavery and its accompanying aristocracy. The slave power's hold on policy making had, according to one Massachusetts reformer, turned America into an oligarchy like that of Athens under its thirty tyrants. And the Constitution's three-fifths clause, which enhanced the political influence of that Southern clique, found an "exact parallel" in the Roman emperors' practice of proclaiming themselves tribunes of the people.[42]

Classical history also provided more hopeful analogies. The American Anti-Slavery Society distributed an essay that associated the modern emancipation movement with Tiberius Gracchus's efforts in the second century B.C. to combat the infection of slavery. The Roman statesman recognized that slavery's concentration of wealth, debasement of free labor, and corruption of morals not only contributed to social and economic dislocation but more importantly shattered the underpinnings of republicanism. In response, he tried to eradicate the chains of bondage indirectly, promoting agrarian reforms that would create a strong Roman yeomanry to serve as a secure base for liberty.[43]

The reformers' historical analogies proceeded up through more recent times as well. Abolitionist and nonresistant Anne Warren Weston linked the work of "The Come-Outers of the Sixteenth and Nineteenth Centuries." Others observed similarities between their campaign against slavery and the Roundheads' conflict with Cavaliers. The episodes demonstrated to reformers the truth of whig thought: that power constantly threatened liberty; that luxury, idleness, and immorality weakened republican institutions; and that tolerance for oppression would propel a nation "forward in the same course of degeneracy that ruined the proudest of ancient, and threatens to destroy the happiest of modern republics."[44]

Reformers saw the clearest parallel to their cause in the efforts of American Revolutionaries. Comparisons often came in the form of direct correspondences: advocates connected their Philadelphia meeting hall, bearing the inscription "Virtue, Liberty, and Independence," with the Founders' temple; they equated abolitionism's Declaration of Sentiments with the Declaration of Independence; they linked Harper's Ferry with the Battle of Lexington; and they identified Wendell Phillips with James Otis and Charles Sumner's attacker, Preston Brooks, with Benedict Arnold.[45] Yet abolitionists forged the most convincing links not through events or individuals but through language. Abolitionists proclaimed that eighteenth-century Revolutionaries not only fought for but repeatedly articulated the very goals nineteenth-century reformers sought. Recall Parker's admonitions to Bostonians on the anniversary of the Sims rendition. After pointing to John Hancock's invocation of forebears as a precedent for his own commemorative act, Parker quoted from a 1775 address by Joseph Warren to illustrate the paramount concerns of Revolutionary leaders. Parker cited portions of the talk that dealt with arbitrary government and tyranny, the potential for mass enslavement, and the possibilities for restoring liberty – categories of analysis familiar to abolitionists. Parker's history lesson taught one central point: that the problem of slavery sparked the independence movement. Warren did not merely sympathize with antislavery beliefs; his words did not simply imply that bondage was intolerable. Rather, slavery was the direct and primary object of his attention.[46]

Nineteenth-century abolitionists described their own activity as a reenactment of that past experience. Phillips declared that having known the heroes of 1776 he could recognize "the Adamses and Otises, the Dyers and Hutchinsons, whom I met in the streets of '35." In 1861, with three decades of agitation to consider, he characterized the state of the nation as one in which "we stand . . . just as Hancock and Adams and Jefferson stood when stamp-act and tea-tax, Patrick Henry's eloquence and the massacre of March

48

5th, Otis's blood and Bunker Hill, had borne them to July, 1776."
Brought back to the terms of the Revolutionary debate, reformers
engaged once again in the contest between liberty and slavery. As
one American abolitionist in England observed, "Anti-Slavery was
the principle of the Independence, and this reform is identical
with, a lineal succession from, the better days of the Republic."[47]

Believing that they reoccupied Revolutionary ground while the
nation remained distant from its original commitments, abolitionists commonly invoked a fifth whig historical theme: the need for
Americans to recover the republic's first principles. Evangelical reform leader Lewis Tappan of New York City summed up a carefully worded review of slavery in the early republic by stating that
"we should recur to the original principles upon which the Government was established." The 1853 Colored National Convention declared that its purpose was to "enforce anew the great principles and self-evident truths which were proclaimed at the
beginning of the Republic." The recovery was of special importance among a people whose political destiny had fallen under the
control of the tyrannical slave power. A Unitarian ally of Garrison,
Rev. Samuel Willard, asked his readers if it was not "frequently
recommended that in political discussions and transactions we often recur to first principles, in order to prevent or correct abuses?"
Rev. George B. Cheever, an associate of Tappan, also advised that
any people trapped by political corruption "must revert to the
original elements and covenant of power." Douglass explained
why the effort was so important: "the safety of a Republic is found
in a rigid adherence to principles."[48]

Advocates believed that the appeal to first principles had a particular bearing on the slavery controversy. As Edward Coit Rogers
traced the worldwide conflict between freedom and despotism, he
observed a constant in history: "the nearer we approach to the
primitive period of a nation, the less evidence do we find of slavery." At the beginning of a nation's life, in the corpus of its fundamental law, slavery simply had no place. Rev. Cheever found that
this claim held true in the New England roots of America. In the
first Pilgrim community, "God kept the most remote possibilities
of this sin [of slavery] out of the compact there, out of the first

foundations, and set personal liberty as the corner-stone." Cheever sensed that America's contemporary subservience to the chattel system presented the picture of a people "contradicting and repelling the very first elements of liberty." Political abolitionist and editor Seymour Boughton Treadwell concurred, locating the roots of the chattel system in the defiance of first principles: "involuntary slavery commenced, and has ever been, and ever must be, carried on by grossly violating all the first great principles of equal justice, between man and man."[49]

The contradictions between America's promise and practice had been so steady that Wendell Phillips feared more than an erosion of fundamental ideals; the nation had to fight for its first principles all over again. The Congressional gag on antislavery petitions, for example, proved to Phillips that "the time-honored rights which had been fought for on British ground, and which our fathers had inherited, not won, were again to be struggled for. The car of Liberty had rolled back four centuries, and the contest whose history is written on the battlefield and scaffolds of England had been all in vain."[50]

The thread connecting these varied observations was noted by Henry David Thoreau as he observed the Northern response to the trial, imprisonment, and execution of John Brown. "Commonly," Thoreau wrote, "men live according to a formula, and are satisfied if the order of law is observed, but in this instance they, to some extent, returned to original perceptions, and there was a slight revival of old religion." Phillips described the issue in much the same way twenty-three years earlier after the murder of abolitionist editor Elijah P. Lovejoy in Alton, Illinois. Starting with the abolitionists themselves and then with ever-greater numbers of the public, "men begin, as in 1776 and 1640, to discuss principles, to weigh characters, to find out where they are."[51] As an American Anti-Slavery Society committee proclaimed, even a gradualist program of emancipation such as one presented by John Quincy Adams in 1839 was "virtually a resolution of things into their original elements."[52] By challenging the antirepublican menace of slavery, a people not only reordered the practices of the present but also recovered the fundamental commitments of the past. The project took on special urgency among a people who had so badly misread their first principles, as ex-Virginia reformer Moncure Conway noted in an 1857 essay. "To a real freeman," he wrote, "this association with liberty of the advantage of free labor or equal power of the general government, is as low as one who should mingle with vows of love inquiries as to the bulk of his lady's purse, or the extent of the betrothed larder." In Conway's view, the problem demanded the type of response abolitionists commonly prescribed: "That brotherhood of freemen, who join hands through all lands and ages, must teach others the RUDIMENTS."[53]

The appeal to first principles clarified a number of issues for the abolitionists. It demonstrated to James Russell Lowell the people's estrangement from their own intentions. Asking "Shall We Ever be Republican?," the poet, essayist, and editor declared, "We are afraid of our own principles, as a raw recruit of his musket." Had Americans adhered to the original policy and principles of their government, announced the Liberty Party, national power would now rest squarely on the side of Freedom. But "how different – how sadly different are the facts of History!"[54]

Abolitionists believed their review also proved that the chattel system altered republican first principles. As Douglass contended, it was not simply a recent enactment like the Fugitive Slave Act of 1850 that stood as "a *modern* invention"; slavery as a whole represented a complete and dangerous departure from original designs. Unfortunately, the chattel system had gained such wide acceptance that, in common parlance, liberty rather than enslavement connoted novelty. In an 1858 speech, Douglass addressed these issues by commenting on the West Indies's so-called "experiment" in abolition, asking his audience to consider their own language in the light of history:

> There is obviously no more reason for calling West India Emancipation an experiment than for calling the law of gravitation an experiment. Liberty is not a device, an experiment, but a law of nature dating back to man's creation, and if this fundamental law is a failure the responsibility is not with the British people, but with the great author of this law. Slavery is the experiment in this

case . . . by which men seek to live without labor, to eat bread by the sweat of another man's brow, to get gold without digging it, and to become rich without using one's own faculties and powers to obtain riches. This is the real experiment.[55]

The point was an important one to make according to William Goodell: the people "need to be disabused of our vague impressions and educational prejudices, if we would understand the relation of slavery to our political institutions, as at first established." For Goodell, the record of the past demonstrated that slavery, rather than antislavery, grew out of new sets of maxims and relations. Yet popular opinion held just the opposite to be true. If Americans had indeed formed a nation premised on liberty, Goodell concluded, "may it be assumed, without scrutiny, that the usages and expositions with which we, in *this* age, have become familiarized, are trustworthy?"[56]

Abolitionists even turned appeals to first principles against other reformers. Faced with fissures in the antislavery movement, particularly after 1839, reformers from different factions urged opponents to adhere to their own campaign's original goals. Writing on divisions among Massachusetts reformers, Garrison declared that only one reason justified the creation of new abolition organizations: "if any existing state anti-slavery society shall at any time depart from the original ground of union, – change its principles, or corrupt its doctrines." Some advocates eventually directed the same appeal against Garrison himself. A long-time ally, Stephen S. Foster, criticized Garrison's firm stands supporting nonresistance and opposing political action. Foster explicitly stated the purpose of his remarks: "My present aim is to bring the Anti-Slavery Society back to 'our old method'; to restore the 'ancient landmarks'; to bring together, and unite in one solid phalanx, the scattered factions of Freedom's contending host." Goodell reported that opponents of the Liberty League party in the mid-1840s also drew on the language of first principles to explain their stance: "a party with so wide a platform was, in this case, pronounced impracticable, and abolitionists were warned to adhere strictly to their 'one idea,' as the only antidote against apostasy from primitive abolitionism."[57]

Whether appealing to themselves or to the public on the importance of renewing first principles, reformers insisted that their purpose was not simply to recreate a past moment. After the raid on Harper's Ferry, Thoreau observed how his neighbors "returned to original perceptions," how they came to see that "what was called order was confusion, what was called justice, injustice, and that the best was deemed worst." Evaluating the public's stirrings, Thoreau wrote that "this attitude suggested a *more intelligent and generous spirit* than that which actuated our forefathers, and the possibility, in the course of ages, of a revolution in behalf of another and an oppressed people."[58] Though regaining an earlier generation's informing ideals, contemporary men and women surpassed the founders' achievements and reestablished the groundwork for a more extensive alteration of power. The revitalization of first principles did not mean a return to some previous condition but the potential for a wider reformation. Such recovery, as Phillips also suggested, marked advance rather than regression. Hoping to see Boston "purged and cleansed" of its fugitive slave renditions, he urged citizens to reinstate a 1646 statute that protected fugitives who were fleeing oppression. Phillips insisted that this action did not represent a step backward; rather, it would enable his listeners "to lead the van of progress in the nineteenth century."[59]

Phillips, Thoreau, and other abolitionists appealed to first principles in order to recall past ideals and project future tasks. They pointed simultaneously to a review of what had been and a forecast of what was yet to be, to the need for both recapitulation and transcendence. The American Anti-Slavery Society opened its 1833 *Declaration of Sentiments* with a call to invoke and surpass the work of republican founders: "We have met together for the achievement of an enterprise, without which that of our fathers is incomplete; and which, for its magnitude, solemnity, and probable results upon the destiny of the world, as far transcends theirs as moral truth does physical force." The 1837 Anti-Slavery Convention of American Women honored the "exemplary" self-denial of Revolutionary mothers and fathers, but the conferees insisted that their own project was a *"far nobler work."* The 1845 Southern and Western Liberty Convention sought "to carry forward and perfect

principles of the Declaration of Independence, would to-day be banished from the councils of the nation," replaced by "Buchanans, Casses, Touceys, and Cobbs" who had neither the ability nor inclination to expand republican ideals. Liberty had taken refuge in the antislavery movement which, according to Rev. Frothingham, struggled for "higher" republican goals. As eighteenth-century forebears achieved the independence of a nation, their abolitionist descendants, trained in whig habits of historical inquiry, took the next republican step toward "the independence of *man*."[62]

Advocates viewed their campaign in the context of a sweeping historical design; they sensed that their language, commitments, and struggles all derived from past experience; they measured success and failure through comparisons with earlier projects. Little wonder, then, that reformers did not expect to create a world *de novo;* rather, they anticipated an all-too-familiar set of conditions and conflicts in society. Abolitionists defined their project more in terms of derivation than invention.

One indication of this attitude was the identity reformers fashioned. Abolitionists thought of themselves as heirs or inheritors, individuals who alone possessed legitimate claims to past achievements or honors.[63] Others saw themselves as a remnant, a small, select group that kept alive the vestiges of certain ideals abandoned or subverted by the rest of the nation.[64] Advocates also referred to themselves as the sons or daughters of illustrious parents who had enunciated (but only partially realized) principles of human liberty. To call these figures "Fathers" and "Mothers" was to do more than merely reassert their status in folklore; it also reaffirmed a perceived kinship in spirit and ideology.[65]

The sense of memory and connection that informed the abolitionists' identity carried over to their relation with the larger political culture. Reformers heatedly denied that they engaged in an unfamiliar and unprecedented cause. They saw their movement as part of a larger pattern of historical experience in which power's expansion had led a venerable line of predecessors to defend and extend human freedom. Advocates declared that antislavery efforts simply reasserted commitments to liberty that lay dormant in the modern republic.[66] Their work enhanced rather than eroded the virtue and harmony that made a republican order possible[67] Convinced that America had both promised and betrayed liberty, and confident that their movement would rise above that sorrowfully mixed record, reformers proclaimed their own form of allegiance to the nation. Advocates stood, as Garrison once said of Phillips, "encircled by the drapery of stars and stripes without compromising [their] abolitionism."[68]

Reformers held that their historical arguments offered proof of abolition's commitment to the nation. The advocates' whig interpretation of the past not only identified a chronic struggle between tyranny and liberty but also provided a much needed warning of the republic's inherent weaknesses: the fragile nature of its liberties; the peculiar susceptibility of a republic to power's aggression; the forgetfulness of republican citizens; and their complacency in the face of imminent dangers. As Philadelphia lawyer David Paul Brown noted, a proper understanding of history illuminated the wide variety of threats faced by a republic. "Experience proves," he said, "that there is no affinity between Liberty and vice. Man has been free and happy in proportion as he has been virtuous; slavish and miserable, as he has disregarded the principles of morality. Republican institutions derive no support from habits of luxury and idleness. Temperance and industry alone can protect them from the effects of premature debility on the one hand, and the ascendancy of despotic power on the other."[69]

The knowledge of past experience clarified these problems as it stressed their persistence. After reviewing the legal systems of Greece, Rome, and America, lawyer and legislator David Lee Child of Boston commented that republicans could not escape history: "I do not perceive that we republicans are free from the passions and vices to which all men are liable, or that we have as yet discovered a *panacea* for the diseases of the soul and state."[70] The nation had to prepare itself for the calamities that past republics endured. The abolitionists' task was, in a sense, to warn that the republic still had to face its own temporality.[71]

Reformers cautioned that "liberty has flourished only where a struggle has been kept up for it – only where its great principles have been constantly flashed in the face of the oppressor – only when the subjects of oppression have been kept alive to their rights."[72] Abolitionists viewed historical inquiry itself as an act of republican oversight. Their historical arguments chronicled and enacted the scrutiny they deemed necessary for republican health.

3

"A FAITH FOR FREEDOM"

THE POLITICAL GOSPEL OF ABOLITION

HISTORIANS HAVE LONG HELD that the roots, character, and conduct of the abolition movement grew out of evangelical Protestantism. In his 1853 history of the movement, reformer William Goodell wrote that "missionary and evangelizing orators . . . were God's instruments for putting into the minds of others 'thoughts that burned,' for the emancipation of the enslaved." Dwight L. Dumond echoed this point almost nine decades later, describing abolition as "a powerful religious crusade" in which "[f]rom first to last churches were the forums, preachers the most consistent and powerful advocates, and the sin of slavery the cardinal thesis of the new social philosophy." Bertram Wyatt-Brown's 1969 study of Lewis Tappan supported the line of argument, noting that "[t]he abolitionist movement was primarily religious in its origins, its leadership, its language, and its methods of reaching the people."[1]

A large body of work has examined the relationship between abolition and evangelicalism. One set of studies focuses on the doctrinal influence of religion on antislavery, emphasizing the importance of beliefs in human efficacy and millennialism for the life of faith as well as for acts of reform. Believers capable of accepting the grace of God could also prepare the way of the Lord; the faithful body that detected and immediately denounced sin, especially the sin of slavery, purified not only themselves but also their churches and world in anticipation of Christ's coming.[2] A second set of studies examines the organizational role of religion in abolition, describing the institutional base of evangelical churches, the schisms that rocked religious groups, the tactics drawn from the "Benevolent Empire" of reform, and the leadership cadre that emerged out of seminaries and congregations.[3] A third group of works draws attention to the personal dimension of religion and reform, exploring the powerful, transformative effects of the conversion experience and analyzing the responses of individuals caught in generational conflict or vocational crisis.[4]

Together, these works demonstrate the guidance that abolitionists took from faith and the depth of their religious convictions. It is also important, however, to examine how reformers actually expressed their religious beliefs. Advocates formed and conveyed their assumptions about God through particular sets of words and images. Their religious experience, in common with that of others, involved beliefs held as well as beliefs structured: reformers renounced sin as they defined its substance, feared divine wrath as they determined God's punishments, and embraced Christian duty as they ranked their own obligations. The abolitionists' religious understanding, in other words, grew not only from the intense inspiration of faith, but also from their purposeful formulation of faith. A study of the choices advocates made to express their religious convictions moves historical analysis beyond the consideration of theological, organizational, and psychological factors alone to an ideological understanding of evangelicalism and abolition, focusing on the language, ideas, and values that made up the reformers' mode of religious discourse.

The particular circumstances in which advocates outlined their beliefs varied considerably. Important differences also marked the reformers' backgrounds, tactics, intentions, and anxieties. But a common thread ran through such disparate experiences, made evident by a range of voices, over an extended period of time, in both public and private expression. The appeals made by abolitionists from the 1830s through the Civil War reveal a clear pattern in the way advocates articulated their religious beliefs and priorities. In discussions of formal doctrine, ecclesiastical mission, or individual responsibility, reformers at different periods and in various situations presented their creed through a constant and distinctive set of terms: abolitionists commonly framed their understanding of faith in the vocabulary, values, and expectations of republican thought. Advocates pointed repeatedly to the harmony that they believed existed between Christianity and republicanism and proclaimed their work for the slave as a sign of fidelity to both piety and politics.[5] More importantly, abolitionists found in republican ideology a language and conceptual framework that meaningfully explained the will of God, the objectives of his churches, and the duty of his followers. The reformers' expressions of religious conviction and the context within which they placed their beliefs demonstrate an important point: that the relationship between faith and reform was one shaped not only by evangelicalism and abolition but by political culture as well.

In asserting their commitment to republicanism, abolitionists emphasized the struggle of freedom against mastery, the links between individual character and constitutional health, and the need for scrutiny over personal and national conduct. To reformers, themes of independence, morality, and exhortation meshed smoothly with religious convictions that stressed a similar set of ideas: freedom of conscience, high standards of conduct, and critical self-examination. The Kentucky-born and Oberlin-trained abolitionist James A. Thome remained convinced that the principles for which he worked "brought heaven and earth together."

The comments of other advocates reveal a similar frame of mind. The 1855 Colored National Convention in Philadelphia heard the call to work "in behalf of the sacred cause of HUMAN FREEDOM." Sarah Grimké, who had been drawn to Quakerism, agreed. She noted that abolitionists carefully maintained "the holy principles of freedom." To Maria Weston Chapman, who had broken away from Unitarianism, liberty's values and standards "were identical to those of Christianity herself." And work in the abolition campaign, as an 1833 pamphlet declared, derived from "a duty we owe to our common Creator, to our fellow-men, and to ourselves, as republicans and Christians." A sense of duty brought reformers to challenge what Angelina Grimké viewed as an intolerable menace: "The doctrine of blind obedience and unqualified submission to *any human* power, whether civil or ecclesiastical, is the doctrine of despotism, and ought to have no place among Republicans and Christians." Rev. Orange Scott, a Methodist abolitionist, spoke to the same concern in an 1837 convention address: "*The condemnation of American slavery* is equally demanded by our professions as republicans and as Christians." Indeed, as Rev. Arthur B. Bradford wrote in 1852, "Our principles must advance or Christianity and Republicanism must go down."[6]

The conjunction of the spiritual and secular also appeared in reform attacks on national hypocrisy. Two abolitionist leaders who were critical of the clergy and unaffiliated with a church voiced such concerns. William Lloyd Garrison condemned Independence Day as America's "great carnival of republican despotism, and of christian impiety." And Frederick Douglass, once aligned with and then alienated from the Garrisonians, warned countrymen boastful of America's liberty and Christianity that "your republican politics, not less than your republican religion, are flagrantly inconsistent."[7]

Abolitionists mixed their references to religious and republican heroes so freely that the figures invoked seemed to speak with one voice in reform appeals, providing another example of the harmony advocates saw between the spirit of Christianity and the spirit of Liberty. Seymour Boughton Treadwell, a political abolitionist active in New York and Michigan, defended the reformers' inflammatory language by recalling the rhetoric of early church and Revolutionary leaders. He argued that those who were indifferent to the great crisis of an age always denounced as abusive and offensive "the impassioned eloquence of a Paul or a Stephen; or of a Hancock, an Otis, or a Patrick Henry of modern times." Wendell Phillips, whose roots lay in orthodox Congregationalism, also summoned a mixed litany of heroes in arguments for disunion: "A Union whose despotism is so cruel and searching that one-half our lawyers and one-half our merchants stifle conscience for bread – in the name of Martin Luther and John Milton, of Algernon Sidney and Henry Vane, of John Jay and Samuel Adams, I declare such a Union a failure.[8]

Reformers felt their religious and political ideals were compatible, and they remained confident that the Lord looked favorably on their labors. But as they explained the reasons for God's blessing and discussed key components of their religious belief, abolitionists revealed an interesting habit of mind: the principles they held as central to republicanism guided the way they expressed the tenets, priorities, and fulfillment of faith. At the heart of the religious consciousness that reformers articulated lay the problem of human freedom. In the abolitionists' view, God and Scripture served to clarify power relations among mortals. Reformers maintained that in a reconstructed political order the religious obligations of mankind could be realized and God's design for the world would be achieved. On such a field, through a distinctive "political" gospel, personal holiness and divine intention intersected and became manifest. Republican liberty was a cardinal principle of Christian belief for the abolitionists, reflected in the ways they discussed a wide range of religious subjects: the purposes of God; the message of Scripture; the qualities of faith and duty; the character of divine justice; and the course of redemption.

In their descriptions of God's nature and intentions, abolitionists demonstrated the pattern of thought they applied to religious inquiry. In an 1838 Fourth of July oration delivered to the people of Dover, New Hampshire, Enoch Mack, a Freewill Baptist minister, spoke of God as the author of freedom and described the Son of God by reference to a passage from Isaiah, as one sent to earth "to proclaim liberty to the captives and the opening of the prison to them that are bound." Speaking before a Boston audience the same day, Garrison also cited this passage to explain Christ's role in the world, asserting that "God WILLS ALL MEN TO BE FREE!"[9]

In an 1843 address, Philadelphia Unitarian pastor William Furness took a similar perspective on the character of Christ. To understand Jesus' ministry properly, one had to appreciate first the particular evils that infected his world, evils such as despotism, bondage, and selfish passion which any good republican would readily recognize and abhor. Jesus expressed the word and will of God in this specific context, and in the process delivered a message that "shook, as with a voice of thunder, the foundations of unjust power, and threatened to topple it to the dust." His teachings were clearly seditious and treasonous, Furness continued, and thrust Jesus into a tumultuous contest on the side of revolution and against tyranny and oppression.[10]

Ministers gathered at the 1846 Religious Anti-Slavery Convention in Boston agreed. Jesus declared that he had begun the prophesied reconstruction of society, and all who professed belief in him were bound to promote this work. No cause in the divine campaign was of greater importance than abolition: "No sight could be more pleasing to God, more honorable to the Christian religion, more cheering to the slave, more hopeful for the universal extension of Christ's kingdom on earth." Indeed, the abolition of slavery had to be accomplished "before the Gospel can exert its full influence here." The *Liberty Almanac* of 1850 stated a common theme in antislavery reform when it proclaimed that "the cause of the oppressed" had to be understood as "the cause of God." As Garrison argued, Jesus' mission in dwelling among us was, simply enough, to overturn "every hold of tyranny."[11]

Standing at the center of creation – and at the center of the struggle against despotic power – the abolitionists' God manifested a political will of a decidedly republican stripe. A tract by evangelical theologian Charles Beecher expressed, in both the content and arrangement of its argument, the distinctive character of divine political intentions. Beecher's essay opened with a list of "the revealed attributes of the true God." The first entry described God as "the Author of all really good social organization, and the only cause adequate to preserve it from corruption. He was the Founder and manifest Executive of the Hebrew Commonwealth." Beecher went on to describe God as "eminently undespotic; the opposite of the usual character of earthly monarchs." It was not until the sixth and final point in the series that Beecher discussed the relation of God to the human soul and salvation. To judge from Beecher's rankings, God was first and foremost a republican, the champion of liberty, and the defender of civic virtue, who was engaged in a continuing battle with the demonic force of oppression.[12]

Abolitionists commonly understood the work and goals of God in the terms Beecher outlined. Angelina Grimké identified God's project as the construction of a *"temple of liberty."* To achieve this goal, one reform periodical noted, "Christianity says, that the Creator gave rights and imposed duties, and prescribed republicanism as the best means of guarding one and enforcing the other." Boston Unitarian pastor John Weiss concurred: "The Divine object in the settlement of this republic [was] to guarantee the enlargement of liberty, and to formally vindicate the rights of man." "Philalethes" explained to readers of an Oswego, New York, newspaper how God fulfilled this design in America. The author pointed not to divine acts that might have produced a transformation of spirit but to intervention which "vouchsafed us from monarchical thraldom and oppression." The Revolution, like all other events in history, announced "the great truth, that human liberty is as the apple of his eye." The eradication of slavery from the Republic, Theodore Parker announced, would allow God's blessing to descend, a blessing that would generate a distinctive political order: in the age to come, the Unitarian minister declared, "we shall have a commonwealth based on righteousness." The vision was one outlined by the liberal orthodox novelist, Harriet Beecher Stowe. At the conclusion of *Uncle Tom's Cabin,* the heroic ex-slave George Harris pictures the fulfillment of God's plan for freemen in the establishment of a particular type of black nation: "On the shores of Africa I see a republic, – a republic formed of picked men, who, by energy and self-educating force, have, in many cases, individually raised themselves above a condition of slavery." The new nation, Harris continued, would exist not only for the benefit of its own citizens but for the propagation of God's political designs: "*Our nation* shall roll the tide of civilization and Christianity along its shores, and plant there mighty republics, that, growing with the rapidity of tropical vegetation, shall be for all coming ages."[13]

The abolitionists' God only infrequently worked in mysterious ways. His program for mankind was (or should have been) familiar enough to the sons and daughters of liberty. The Deity did not speak in tongues. Rather, God addressed humanity in a Revolutionary vocabulary. As Ohioan Charles Olcott explained, "The Law of Nature which is the Law of God revealed in His Works and Providence only, is wholly republican in its structure and operation, and vindicates the natural equality of Human Rights, as clearly as the Law of God revealed in His Word does."[14]

For Olcott and other reformers, the political commitments that explained the will of God also clarified the nature of Scripture. Rejecting claims that Holy Writ did not teach politics or political action, Presbyterian minister George Bourne declared that "the Bible is the strongest and best political book in the world. A book which utterly condemns all sins, political as well as others, must necessarily be a political book." Believers who acted on that book and who attempted to transform its words into deeds would find themselves, of necessity, engaged in work of political renovation. As members of the 1846 Religious Anti-Slavery Convention proclaimed in their declaration and pledge, "the Gospel properly administered is the great charter of human freedom and equal rights."[15]

Properly understood, the Bible announced not only the path to salvation in the next life but also a specific plan for liberation in this world. According to Bourne, Scriptures indicated general divine favor for "righteously and wisely administered" government. Yet God's revealed words made "a just distinction between forms of government, because they plainly teach a preference of the republican form over all others." A contributor to the *Emancipator* in 1837 noted that "the scriptures have been appropriately called a *republican book,* and with good reason, for they teach the natural equality of men, and that God is no respecter of persons." While abolitionists might find comfort and direction in this message, one particular group of individuals feared and condemned the republican character of Scripture: "for this reason probably crowned heads, in proportion to their despotic dispositions, have been the enemies of Bible Societies."[16]

America's tyrannical equivalents of crowned heads also tried to suppress the holy call for freedom. As Charles Olcott noted, slaveholders kept the Bible from their slaves because of the good book's informing political spirit. Masters "well know," Olcott wrote, "there is not another book in the world, that vindicates and establishes the equal rights of all men, and denounces their infringement, with half the energy, severity and copiousness, that the Bible does. They know it is the most republican book in the world." One did not have to strain to see this message in Scriptures, he continued. "If there be one doctrine more plainly and clearly taught in the Bible than another, it is the doctrine *of the utter condemnation, reprobation and denunciation of every kind*

66

and degree of Human Oppression, especially all slavish oppression. It is a *leading, prominent,* principal doctrine of the Bible." Furthermore, Scripture not only forbade political authority from acting in a tyrannical fashion but also prescribed the shape of government and the mode of governance. Like Bourne and other reformers, Olcott believed that "the spirit of the Scriptures not only enjoins good civil government, as a Divine institution, but it plainly teaches, that such government should be *republican,* in its *form* and structure."[17]

Abolitionists discerned a simple and compelling reason for the Bible's focus on republican liberty: Scripture taught that faith required freedom. In the absence of liberty, reformers argued, genuine religious understanding and practice could not be attained; an individual would lose the very capacity to receive God's message and saving grace. In an 1839 essay, Mary Robbins of the Lynn, Massachusetts, Female Anti-Slavery Society defined a direct relationship between a person's political state and spiritual condition: "Once believe man to be an incarnation of the Divine Mind, the 'Word made flesh,' and liberty becomes at once a necessary *element* for the soul *to be in.* It is the only conductor through which *soul* will consent to pass. It cannot exist without it. You might as well talk of animal life without atmosphere, as a man without perfect freedom."[18]

Although faith required the purity and receptivity of the soul, it depended fundamentally on the *survival* of the soul. The soul endured, in turn, only through the guarantee of liberty. The substance of Robbins's argument found expression in a variety of other reform appeals. Daniel Foster, pastor of the Free Evangelical Church of North Danvers, Massachusetts, condemned the chattel system because it repudiated "the highest, holiest of all rights, a man's right to himself," thereby denying slaves knowledge of their God and of their place in the divine order. The tyranny that enchained action and movement also enfeebled religious understanding. A Poughkeepsie, New York, minister, H. P. Cutting, declared that the promotion of liberty was the precise reason for rekindling Christian zeal: "We want the revival of the religious sentiment in this nation in order to place the government perpetually on the side of Freedom." Lewis Tappan, an evangelical Congregationalist, explained that "independence of thought, speech and action" provided the "liberty where with Jesus Christ can make men free." And Tappan's associate, George B. Cheever, pastor of New York City's Church of the Puritans, maintained that "the sum of the argument" resided in Psalm 119:134: "DELIVER ME FROM THE OPPRESSION OF MAN; SO WILL I KEEP THY PRECEPTS."[19]

Cheever and his fellow reformers viewed injustice and oppression as particularly ominous threats to the life of faith. All agreed that the faithful had to strive for a state of liberty in order to keep themselves and others open to the influence of God. And all held that freedom served as a critical precondition for the full flowering of divine grace. For these reasons, Cutting hoped for the renewal of a distinctive scriptural message, one he claimed was heard throughout the land during the Revolution. It was time, he declared, for ministers to preach "the gospel of human liberty." Garrison noted that the call came directly from Jesus, although a slight embellishment to Mark 16:15 made the point clearer: "Go ye into all the world, and preach the gospel *of freedom* to every creature."[20]

Abolitionists pointed out that faith originated and flourished in liberty. William Furness argued that freedom marked the beginning – a new birth and starting point – for spiritual regeneration.[21] Such a belief, advocates insisted, did not arise from tortured exegesis but from the unambiguous commands of God. Frederick Douglass reminded an abolitionist convention in 1849 of the specific sequence of steps God had outlined to bring his people to a life of faith: "God did not say to Moses 'Tell my people to serve me that they may go free,' but 'Go and tell Pharoah [sic] to let my people go that they may serve me.' The first thing is freedom. It is the all important thing. There can be no virtue without freedom – there can be no obedience to the Bible without freedom."[22] Douglass maintained that liberty undergirded piety, not the reverse. The divinely inspired order of events he recalled made this fact abundantly clear: Moses would lead his people to God by first liberating them in the political realm.

In the same sphere, reformers argued, nineteenth-century Americans fulfilled their own divinely appointed tasks. The abolitionists' understanding of religious duty, like the other components of their faith, centered on the establishment of proper power relations within the human community. Upon hearing the gospel of liberty, Unitarian minister Samuel May, Jr., argued, all would come to realize that the cause of emancipation displayed and defined devotion in the nineteenth century. The reform movement was "the true touchstone which determines the character of every soul, for there is nothing else which tries 'as by fire' now." Because the abolition of slavery was a holy cause, a ministerial conference declared, "every friend of Christ is bound to be engaged in it, as a proof of his love to his Saviour." Freedom, as John Weiss argued, was "God's project, the long-cherished intention of the infinite wisdom." To honor the divine commitment to liberty, he continued, "it shall be so interwoven with our creeds, that whoso accepts religion accepts freedom, and is consecrated to the idea of a pure republic." In Daniel Foster's view the pursuit of liberty stood as "the Christian's first and most sacred duty in the vineyard of his Lord, *now*."[23]

Even the task of separation and purification, so central to evangelical revivalism, found expression within this context. Lewis Tappan urged his brother, Ohio senator Benjamin Tappan, to follow traditional republican injunctions, move beyond petty partisan concerns, and stand foursquare against slavery. Benjamin would thereby rise to the stature of a great national "patriot," concerned with the best and broadest interests of the nation. Giving a twist to a familiar evangelical phrase, Lewis wrote: "Oh, that you, my dear brother, would, this session . . . eschew the paltry democracy of the day and *come out* such a democrat as the 19th century demands."[24] "Come-outerism," the act of withdrawal from impious churches, took on an important political meaning in Lewis Tappan's mind. It still stood as a commitment realized through separation, though not, in this case, from theological enemies. Rather, Tappan implored his brother to come out from aristocratic and authoritarian foes, from the allies of the slave power.

Other reformers extended Tappan's argument, insisting that the dutiful believer must do more than withdraw from the evil influ-

ence of the chattel system. Advocates of nonresistance and dis-
unionism, for example, argued that one was also obliged to come
out from all forms of oppression and corruption – even the tyranny that could infect an institutionalized republican order.[25]
Only then could society secure the liberty required for obedience
to God. The theology of these critics, once again, revolved around
questions of sovereignty, legitimate authority, and individual au-
tonomy.

William Lloyd Garrison and utopian reformer John Humphrey
Noyes provide illustrations. Both renounced the existing government and proclaimed an end to their cooperation with it. Their
reasons coincided: the prevailing political order and its Constitutional base were inconsistent with the higher government of God.
Yet Garrison and Noyes structured their own mode of protest –
and the form of argument they attributed to their God – on the
model of Revolutionary founders. Noyes announced: "I have sub-
scribed my name to an instrument similar to the Declaration of
'76, renouncing my allegiance to the government of the United
States and asserting the title of Jesus Christ to the throne of the
world. . . ." As a nonresistant, Noyes could not meet force with
force, but an alternative course did have divine sanction: "I must
. . . either consent to remain a slave till God removes the tyrant, or
I must commence war upon him, by a declaration of independence
and other weapons suitable to the character of a son of God." Although Revolutionary forebears relied on violence and came to decisions that eventually led to an oppressive political order, Noyes
recognized that their initial act, a declaration of the principles of
liberty, was a valid and exemplary precedent, one defined as God's
recommended course of action.[26]

In similar fashion, Garrison explained that he merely appropriated the arguments of eighteenth-century patriots. He distrusted
power, defended liberty, and respected the right of resistance. He
attacked the modern-day tyrants whose despotism had been fore-
seen by the Revolutionaries. And his abolition efforts reenacted
the noblest national virtues – which stood as the strategic choices
of the divine mind itself. Challenges to human government in general and to the Union in particular were the logical, though popu-

larly unexplored, extensions of this republican critique. Garrison perceived disunion and nonresistance as effective *and* divinely ordained means of broadening the field of liberation. The God he worshipped vigilantly observed the status of human liberty and expected believers to demonstrate their faith through similar exertions. Garrison assumed that following in the ways of the Lord in the nineteenth century meant applying a republican analytic to an existing republican order.[27]

Those who broke with oppression and engaged in emancipation believed that their efforts determined the true meaning of religious fidelity. Although spiritual exercise, material sacrifice, and formal ritual might appear the clearest demonstrations of piety and duty, reformers held that the establishment of freedom was the genuine and definitive mark of faith. Charles C. Burleigh, a Garrisonian committed to perfectionist principles, argued that "true veneration" expressed itself "in doing good to our wronged and oppressed brother, in laboring for the overthrow of every system of injustice which is oppressing and degrading him."[28] Furness expanded on this theme in 1856 by declaring that

> [l]iberty, . . . is the indication of the Spirit of the Lord. It is the sign of the influence of that Spirit in the hearts of men. Not cathedrals and costly churches, not pompous ceremonials, not Sabbaths and feast days and fast days – Easter and Lent – not morning and evening prayers, not the ringing of church bells, not baptism and sacraments – not these are the indubitable signs of the presence and power of the Spirit of the Most High; but liberty, liberty to think and to speak what we think; personal, civic, religious liberty, . . . – this it is that bears witness to the Spirit of the Lord dwelling in individuals and in nations. This is the grand test of the prevalence and power of religion, pure and undefiled, . . . In fine, liberty is divine – the Spirit of the Lord.[29]

The campaign for freedom did more than merely exemplify a creed. For reformers, the cause expressed the will of God. Emancipation realized the informing doctrines of Scripture. By advancing liberty, one not only testified to faith but also established the very possibility of faith.

The standard of liberty by which abolitionists defined faith and duty also clarified the nature of sin. Reformers held that the highest form of obedience to divine will rested in the promotion of liberty over power; the basest form of disobedience to God lay in the expansion of power over freedom.

The sinfulness of slavery stemmed from its challenge to "the laws by which God has regulated human society." The chattel system condoned man stealing, turned people into property, exacted labor without compensation, inflicted cruel punishment, violated the sanctity of marriage, separated families, and hindered religious instruction. Slavery, the American Anti-Slavery Society declared, formed nothing less than "a presumptuous transgression of all the holy commandments."[30]

Yet reformers such as John G. Fee, a Lane Seminary graduate and founder of Berea College, urged audiences to step back from these particulars and understand slavery's transgression in broader, comprehensive, *and* politically charged terms. In Fee's view, the various evils of the chattel system all served as examples of its principal and informing sin: slavery was an act of "usurpation." Slavery was a sin against God chiefly because "it is a usurpation of his authority – an invasion of his rights" and "a usurpation of man's rights." Speaking to a black convention, Presbyterian minister Henry Highland Garnet placed the many "direful effects" of enslavement in a similar context, describing the chattel system as a crime against God and humanity because it attempted to obliterate "the good seeds of liberty." Addressing listeners in Rochester, Frederick Douglass based the sinfulness of slavery in its "monstrous violation of the great principle of human liberty" and its "direct war upon the government of God." In sermons to New Hampshire and Massachusetts assemblies, Congregational pastor David Root struck the same theme. He reduced the multiple evils of slavery to the sin of "oppression," the one central transgression which fed injustice and extortion, generated "the very worst forms of tyranny and despotism," and "provoke[d] the Divine vengeance."[31]

Root argued that slavery was a "sin" and that its "sinfulness" consisted of oppression. He and other reformers also raised three other concerns about the transgressions of the chattel system. First, advocates noted, slavery stood as the *worst* of all possible sins, specifically because of its abuse of power. James T. Dickinson, pastor of the Second Congregational Church in Norwich, Connecticut, reminded his listeners that slavery's "sin of oppression" stood condemned throughout the Bible "in terms of unmeasured severity." Fee wrote that slavery's form of oppression "is not only sinful, but classed with sins of the most aggravated character." The pastor of Cincinnati's Sixth Presbyterian Church, Jonathan Blanchard, told an audience that "the sin of oppression, is, throughout the scriptures, more denounced than, perhaps, any other form of transgression, and, as we have seen the worst possible form of oppression is slaveholding."[32]

Reformers insisted, secondly, that slavery's abuse of power elicited God's mightiest wrath. Baptist minister and ex-slaveholder William Henry Brisbane argued that in the past God angrily responded to the chattel system's oppression by bringing about the Flood, the captivity of Judah, and the punishment of Pharaoh. "The Old Testament," Brisbane wrote, "abounds in the strongest expressions of God's indignation at any system, by which the brotherhood of man is disregarded, and the poor are kept poor by the oppression of the wealthy and the powerful." Rev. Root also cautioned his congregations that the tyranny of slavery provoked the sternest Divine vengeance: "How he has peeled and scathed and annihilated the nations who have dared to oppress and crush the helpless and unoffending."[33]

The abolitionists' third concern about the sin of slavery was the most ominous. Reformers argued that when a community subjected others to oppression, the Lord expressed his wrath in a particularly fitting way. Those who acted despotically or acquiesced in despotism faced *political* punishment from God. Writing in 1836, Presbyterian James Birney warned that a slaveholding nation had to recognize the consequences of accepting and supporting the chattel system. Its people deeply offended God by such actions and caused the Lord to apply his particular calculus of crime and punishment to them. "A God of Justice," he predicted, "is bringing down on an impenitent nation retribution, in the loss of

73

our own liberty." The convention of Radical Political Abolitionists held in Syracuse, New York, in 1855 argued the same point. Reformers feared that a people who upheld or tolerated slavery would suffer a terrible fate: "God will punish us by the loss of our liberties." A Congregational minister from Connecticut, William W. Patton, stated that he already detected freedom's decay in America. Slavery, Patton said, was nothing more than a "giant usurpation," a force which proceeded in "a career of usurpation" until it subjugated all institutions and all society. At the moment, "God is allowing event after event to occur in our land, which shall illustrate the power of slavery in church and state and exhibit its true spirit and tendency." America's punishment was to bear witness to the steady erosion of fragile republican liberties.[34]

Unitarian minister Edmund H. Sears also saw slavery's oppression as the root of American sinfulness and believed that God would respond in kind. The nation had to recognize the distinctive character of its sin and confront "the despotism that is submerging us." A final, special sentence would come to pass if the nation did not choose justice over self-interest: "Revolution is God's remedy, when a people are past reformation and need punishment. It is the cup of the Divine anger."[35] All revelation and all experience demonstrated the validity of this claim, as the *American and Foreign Anti-Slavery Reporter* noted. Americans had to see slavery as a national sin, the type of offense to which God responded in a particular way:

> The Israelites sinned as a people, and the Almighty took away their republican liberties, and gave them the political bondage of monarchy for a punishment. . . . Spain sinned as a nation, and fell from the summit of power to political insignificance and social anarchy; and her colonies, founded in blood, have waded through blood from despotism to disorganization. France sinned, and has passed through every modification of political mischief, from the tyranny of one to that of a million.

America's toleration of slavery was a national sin of similar magnitude, and "its consequences will come in that general corruption which infallibly leads to political slavery, and to all those moral deformities which are its inseparable companions."[36] For the abolitionists, sin, suffering, and penance all assumed a clear political complexion. God's wrath would visit a tyrannical and unrepentant America in the form of a new plague, one of political turmoil.

God's word and will offered abolitionists one form of instruction in the cause of liberty. The acts of God's chosen peoples in the history of redemption provided another apparent demonstration of the Creator's commitment to republican principles. God's appointed agents earned distinction and honor by advancing the work of salvation, fulfilling their tasks in what reformers saw as a divinely inspired political framework. Olcott pointed to the history of the ancient Israelites as an example. He argued that "a critical examination of the Jewish theocracy, the only form of civil government that God ever directly established unveils a beautiful system of republican government, best adapted to protect the equal rights of all its subjects."[37]

The achievements of God's Christian agents also grew out of their divinely appointed political acts. Wendell Phillips attributed John Calvin's prominence to distinguished statesmanship. To Calvin, we owe "republicanism – the republicanism of the Church," which created a religion of the people that trusted in the people at large and asserted that the masses were closer to God than scholarship or priestcraft. Similarly, Phillips described the lesson of Puritanism in terms more congenial to an analysis of power than to theological distinctions. He focused not on triumphs over infidelity or impiety but instead discussed the Puritan as one who exposed despotism and challenged institutional constraints.[38]

Sears presented Puritanism in a similar light in a scathing 1856 address entitled *Revolution or Reform.* He explained the contest in his own day between the "slave-despotism" and freedom as "the old conflict renewed between the Cavalier and the Puritan," the latter characterized by the Anglo-Saxon "element of liberty." The continued aggression of the slave power royalists challenged the North to raise up from its own Puritan element "a Milton, a Pym, a Hampden and a Cromwell" to battle once more against ever-encroaching, oppressive power. Sears chose to bypass the New England religious communities of the seventeenth century in his depiction and application of Puritan history, focusing instead on their English brethren's republican struggle against monarchical injustice, authoritarianism, and centralization. In doing so, he shaped a distinctive memory for his audience, one that analyzed the Puritans through their concepts of power and their exercise of political, rather than spiritual, weapons. In the pictures presented by Sears and Phillips, the Puritan stood as a historical and political type, known by and for the defense of republican principles.[39]

Theodore Parker carried this interpretation further by placing God's agents of salvation within a sweeping historical context. Parker called attention to a modern alteration in the course of redemptive history, a divine plan that would itself be achieved through human freedom. The key events in this unfolding design were the birth of Christ, Luther's ninety-five theses, and the Plymouth settlement. The fourth moment, "indissolubly connected with the three preceding," came in 1776 with the crystallization of the "American Idea," based on the natural, equal, and unalienable rights of mankind. "The Idea was Christian, was Protestant, was of New England. Plymouth was becoming national; Protestantism going into politics . . . . The Declaration of Independence was the American profession of faith in political Christianity."[40] It was precisely this faith, shaped by the values of Revolutionary republicanism, that Parker and other abolitionists carried into the battle against slavery.

Because its core principles had formed around the issues of freedom and tyranny, Protestantism offered special insight into the uses and abuses of power. So argued Thomas Treadwell Stone, a Salem, Massachusetts, Unitarian minister who anticipated a "Second Reformation" that would apply the lessons of Protestantism to the state as well as to the church. In a brief historical sketch, Stone located the origins of Protestantism in Luther's attacks on "popery," describing the reformer's critique as one focused more on problems of worldly despotism than spiritual blindness. Protestant discontent in the sixteenth century sprang from the "assumption of divine authority to which men are religiously bound to submit"; in the nineteenth century, "the Second Reformation shall expose the falseness of the same claim in behalf of political institutions." In Stone's view, contemporary Protestantism would realize its goals in the realm of secular power relations, the new and true field of religious endeavor. As Luther and his followers taught mankind to resist concentrated authority in the Church, "so must a broader Protestantism teach us to say to all Power." The lesson extended to republican institutions that had become unfaithful to their own founding principles. Stone's fellow citizens, descendants of rebels and traitors, had slipped back into "the old doctrines of absolute authority and unquestioning obedience," creating within the Republic a "Popedom of State."[41] Such conditions called for a reinvigorated religion of human liberty, a faith tested and proven in the struggle against tyranny and usurpation. Protestantism had originally formed through such a contest in the Church; it would now be fulfilled through its efforts in politics.[42]

Republican principles suffused the reformers' expression of religious beliefs. Through the language of liberty, advocates ordered past events, compelled action in the present, and clarified expectations for the future. In describing the intentions of their God, his actions in time, the commandments of Scripture, and the responsibilities and priorities of a Christian, in locating the seat of sin and outlining the route to salvation, abolitionists demonstrated the extent to which they embraced a "political gospel."

Differences existed among advocates on the exact nature of their creed. Did, for example, their faith represent the word of God for all peoples in all times; or did it describe the appointed work of their particular "season"? Yet, even among those who perceived a special task for their day and nation, the struggle for liberty over power transcended all other divine assignments. As Anne Warren Weston, a critic of Boston's Unitarian churches, noted, "never to the nations yet /a Holier work He gave /than that appointed to *our* time – / THE FREEDOM OF THE SLAVE!"[43]

The abolitionists' confession of a distinctive political, social, and institutional order remained a constant. "Genuine Christianity," Charles Olcott wrote, "is a system of republican liberty and equality; . . . it grants and guarantees equal rights to all mankind." William Goodell carried the same set of ideas into his own writing, particularly in his account of the "religious" influence on abolition. Goodell, a Calvinist who had been part of the nonsectarian, antislavery Union Church movement, acknowledged the importance of evangelical millennialism in the origins of antislavery reform; but he described the distinguishing feature of the approaching millennium as the security of rights. For Goodell, as for other reformers, the religious impulse operating in America was informed by republican commitments: "To be 'up and doing' was the watchword, and our American love of liberty, equality, and 'free institutions,' was gratified with the assurance that all the despotisms of the earth were to crumble at the Prince Emanuel's approach!"[44]

In whatever terms the abolitionists chose to express religious principles, their faith remained authentic and vital. The republican understanding they brought to Christianity animated religious zeal, channeled the energy of their beliefs, and identified a transcendent imperative to complete secular obligations. Advocates assumed that the measure of a people's worthiness rested in their dedication to freedom against despotism. They portrayed God as the enemy of tyrannical rule and the champion of liberty. They declared independence as the basis of both humanity's condition and its salvation. The triumph of "a faith for freedom" would seal the fate of satanic enslavement; a "pure and liberty loving religion" propagated at home and abroad would overcome the evil of oppression.[45] The sign of God's presence and favor lay in society's configuration of power, authority, and freedom, lending a republican slant to Paul's statement in II Corinthians: "Where the Spirit of the Lord is, there is Liberty."[46]

4

POWER, PASSION, &
PERSONALITY

ABOLITION & AMERICAN POLITICS

THE REPUBLICAN PERSPECTIVE that abolitionists brought to historical and religious matters also manifested itself in their handling of political questions on power and governance. In its 1835 *Annual Report,* the American Anti-Slavery Society touched on all three subjects as it discussed why the tyranny of slavery was the "*dry rot* to all the props that can sustain a good government." The "awards of Divine Justice" insured that acts of enslavement would lead to the collapse of liberty. Past experience demonstrated that chattel-based societies like that of ancient Greece would find themselves "engaged in endless broils [because] they were *Slaveholding* states." Both God's intentions and history's direction revealed to the Society a fundamental principle of political order and administration: it was simply "impossible for a pure republican government to subsist long upon a foundation of tyranny" before it descended into despotism.[1] The logic of republicanism ran steadily through these categories of thought, justifying the necessity and urgency of abolition.

The American Anti-Slavery Society's view of republican government illustrates abolitionism's informing political logic. Reformers conceived of power's structure and uses in terms of a coherent body of republican assumptions. Through this frame of reference, abolitionists defined three critical issues: the key forces operating in American politics; the role reformers ought to assume; and the proper course of action their movement should follow. Ironically, the abolitionists' shared body of assumptions generated a considerable degree of confusion, misunderstanding, and debate. Their professedly republican mode of analysis did not in the end lead to a uniform set of political positions but instead legitimated a variety of stances. Purposely recapitulating past republican ideals, reformers unintentionally reenacted past republican debates.[2]

Abolitionists continually expressed two basic assumptions about the nature and tendencies of political relations: that power held fearful consequences for a political order; and that, as a defense against such threats, a people needed to exercise the highest standards of character and morality. These were not marginal reflections on the problem of slavery but the informing ideas of abolition.

The abolitionists' concern with the disposition of power served as an organizing principle of key reform arguments. Evangelical advocate Theodore Dwight Weld opened the second half of *American Slavery As It Is* by outlining the course of power in history. Responding to readers who may have doubted the frightening claims he raised earlier in the book, Weld observed that the "nature and history of man" demonstrated the truth of the ancient maxim that power corrupts. The love of power "is perhaps the strongest human passion," he noted, "and the more absolute the power, the stronger the desire for it; and the more it is desired, the more its exercise is enjoyed: this enjoyment is to human nature a fearful temptation, – generally an overmatch for it." Such issues had long been settled, he claimed: "The possession of power, even when greatly restrained, is such a fiery stimulant, that its lodgement in human hands is always perilous." Power's use generally turned into power's abuse, opening the door to the unrestrained, absolute, and arbitrary exercise of authority. Such power had proved itself destructive both to its victims and to its wielders.[3]

The anxieties Weld expressed in 1839 appeared regularly in the appeals of other abolitionists. In an 1846 letter, New York lawyer and Tappan associate William Jay ordered his reflections on Constitutional law around a core observation: "Wherever there is power, in the family, the church, or the State, it may be used for evil as well as for good." The *National Anti-Slavery Standard* warned readers of power's dangerous course, arguing that "the natural and necessary tendency of power is to consolidate and perpetuate itself." The record of power demonstrated to Ohioan Charles Olcott the fragility of basic human rights, "in constant danger of being infringed and trampled on." All experience pointed to power's characteristic potential for ever-expanding evil.[4]

Of the many forms taken by unlimited, unaccountable power, none was more calamitous than slavery. The reason was simple, according to Weld: by legally granting masters absolute authority over slaves, the chattel system stimulated the desire for even greater power. Other abolitionists concurred. In an 1855 work, Edward Coit Rogers argued that slavery was both the clearest example of despotism and a critical step in the fulfillment of wider and more malicious designs. Proslavery forces sneered at appeals to justice, "primal law," and limits on power; they supported a variety of tyrannical causes such as "kingship, lordship, mastership"; they sought to replace the fundamental principles of republican government with the establishment of absolute despotism. The slave interests that exercised power over plantations had already gained wide authority over the nation, according to reformers. Slavery's promoters enjoyed an ever-increasing ability to subordinate the entire apparatus of government to their purposes, advancing what the *National Anti-Slavery Standard* described as the growing centralization of power that was "at once the natural tendency and the certain curse of modern governments." The reform journal noted the immediate cause of the problem: "Power delights to lie ensconced in the centre of its domains, like a spider at the citadel of his radiating lines of entrenchment, ready to dart with equal ease and certainty upon any cause of offence [sic], near or remote." Slavery offered the perfect vehicle for the realization and extension of these malicious skills. Despotic masters broadly and continually applied the lessons learned in their handling of slaves. As Moncure Conway warned, "The Old Serpent of Slavery has a great way of slipping from one skin into another; and wherever slavery has a new skin Freedom should have a fresh Avatar, ready to bruise its head."[5]

Abolitionists believed that the pattern of absolute power was constant; the exercise of absolute power created new and often unexpected forms of injustice; the fear of absolute power derived both from the uncertainty over where it might lead and from the certainty that no people were immune to its ravages. The last point was particularly troubling to reformers. As David Lee Child pointed out, the republic could be lost if it failed to heed the warnings provided by a republican analysis of power. Speaking before the New England Anti-Slavery Society in 1833, Child reminded his audience that their "republican" roots had not generated "a new edition of man" relieved from the burden of the past. The craving for despotic power was still present; in the American republic as elsewhere, it would inevitably lead to the abuse of power. Sufficient evidence could already be gathered, Child said, to show that ostensibly republican governments in the Southern states had secured tyranny rather than liberty for their people. Almost two decades later, Samuel J. May noted that the problem had spread far beyond a region to encompass the entire nation. With the passage of the Fugitive Slave Law in 1850, it became clear that power arrangements intended to serve freedom did nothing less than establish in-justice for all. May urged disobedience to such laws, based on arguments he attributed to Revolutionary leaders: that "men were not made that they may be the subjects of an oppressive political compact called a Republic, any more than they were made to be the creatures of a despot." Rev. William Furness warned that the danger extended beyond America's boundaries. The subversion of true republican commitments had taken its toll in foreign as well domestic affairs. "A republican form of government like ours," Furness argued, "is and must be, of all forms of government, the most pacific." Yet, the "anti-republican power" of slaveholding had fostered such unrestrained despotism and aggression that the world's most reliable preserver of peace had become its most dangerous agent of war.[6]

Power was an institutional leveler of sorts. It ran its course through all political orders, varying only in its concentration and cruelty. A well-constituted republic might withstand power's blows more effectively, but it could not eliminate power's stimulation of base human appetites.

It was this last aspect of the problem, however, that offered some grounds for optimism. Power posed external, institutional threats that could be contained structurally by a republican form of government. But power also had an internal, temperamental dimension that could be checked ethically by a commitment to virtuous self-discipline and self-sacrifice. If the disposition of national office did not offer complete security in the struggle against power, then perhaps the disposition of national character could lend assistance in the effort.

The outer framework of the state was not completely dispensable. Republican structures could still inspire republican behavior. As Rev. Furness recognized, "the political forms of a people, which, while they are the people's work, become, in return, the creators of the people, forming the popular character."[7] Since politics and morality remained intricately intertwined, the glorious cause of liberty depended on the preservation of republican forms as well as republican character.

Yet abolitionists commonly emphasized the latter. The task before the nation called more for ethical, rather than institutional, exertion. Reviewing the nature of "true liberty," Alonzo Ames Miner, a Boston minister, instructed his audience to take special care not to substitute mere forms of freedom for the genuine article. Liberty's deepest qualities, he argued, were not so much social or political as moral; law alone would not guarantee freedom. Other abolitionists echoed Miner's thoughts, convinced that industriousness, frugality, and other virtuous behaviors best secured liberty. Unitarian minister Edmund H. Sears feared that government would not serve the cause of freedom "until the tone of virtue and moral sentiment here at the north be brought up to its ancient manliness and glory." For the protection of basic rights and the defeat of tyranny, Samuel J. May noted, "we are very much less indebted . . . to our government, than we are to a correct moral and human sentiment, prevalent throughout the community." Schemes to colonize ex-slaves or to compensate masters financially would never work, Bostonian Maria Weston Chapman argued, because such plans overlooked a basic truth: "Slavery can only be abolished by raising the character of the people who compose the nation; and *that* can be done only by showing them a

higher one." The reformers' key purpose, as nonresistant Adin Ballou believed, was to teach that "the only government that can meet
the wants of man is one founded in the moral sense of the people –
sustained by an enlightened public conscience." Government
without such moral resolve simply invited collapse. Institutional
remedies alone could not save the Republic; the task of preserving
liberty had to draw upon individual and collective character.[8]

Reformers approached the problem of despotism with a similar
set of assumptions, viewing it as a political force manifest not only
in the distribution and exercise of power but also in the ways individuals conducted their daily lives. Tyranny represented the corruption both of government structures and of ethical codes. A republican people had to bear in mind, as Gerrit Smith stated, that
"despotism has a moral character, and a bad one." It was to this
very point that Charles Follen addressed his 1836 examination of
"The Cause of Freedom in Our Country." Follen urged his readers
to recognize the effects of arbitrary power and to form a united
front against its agents:

> I wish to direct public attention to the fact that the *tendency to
> oppression,* of which slavery is only the grossest manifestation, is
> apparent in our manners and habits as well as in our laws; and
> that when we see the anti-republicans in every walk of life and
> line of business endeavoring to strengthen their natural connex-
> ion by actual alliance and co-operation, it is high time that the re-
> publicans of every description, the friends of universal freedom
> . . . should recognize each other as fellow laborers.[9]

Republicans ought to find that common cause, Follen argued, in
something beyond a framework of codified political procedures;
they should also act in concert against the signs of tyranny that
arose from race prejudice, aristocratic pretense, blind ambition,
and intemperance. These problems affected Northerners as well as
Southerners. Structurally or behaviorally, the quest for power was
sure to grow and corrupt. The *Liberator* agreed, declaring that political accommodation with slavery led to "the deterioration of our
national morals, and the degradation of our national character,"
hampering the development of a "true Republic." Philadelphia

lawyer and reformer David Paul Brown also noted that the great
curse of the chattel principle lay in the "moral contagion which is
the fruit of slavery, and which by its silent encroachments upon the
true principles of republican government, has already tarnished
the brightness of our fame, and destroyed the force of our example."[10]

Abolitionists not only relied on their own explanations to show
the link between moral decay and tyranny but also cited a statement of unusual historical weight to express the same reading of
power: Thomas Jefferson's observations from *Notes on the State
of Virginia* on moral degradation and oppression. In Query XVIII,
Jefferson wrote: "There must doubtless be an unhappy influence
on the manners of our people produced by the existence of slavery
among us. The whole commerce between master and slave is a per-
petual exercise of the most boisterous passions, the most unremit-
ting despotism on the one part, and degrading submissions on the
other. . . . The man must be a prodigy who can retain his manners
and morals undepraved by such circumstances."[11]

Abolitionists cited Jefferson's comments to show the relation of
morality and law to the specific problem of slavery. Direct or indirect reference to Jefferson as a republican slaveholder demonstrated a cardinal element of abolitionist political thought: that
power contained the potential for abuse in all political orders, including republics, and among all political leaders, including key
republican exponents. The discrepancy advocates perceived between Jefferson's own words and deeds warned of oppression's
constant presence and of humanity's tragic fallibility.[12]

In broader terms, Jefferson's comments confirmed the evil slavery created in the conduct of masters in general and the threat slavery posed to the civic virtue of the entire people.[13] The quote demonstrated to New Hampshire reformer William Claggett that the
tyranny of the chattel system led at once to "the foundation of an
Aristocratic form of government" as well as to "vice and all manner of criminal indulgencies [sic] – to a general degeneracy of the
public morals." In law and in habit, the republic declined. Its
downward course would continue because the decay of character
itself further undermined institutional health: "When the great

mass of the people become corrupt, it is in vain to expect, that they will elect the most virtuous and enlightened citizens to office, as their law-makers. The public officer will generally be actuated by the same motives, which govern the main body of his constituents."[14]

While the abolitionists' descriptions of Southern depravity may have piqued the curiosity of audiences, advocates had other reasons for emphasizing the importance of personal character in their analysis of slavery. Claggett's words summarized the abolitionists' perspective on political relations: power was dangerous because of its tendency to expand; human beings were deeply flawed because of their often uncontrollable drives; and when these two forces joined – when a political structure allowed the exercise of excessive power and a people could indulge their base cravings – a process of mutual degeneration ensued. The "legal" legitimation of vice stirred deeper desires which further infected the conduct of public affairs and gave play to greater immorality.

The reformers' understanding of character and constitution informed their central arguments on the origins, dangers, maintenance, and defeat of slavery. Claggett, Child, Olcott, and others traced the roots of the chattel principle beyond economic, social, or racial conditions alone to passional causes, to humanity's malevolent desire for power. Though this character flaw was universal, a particularly virtuous people might contain it. If they did not, the passion for power would surely grow uncontrollable.

The abolitionists' reading of moral and political experience explained the threats of slavery. Advocates assumed that the chattel system's effects would become manifest not only in a single region or in the halls of government but also in the popular temperament, a condition vital to the republic but unaffected by normal constitutional treatment. Indeed, a fully corrupt people would likely choose to wallow in their vice rather than remedy it. The chattel system, in other words, threatened the enslavement of some and the corruption of all.[15]

The links between morality and political policy called attention to the slave power's methods for sustaining their authority. As James Birney and the Reverend George Bourne argued, slaveholders insisted that the chattel system was a purely political issue and not a moral concern at all. Political questions did not, in the masters' eyes, involve moral choices. Therefore, slavery presumably stood outside the formal and critical domain of its greatest potential critic, the church. In fact, Birney and Bourne claimed, masters insisted that the clergy's *interference* with the slave system stood as the greatest moral evil the South faced. By repudiating the connection between morality and public health, the slave interest did nothing less than repudiate a key premise of republicanism.[16]

The reformers' understanding of ethics and politics illuminated a broad strategy for abolishing slavery. If the forces of despotism and liberty each contained a crucial moral component, then the defeat of tyranny and preservation of freedom depended on something more than formal, procedural, or bureaucratic measures alone. Some inner renovation had to accompany, if not precede, institutional reformation. As the *Liberator* stated in an 1847 editorial, "the politics of a people will always be shaped by its morals, as the vane on the steeple is ever indicating in what direction the wind blows." Samuel Johnson told a Lynn, Massachusetts, congregation that they could neither depend on laws alone to safeguard freedom nor expect any mechanisms of state, religion, or the marketplace to take the lead in denouncing despotism. In a republic, he argued, "the popular character is the only reliance."[17]

In order to form that popular character, advocates stressed the importance of training the minds as well as the manners of republican citizens. For too long, political reformer Seymour Boughton Treadwell argued, the people, "'while priding itself in the education of the *head,* have lamentably neglected the education of the *heart.*'" Unfortunately, he noted, "'crime and intellectual cultivation *merely*'" went hand in hand. The refinement of moral sentiment had to accompany the exercise of analytical skills: "Our only hope as a nation must forever be in the intelligence and virtue of the great body of the people." Claggett reminded an audience that this resource was well appreciated by republican forebears: "The patriot founders of our government gave their solemn assurance, that knowledge and virtue, generally diffused, are the main pillars in the support of our political edifice." The republican utility of such an education derived from the particular kind of authority it offered the instructed, as former leader of the black Wilberforce colony, Austin Steward, explained: "Truly has it been said, 'knowledge is power.' But it is not like the withering curse of a tyrant's power; . . . but a power that elevates and refines the intellect; directs the affections; controls unholy passions; a power so God-like in its character, that it enables its possessor to feel for the oppressed of every clime, and prepares him to defend the weak and down-trodden."[18] Ignorance emboldened the despot and subdued challenges to tyrannical rule; an education grounded in self-control and public service empowered a people to fulfill the tasks of republican reform.

Calls for the cultivation of the intellectual and moral sense did not, from the abolitionists' perspective, sidestep pressing problems but addressed them directly and promised dramatic change. Charles Olcott recognized that many people, long conditioned by "habitual aristocratic prejudices," would likely view such a prospect as "incredible and impossible." He insisted, however, that moral education and the liberty it realized were "all that will ever be necessary, to insure the greatest prosperity and happiness to both races, living together unamalgamated, in a state of perfect republican equality of rights."[19] The success of reform efforts did not depend primarily on control of official channels of power; indeed, if efforts had depended on such control, abolitionism was doomed to failure because of the inroads slave interests had already made over politics, law, and religion. The republic's hope lay instead in its citizens' recognition of the passion for power, their knowledge of tyranny's morally degenerative consequences, and their commitment to virtuous behavior. Remedy would best be found in free agency rather than formal agencies.

Advocates believed that they rendered republican political instruction in a particularly fitting manner. Speaking at a July 4 celebration in 1836, Vermont abolitionist and anti-mason Edward Downing Barber warned his audience that "if the *spirit* of liberty is not maintained with its *forms*, it is but a mockery." That spirit and its rigorous conditioning had already departed the South, where "the sentiment and moral sense of the people are vitiated" by slavery and where the chattel system "has incorporated itself into their habits of life and their modes of thinking." Barber believed that a campaign to rehabilitate public character could be launched and would be successful; the elimination of slavery's republican "heresies" was at hand. It was up to Northerners to rouse themselves from their own advancing lethargy and preserve these resources for the defense of freedom.[20] To halt the enervation of liberty, Barber and other advocates sought to upset complacency, expose iniquity, revitalize virtue, and promote authentic republican principles. Reformers cast themselves in the appropriate and ideologically meaningful role of republican agitators.

Wendell Phillips reviewed the nature of abolitionist agitation in an 1852 speech before the Massachusetts Anti-Slavery Society.[21] He reported the spread of antislavery sentiment and attributed its growing influence to reformers who had accurately read the political condition of the nation. Advocates appreciated the fearful consequences of power, even within a republican order; they recognized the inadequacy of institutional protections alone against the expansion of tyranny; and they understood the need for an informed citizenry to defend freedom. The reformers' concerns led them to a disturbing realization: because power posed an ever-present threat, the security of the republic could never be finally settled. It was not within the nature of republics – even those attentive to the subtle encroachments of power – to achieve repose. Such carelessness was more the mark of a nation corrupted by despotism than of a people devoted to liberty. The tyrant urged calm among subjects, the better to entrap his victims; the patriot urged wariness, the better to detect oppression. In vigilance lay the protection and perpetuation of a republic. Abolitionists knew, as Phillips said, that "there is no Canaan in politics." To the contrary, "Republics exist only on the tenure of being constantly agitated. The antislavery agitation is an important, nay, an essential part of the machinery of the state. It is not a disease or a medicine. No; it is the normal state, – the normal state of the nation."[22]

To consider agitation aberrant was to misunderstand the very nature of republicanism. Far from representing anything extraordinary or destructive, abolitionist agitation was a requirement of the republic, part of the routine maintenance of liberty. The greatest threat to the republic's stability, as Theodore Parker argued, came from injustice, not from agitation on behalf of rights and equality. The very "life of liberty," New York minister and Tappan associate George Cheever wrote, lay in the "unlimited freedom of examination, disputation, and conflict of opinion." The public needed to realize that "[a]gitation, the conflict of opinion, the freest comparison and battle of thought, is what we need . . . . [I]f every thing is to be kept close and quiet, it may be a stagnant despotism, but never a LIVING STATE.[23]

Abolitionists viewed the work of agitation not as an end in itself but as a necessary chore to keep their republican house in order. As the *National Anti-Slavery Standard* stated: "Liberty is only to be maintained, and, if lost, recovered, by an active conflict of opposing opinions." The agitator was the "true friend to the peace of the country," exposing the danger a people faced and "the ruin that is working destruction, and is sure to break forth every year with a new desolation." What had abolitionists done, asked a New England Anti-Slavery Society committee, other than "to collect and to disseminate correct information, to argue, to answer objections, and to advise." This activity, far from promoting confusion or disorder, was "the indispensable condition, the conservative principle of every republic." Before complaining of agitation or attempting to quell it, Charles Olcott noted, the public should "first endeavor to suppress all republican institutions and publications, and abolish republican principles entirely; on account of their 'inflammatory tendency,' to disturb the peace of tyranny." The settled pattern of republican life ought to leave citizens purposely unsettled.[24]

Advocates proclaimed that the work of agitation followed the model established by republican forebears. While critical of founders who did not extend liberty to all, Douglass nevertheless praised those who "preferred revolution to peaceful submission to bondage," who "did not shrink from agitating against oppression," and "who believed in order; but not in the order of tyranny." In an 1838 Independence Day oration, Garrison linked his fellow reformers with James Otis, Joseph Warren, Patrick Henry, and other heroes of the founding. These illustrious figures, Garrison said, would hardly be angered to hear scorching criticism of the nation, even on occasions of nominal celebration; they, of all people, understood the Fourth as a celebration of agitation. Phillips extended the argument, noting that "'agitation was commenced when the Declaration of Independence was signed; it took its second tide when the Antislavery Declaration was signed in 1833.'" Rev. Cheever pushed the reformers' "war of thoughts and words" further back in time, tying their agitational efforts to the "noble Algernon Sidney." Abolitionist and nonresistant Charles King Whipple also invoked a long line of agitational heroes, ranging from Brutus to Sidney to Kosciusko to Washington, all "resisters" of tyrannical authority. These were "the predecessors," Whipple wrote, "whose traitorous footsteps we follow."[25]

However much abolitionists meant to continue the founders' agitational legacy and to challenge the public mind, reformers argued that their exhortations did not signify distrust of the masses. Rather, advocates conceived of their agitation as a tactic justified and required by the distinctive role public opinion played in a republic. Reformers claimed to take seriously the belief that government's "foundation rests on public opinion." The abolitionist's task was "to purify the public opinion" and to restore the "seat of sovereignty" to its rightful holders, the people at large. Their will would be reached and properly instructed by the "inquiry," "exhortation," "warning and admonition" that lay at the heart of abolitionist agitation.[26] Edward Barber wrote that this was precisely the reason why abolitionists engaged in their efforts: "If slavery existed in despotic governments . . . , we should have no means of reaching it – it would then be controlled by an Autocrat or an Aristocrat whom discussion or the public voice would not affect. . . . But where the people are the source of power, you have but to obtain their voice in favor of any measure and the object is accomplished. Their will is law."[27] Reform activity, Phillips argued, purposely sought to acknowledge the republican principle of popular rule by setting all "*thinking* on the subject of slavery," anticipating that "[t]he moment we have the control of public opinion, – the women and the children, the school-houses, the school-books, the

republican institutions, even for the educated yeomanry of New England, without the protecting shadow of a royal throne, or its equivalent in some form."[30] Leaders who harbored such deep suspicions of whites could hardly be expected to champion the cause of blacks. The chattel system that emerged had a doubly tyrannical face: slavery explicitly subjugated an entire race while it implicitly denigrated a republic's most reliable power, "the unfettered average common sense of the masses."[31]

Reform would come about only through the efforts of those who fully assented to the principles of the Declaration "which must lie at the basis of any consistent and thorough agitation for the present removal of slavery."[32] Abolitionists believed that their agitation endorsed rather than assailed republican principles; it upheld rather than upended genuine republican order. Agitation was needed because of power's continuing threats to liberty; agitation was valid because of its status as a long-standing republican ritual; agitation was incumbent upon those who located the seat of ultimate authority in the people rather than in political institutions.

Abolitionists shared both a common framework of political assumptions and a distinctive part in political debate. Yet advocates so united by their convictions and their role differed sharply on the way republican agitators ought to shape the political order. One issue that brought these matters to a head involved the formation of an abolitionist party. The proposal struck some as the logical extension of the agitators' responsibilities and others as the shameful abdication of those tasks. The controversy demonstrates how abolitionists assigned multiple meanings to key republican principles. Their informing ideology could both unite and divide the reform movement.

Before sharp disagreements over an antislavery party arose in 1839–1840, the question of political action generated little debate within the reform movement. Advocates who petitioned officials and questioned candidates had little difficulty squaring their activity with abolition goals set out in the 1833 Declaration of Sentiments and Constitution of the American Anti-Slavery Society. The Declaration stated "that there are, at the present time, the highest

93

obligations resting upon the people of the free States, to remove Slavery by moral and political action, as prescribed in the Constitution of the United States." Article II of the Society's constitution held that abolitionists "will also endeavor, in a constitutional way, to influence Congress to put an end to the domestic slave-trade, and to abolish slavery in all those portions of our common country which come under its control, especially in the District of Columbia, – and likewise to prevent the extension of it to any state that may be hereafter admitted to the Union."[33]

The party proposal, however, involved significant changes both in tactics and in obligations. Advocates would no longer simply carry their message to the unsympathetic Whig Party and Democratic Party in hope of one day building a base of support among government officials. By running slates of abolitionist candidates, reformers would be *among* those officials, making their presence felt inside as well as outside the halls of government.

Key sponsors of the project, including James G. Birney, Alvan Stewart, Gerrit Smith, Joshua Leavitt, and Elizur Wright, Jr., believed in the propriety and necessity of political action. Proponents pointed to the inadequacy of earlier antislavery tactics, the political potential of a tightly organized minority, and the need to attack slavery on several fronts. Such proposals struck others in the movement as both misguided and unprincipled. A diverse group of abolitionists, ranging from supporters of William Lloyd Garrison to anti-Garrisonian critics, condemned the idea of an abolitionist party and feared it would weaken, if not destroy, the reform movement. According to opponents, the campaign sacrificed the purity of abolition appeals by courting voters unchanged in their attitudes toward slavery; party activity diverted attention away from the project of social reform to the daily business of political organization; the effort created dissension within antislavery ranks; and the venture exposed abolitionism's numerical weakness in the political community.[34]

In April 1840 party proponents took two decisive steps, forming the "Liberty" Party and nominating James G. Birney as its presidential candidate with a platform that focused on slavery alone. The party drew only 7,000 votes for its national slate and performed, at best, as a balance-of-power pressure group on the state and county levels. In 1844, the organization went with Birney again and received some 63,000 ballots. During these years, low vote totals dismayed many party members; some debated the wisdom of a narrow platform; still others believed that the best hope for the Liberty movement would come from union with antislavery Whigs and Democrats repelled by their own parties.

The Liberty Party floundered until 1848 when it finally broke apart. Many members, such as Henry B. Stanton, Joshua Leavitt, John Greenleaf Whittier, and Gamaliel Bailey, threw their support to the new Free Soil Party organized by Democratic followers of Martin Van Buren and "Conscience" Whigs. Though Free Soilers spoke only to the nonextension of slavery and made few appeals on the national level for racial equality, abolitionist supporters believed their presence in the party would refine and ultimately elevate its platform. Other emancipationists, such as William Goodell, Gerrit Smith, Francis Julius LeMoyne, and Elihu Burrit, created yet another abolitionist party, the Liberty League, which, from 1847 to 1861, openly committed itself to ending slavery and racism. The League fielded fewer candidates for office than the Liberty Party, however, and enjoyed even less electoral success. Meanwhile, debates over abolition parties fed organizational schisms. The party issue played a major role in the breakup of the American Anti-Slavery Society, which, as abolitionism's single "national" organization, had stood for nearly a decade as a sign of reform unity. After May 1840, new national associations, especially the American and Foreign Anti-Slavery Society, vied for the support of emancipationists.[35]

Despite the duration and intensity of the party debate, the two sides grounded their arguments in similar sets of assumptions. Opponents as well as proponents denounced the prevailing state of political organization and invoked themes of antipartyism and moral agitation in their appeals. Both groups assumed that a republican analysis of power provided the most persuasive and comprehensive account of America's political condition.

Opponents appealed to a familiar set of fears concerning the dangers of parties. Conventional republican wisdom from the

Revolution through the first national administrations associated parties with factions, the secretive cabals of special interest that manipulated the many in order to serve the few. Parties were the products of opportunism, selfish advantage, and authoritarianism; they embodied corruption and concentrated power, the principle threats to republican stability. The party appeared to have no legitimate place within a republican order.[36] Those who questioned the abolition party plan found such traditional arguments applicable to their own circumstances. Opponents suspected that parties, by their very nature, sacrificed principle, disregarded pledges, and resorted to "miserable trickery"; citizens could find "no honesty, no humanity" within such bodies. By professing "ultra-republican claims," parties exploited patriotic sentiment and rewarded it with "republicanism [that] is a mockery of human rights."[37] By appealing to self-interest and exclusivity, parties encouraged members to seal themselves off from others in society and from comprehensive, disinterested proposals for national reform, rewarding inwardness and self-centeredness rather than public service. And by concentrating on political victory and organizational expansion, parties cultivated the dangerous love of power. Taken together, these aspects of party activity presented nothing less than the specter of despotism, breeding a passion for personal ambition and aggrandizement that was of particular danger to a republican society.[38]

Rather than strengthening moral fiber, parties were agencies of demoralization and corruption; possessed of no moral character, they encouraged members to dissociate morality from politics. Rather than enhancing freedom among its adherents, parties robbed them of their personal independence; party duty required subservience to the organization and silence in the face of its errors. And rather than fostering a spirit of public citizenship, parties addressed society as a collection of private individuals; the organization thereby divided the wholeness of the community.[39] In the eyes of critics, parties jeopardized virtue, liberty, and civic responsibility, the foundations of a stable republic. Maria Weston Chapman added that party activity not only undermined republican order but also misplaced republican energies: "In a republican land the power behind the throne is *the* power. Save yourself the trouble of calling caucuses, printing party journals, distributing ballots, and the like. Let men who are fit for nothing of more consequence do this little work, which is best done by mere nobodies. . . . Don't drag the engine, like an ignoramus, but bring wood and water and flame, like an engineer."[40]

Others observed that the party spirit even existed in reform associations, representing a danger that vigilant advocates had to monitor. Connecticut minister William Barnes feared that reform societies had the potential for all sorts of republican nuisance: "They excite passion and party spirit, and beget intolerance and proscription and lord it over private judgment and conscience, and rely upon machinery and numbers rather than argument, in the propagation of truth, and prompt men not individually and intelligently, but collectively and blindly to follow dictating leaders, as a flock of wild geese follow their pilot." Charles Olcott argued that the antislavery movement should not perpetuate itself any longer than necessary; the organization ought to dissolve itself once Americans became "abolitionized." In the meantime, Garrison noted, reformers had to steer clear of narrowness, special interest, and tyrannical leadership; by avoiding these errors they would preserve "the *republican* character of the anti-slavery cause." The Massachusetts Anti-Slavery Society offered another piece of republican advice, to decentralize reform efforts: "The less power there is lodged in the hands of any select body of men, – to a certain extent, at least, – whether in Church or State, in any philanthropic or moral reform, the less danger there will be of corruption, usurpation, perversion."[41]

Party activity not only weakened republican principles but also prevented reformers from carrying out their key republican task of moral agitation. One critic charged that party advocates made the survival and expansion of the political organization paramount to all other considerations. "Party abolitionists" followed the path all party members took: "they will go for party, rather than anti-slavery, when the two conflict. . . . It is to party they would mainly owe their elections, and party would govern their action." Immediate emancipation had little chance of success under such arrangements. Another route to abolition held far more promise: to "rely mainly on the creation of moral principle, for the slave's deliverance, and for that purpose we would agitate the country."[42]

Other critics feared that party behavior jeopardized the leadership of reform efforts. Philadelphian Lewis C. Gunn argued that abolition party sponsors placed the critical job of moral agitation in the least capable hands: "Did they suppose that *politicians* would run in advance of the *people* on moral questions?" Such had never been the case. Reform advocates themselves had to "retain and continue to exert our power of moral conviction." The party opponent "Quintius" wrote that "an independent political organization would diminish, if not annihilate, this power" of moral resolve. Even if a party did not destroy moral commitment, even if, by some strange turn, party officials applied themselves to moral agitation, the idea of placing moral leadership in politicians was still a serious error. The motives of politicians were always suspect; the motives of the moral agitator had to be above reproach. However honorable and dedicated a politician might be, the public assumed that office-seekers were not disinterested. Such pervasive doubts could not be erased; who could convince citizens not to hold them? The popular trust that a moral agitator had to enjoy would not be present. The lesson for reformers was clear: parties and their representatives could not provide moral guidance. The party proposal was not just a miscalculation but a fundamentally flawed understanding of the way any moral enterprise progressed.[43]

Party opponents believed that the public had good reason for its mistrust. Wendell Phillips charged that political parties were incapable of moral advocacy since they, like all other political institutions, would eventually come under the control of the slave power. The greater the slave power's influence, the less likely any such organization could act as a moral leaven. A reformer could not expect parties to abolish slavery because, as William Ingersoll Bowditch wrote, "these institutions are merely the manifestation in part of *the very evil which he wishes to overthrow*."[44]

Bowditch, affiliated with the American Anti-Slavery Society, urged reformers to rely "on the exercise of moral power alone," a resource that corrupted institutions did not wield. Such a force would serve "to change the hearts of the people, to make them feel that all men are brethren," and to reform popular ideas and habits. The rehabilitation of character and conduct that would follow offered the only hope for defeating tyranny and its attendant moral ills. The principles of abolition first had to "go down into the hearts of men – they must be urged upon the conscience by other means and on other occasions than a political caucus, before a majority of the voters of the nation, or of any particular section of the nation, will cast their vote for the sole object of electing an abolitionist."[45]

Tyranny's advance rested on virtue's fall, not on political miscalculation. To correct the problem, Garrison wrote, "moral reformation is necessary to produce an enlightened, conscientious, impartial political action." That reformation would come through agitation unencumbered by the restraints and perils of political organization. Garrison insisted that "a man must first be abolitionized" before he would "be able or willing to burst the shackles of party, and give his vote for the slave." Then he would be able to "'take care of himself,'" and could be "'turned loose' with perfect safety." An informed and elevated public opinion, Garrison continued, would grow under the influence of the abolitionists' moral agitation and would eventually pursue a political solution to the problem of slavery. Reformers would not succeed until they abandoned party projects and pursued moral agitation outside the structures of American political life. As Phillips said, "Liberty rises up, as she did in '76, and tramples *forms* under her feet, and says, 'By the living God! I go for the ESSENCE!'"[46]

Changes in public opinion would not take place suddenly. Because citizens had been misled for so long – and because proslavery forces grew ever more brazen in their defense of the chattel system – abolitionists had to expect public sentiment to come around slowly. The key question for moral agitators was not whether their strategy would succeed but whether reformers would maintain their convictions: "It will take but a very short time, comparatively, for the 'little leaven' of anti-slavery to leaven the whole lump of politics, provided abolitionists hold fast their integrity, and have faith as a grain of mustard-seed. *Both political parties will yet be compelled to do homage to the moral majesty of our enterprise, . . ."*[47]

For the present, the *National Anti-Slavery Standard* declared, "The business of the Abolitionists is with the ideas and not with the machinery which those ideas have set in motion." Advocates needed to "strengthen and sharpen the opinions and emotions of the people," alerting citizens to the passional roots of power, the corrupting influence of parties, the critical functions of character, and the trustworthiness of an informed public moved to action by moral exhorters.[48]

Opponents of an abolition party were not alone in their republican concerns. The party's proponents also appealed to traditional republican principles in their assessment – and criticism – of political parties. Party advocates presented themselves as reluctant politicos, approaching the business, form, and policies of parties with considerable trepidation.[49] Proponents claimed to create their organizations as a way of serving republican goals. In their view, the party could act as a republican means to a republican end.

One of the supporters' key themes was their party's avoidance of the antirepublicanism displayed by Whig and Democratic Party supporters. While members of the large national parties considered their organizations as ends in themselves, reformers asserted their dedication first and foremost to the goal of human liberty. By "aiming to base all our laws in a recognition of the rights of man," one proponent argued, abolitionists established "the just foundation of a party in a great republic." While Whigs and Democrats sought "their own and not others' good," satisfying their self-interest through any possible means, the abolitionist party claimed to rise above corruption and selfishness. As Lewis Tappan wrote, "We contend – not for men but for great moral principles, principles infinitely above Tariffs, Banks, or Lands." While the major parties cared little about the virtuous character of the polity, reformers emphasized the close connection between morality and politics. While Whigs and Democrats demonstrated their talent for evasion and expediency, emancipationists promised to stand firm on their stated objectives. And while the largest political organizations proved incapable of defending liberty because of their own subservience to the slave power, the abolitionist party pledged obedience to no force other than the ideals of the republic.[50]

Because they drew on a long-standing tradition of antipartyism, proponents at times echoed the sentiments of other political reformers, conceiving of their work in terms quite similar to those used by leaders of the major political organizations. For example, the abolitionists were not alone in their condemnation of narrow, self-serving political groups; Martin Van Buren had drawn on this theme nearly three decades earlier in his own political arguments. Van Buren's other appeals, however, help demonstrate some of the conceptual differences in the abolitionists' party: while Van Buren emphasized the importance of a mass organization, party loyalty, and the preservation of the Union, abolitionists focused attention on agitational leadership, personal conviction, and the preservation of Revolutionary principles.[51]

Reformers charged that many in politics assumed the name "Democrat" or "Whig" but betrayed the basic tenets associated with those terms. The abolitionists, as Joshua Leavitt and others announced, sought "enlightened and honest men who are true to the principles of republicanism." Those with impeccable republican credentials could be trusted to act in the interest of freedom.[52] Supporters asserted that party members had enacted the founders' ideals in an appropriately republican manner. Their organization did not seek to abolish slavery by expanding government power, a strategy that would only create another source of tyranny. Instead, the party sought to use existing republican guarantees of liberty, respecting at once legislative supremacy, states' rights, and the spirit of the Declaration of Independence.[53]

Proponents who hailed the republican character of their party referred, secondly, to its republican origins. Advocates maintained that their organization was not a novel political exercise or a departure from past standards but one that recalled and surpassed basic republican commitments. Its members followed "the example of our fathers (not of their opposite sons) to pledge to the maintenance of the heaven-born principles of the Declaration of American Independence, their lives, their fortunes, and their sacred honor, and to carry these principles to the polls and the legislative Halls." The party, as Tappan noted, "revived the principles of the leaders of the American revolution"; it sought, as others observed, "to complete their great work, to remove from the republic the great cause of derangement and ruin." The abolition party not only continued the ideals and methods of republican forebears; as Liberty Party leaders proclaimed, their organization grew out of the very processes of human experience identified by republican historical thought: "The Liberty party of 1845 is, in truth, the Liberty party of 1776 revived. It is more; It is the party of Advancement and Freedom, which has, in every age, and with varying success, fought the battles of Human Liberty, against the party of False Conservatism and Slavery."[54]

The comments of Liberty Party leaders pointed to a third theme in the proponents' argument. Because the party fulfilled Revolutionary tasks in such a distinctive manner, advocates held that their organization was not an example of politics as usual; indeed, supporters insisted that their project was not a "party" at all in the conventional sense of the term. Liberty Party members attending an 1845 meeting urged the public not to consider the movement as "factious" but to see it as the defender of "Impartial, Universal Liberty," an organization bound to win favor in the nation. It was nothing less than a "libel upon the intelligence, the patriotism, and the virtue of the American people to say that there is no hope that a majority will not array themselves under our banner." New York conventioneers declared that they had not mounted their effort in order to undercut and eliminate an opposition: "We have organized such a party – not to defeat any proper object of either of the other parties – but to unite with all that is most valuable in the objects of both." Though appearing "in the attitude of a distinct party," an Albany gathering resolved, supporters would not coerce obedience or violate the freedom of members; the organization purposely rejected "what some think implied in party management."[55]

Rather than engaging in the divisive, destructive practices of the Whig and Democratic parties, proponents charted a different course: they would act "in behalf of the Liberty, not the third party, but the first party – the great original party which in 1776 asserted the great principles of Liberty against the despotism of the British Government." Advocates shared one simple obligation – "instead of supporting a first, second, or third *party*, to rise above all party." Ultimately, as American and Foreign Anti-Slavery Society executives wrote in 1848, the Liberty Party did not seek its own preservation above all other goals; rather, the party anticipated the day when abolition principles would be so widely accepted that it could suspend operations. By satisfying its primary objective, the party would cease to exist.[56]

Gerrit Smith declared that party advocates refused to tamper with individual freedom, guarded against the dangers of servility, and promoted disinterested service to the republic. "In a word," he wrote, "such an association is a no-party party." Its sponsors not only announced but applied republican antiparty standards to their work. Because of this, Smith reasoned, party advocates and their opponents actually stood on common ground, united by their hostility to the corrupting influence of traditional political organizations. Party proponents remained confident, however, that a steady adherence to principles of liberty and virtue would keep their organization on the proper republican path. Who was better prepared to take on such a project and maintain moral resolve? As Ohio Senator Thomas Morris wrote, abolitionists presented a "new, strange and cheering phenomenon" to the world: a body of individuals selflessly devoted to the extension of freedom, securing the natural rights "promised to all men as the chief corner-stone of our republican edifice."[57]

The assurance of Smith and Morris spoke to a fourth theme raised by party promoters. Far from weakening their own campaign or endangering the republic, sponsors insisted that an antislavery party was the proper vehicle for moral agitation. Because American politics had degenerated into a festering pool of immorality, there was no better place for moral exhorters to apply their skills. They needed to bestow their uplifting touch directly to those areas of political endeavor most in need of moral renovation.

Once again, party sponsors embraced their opponents' categories of analysis. Advocates agreed that the root of America's political turmoil lay outside institutions. The state of the nation's character primarily determined the direction of the republic: "The great faults of parties and their leaders, arise not so much from politics, as the low intellectual and moral state of the country. . . . Educate the people, elevate their moral standard, and parties will be wiser and more honest, and their leaders act on higher principles." While applying moral pressure outside the republic's institutions, however, abolitionists ought not abandon similar efforts within the political arena. Parties offered little moral guidance in the past, but political organizations led by abolitionists could teach important lessons in character and conduct. A party of such refined purpose provided a model of moral discipline, a clear and compelling example of the goals for which a people should aim: "form an anti-slavery party, – show the nation something worth contending about, . . . and all the moral power of the country will soon be found in our ranks."[58]

As Lewis Tappan explained, those who accepted such a project only implemented the common abolitionist belief in the links between politics and morality. Rather than watching immorality play itself out in political affairs – and rather than allowing politics to debilitate morality even further – some abolitionists had decided to step in and redirect events. Those who rallied under an abolition party banner, Tappan wrote, would be "bearing a testimony against the two great political parties," and encouraging "people to regard moral principle in their political acts."[59] Advocates would establish a higher standard for political behavior and remind citizens of the moral consequences that political acts held. Party proponents thus provided a clear lesson in the work of political morality.

An abolition party did not present an alternative to moral agitation; it did not challenge, weaken, or abandon efforts at moral suasion. Rather it represented another way of "purifying the public mind." Abolitionists engaged in party activity "not as a substitute, or means of greater power than moral suasion, but simply as an adjunct, and a practical commentary upon the doctrines they teach."[60] Proponents intended their party to serve as an agitational force, designed to prod, berate, and exhort those inside as well as outside the organization. Enlisting in such a cause "will purify and elevate the character of those who support it, and purge them from the dross of vulgar politicians. Have not those who have heretofore joined us, had their souls formed and enlightened by the ennobling object which they pursued?"

Even political and moral backsliders attracted to the party for base motives would presumably pose no threat to the party's operation and ideals. As one proponent admitted, some might try to use the party for selfish gain or personal aggrandizement. While such individuals would be welcome in the major parties, they would find neither encouragement nor satisfaction among reformers: "We elevate and improve lower minds when we induce them to unite with us for worthy objects." Such refinement would proceed "as surely and effectually as any course of preaching or moral lectures."[61]

Advocates declared that the moral influence of an abolition party would even reach those who bore no affiliation to it. Members might regret that their numbers were not greater, but the process of building the party's base of support had to take time. The public, so accustomed to the major parties, would be "weaned" rather slowly from the established organizations. While abolitionists waited for a change to occur, however, their own party would have a continuing impact on American political activity. Outsiders who observed the ideals, actions, and courage of the abolitionist organization would come to recognize "the absence of all moral principles in their parties."[62] By showing others how conventional politics violated the best interests of the republic, abolition party supporters believed that they fulfilled in one more way the role of moral agitator.

Party proponents insisted that their project did not moderate abolition goals, did not transform an agitation movement into a political pressure group, and did not force advocates to choose between moral reformation and political action. Rather, advocates conceived of their party as a way to maintain the reform movement's fundamental commitments while expanding the range of abolition agitation.

It appears ironic that advocates who so consistently measured their actions by republican standards found their movement so deeply divided over critical political questions. This might seem the one area where reformers concerned with the disposition of power would find common cause. Should not the abolitionists' informing principles have generated greater harmony in their ranks? Perhaps, unless one looks at the question from another perspective. Considering the diverse readings of Revolutionary ideals and the varieties of republicanism expressed in American life from the late-eighteenth to the mid-nineteenth centuries, the greater surprise may not be how much division existed among abolitionists but, rather, how little.

Advocates found in the language and principles of republicanism a way to make sense of their world; they perceived a distinctively republican crisis in their political order; and they claimed, in the midst of that turmoil, to stand as the true heirs of the Revolution. Common assumptions about the state of politics and the role of reformers underlay disagreements among advocates: both critics and proponents of the party plan presupposed the aggressiveness of power, the influence of character on constitution, the corruption of established parties, and the necessity of moral agitation.

Still, the question of an antislavery party did help spark personal and organizational division within the reform movement. Debate continued for decades over how to transform American political behavior and where to apply moral force. The advocates' republican beliefs may have offered them a common frame of reference. But their quest for republican purity proved difficult and elusive. The reformers' source of unity could also serve as the base of strategic and organizational division. In this respect, advocates shared in the main patterns of American life far more than they may have realized or even desired: as in the nation at large, the society of abolitionists encountered the ominous gap between republicanism confidently invoked and republicanism peacefully secured.

5

THE COSTS OF LIBERTY

THE ABOLITIONIST ARGUMENT

ON POLITICAL ECONOMY

ON SEPTEMBER 21, 1849, Rev. Daniel Foster addressed the people in his home community of Danvers, Massachusetts, on the subject of slavery. In his opening remarks, Foster emphasized the momentous choice facing his listeners, pointing to the particular evil that the chattel system represented: "We exert an inevitable and most important influence in the decision of the one transcendent question, on the right and speedy settlement of which depends, more or less intimately, the well-being of all men. That question is, 'Shall slavery be extended and perpetuated in our land, giving over society to the desolation of unrestrained *selfishness*?'"[1]

Foster's concern may appear unusual or even misplaced to modern eyes. Out of the many conceivable dangers posed by the chattel system, one might imagine that the problem of "selfishness" would not hold a position of such urgency and importance. Yet Foster merely echoed a frequently stated fear among reformers about slavery. His remarks and those of fellow advocates point to a critical – if initially puzzling – component of the abolition argument.

The warnings that Foster and others raised over the chattel system's "selfish" force were part of a larger set of assumptions reformers held about the political economy of slavery. In their critical examinations of the slave system, advocates often directed attention to matters of labor and class relations and reflected on questions of utilitarianism and liberal commitments. But Foster's comments suggest one other important subject of political economy, a theme prominent in reform appeals though relatively neglected in recent scholarship: the interconnections between the economics of slavery and questions of ethics and politics.[2]

In discussions that tended to be long on agitation and short on systematic rigor, abolitionists traced out the links between slavery's material base and the wider society. Although the empirical validity of reform claims remains open for question, the language, imagery, and assumptions of the abolition argument pointed in a clear direction: advocates maintained that their opponents were not only masters of slaves but also masters of the market. Reformers portrayed the slave power as a body that dominated economic relations, internalized the mercenary standards of the marketplace, and sought to institutionalize those codes throughout the nation. The enemy, in other words, hoped to subordinate the polity and society completely to the principles of economic transaction, conducting life according to the ledger book rather than the Good Book. The abolitionists' response to this question of political economy offered them an understanding of how the chattel system had advanced and at what cost to republican liberty the slave power had succeeded in its ambitions.

The reformers' concern with the interrelations of economics, ethics, and politics grew not only from established traditions of political economy[3] but also from the informing ideas of the abolition movement itself. Those who saw slavery as a sin believed that the unrepentant brought the mark of their transgression to every private and public act in their lives. In the words of evangelical reformer George B. Cheever, slavery was "a fountain sin, a germinating sin, an accumulating and multiplying sin, a sin that causes and compels others to sin, a sin that enlarges from generation to generation." The continuous compounding of slavery's evil that Cheever described theologically had its historical equivalent in the passages from *Notes on the State of Virginia* that advocates quoted so frequently. Echoing Jefferson's concerns about "the whole commerce between master and slave," abolitionists feared that the chattel system bred habits of passion and despotism which would infect the wielder of power as it degraded the manners, morals, industry, and liberties of a people.[4] The philosophical assumptions of other reformers also described a world in which a people's shared commitments shaped and united their apparently distinct spheres of life – often in the service of evil. Wendell Phillips argued that a clear and coherent principle of order lay beneath the nation's chaotic surface: ultimately, the bewildering variety of American life was reducible to those elements allied with slavery and those which served liberty. And Theodore Parker maintained that Southern society in particular formed a meaningful whole because of its remarkable harmony of "sentiment," "idea," and "action"; dedication to the chattel principle tied together the region's investments, structure, power, and beliefs.[5]

The "interdisciplinary" point of view that Parker and others expressed suggested that one could not separate economic decisions from matters of morality or governance. "The holy principles of freedom" which reformers embraced suggested that one should not make the distinction. Abolitionists insisted on righteous and republican principles to guide all behavior, including conduct in business and trade.[6] They feared that the chattel system reversed the order: on an unprecedented and ever-widening scale, the slave power made the market the measure of all things.

The issue, as reformers defined it, was not simply one of holding money or desiring wealth; they knew the North had its legions of "mammon-worshippers," too.[7] The slave interest, however, formed a most peculiar sect, one that pursued its creed to an extent unimagined elsewhere.

Reformers outlined several reasons why the slave power's "faith" posed a unique and ominous threat. First, and most importantly, the slave interest's obsessive love of gain led to more than a desire for material goods and intangible assets; slaveholders also sought that which, presumably, could not be possessed. Second, as they engaged in their quest, slaveholders felt free to transgress republican principle, natural law, and even divine command. Third, the slave interests exclusively obeyed the stratagems of the marketplace, their actions guided by self-aggrandizement, shrewd calculation, and pecuniary values.

Abolitionists saw the effects of an enterprising slave power played out in a variety of ways. The first step the slave power took on its perverse course was to redefine the very idea of material resources, radically and recklessly expanding the range of entities that could be conceived of as property. "The very essence and definition of slavery," Illinois abolitionists noted, rested in the fact "that the slaves are considered in law not as men, but as things – as *goods* and *chattels*." The *Anti-Slavery Record* agreed: "The cause which has brought blighting and mildew upon southern hearts as well as southern fields, is the turning of *men* into merchandise." In Frederick Douglass's words, the master transformed humanity into "a marketable commodity."[8] Reformers believed that appeals to benevolent feeling made no impression on the customers for this new breed of property; masters also imaginatively revised biblical warnings about the sin of "man-stealing"; and they dismissed out of hand arguments on equality of natural rights.[9] The slaveholder's sense of "property" had no apparent limit. No moral, religious, or political injunction could serve as a barrier to its inclusive and aggressive expansion. The slave power's first and greatest offense, then, came not simply from engaging in economic exchange but from making human beings the object of economic exchange.

In turn, the "chattelizing" of humanity confirmed the central trait that reformers beheld in the slaveholder. The person who set about "converting his brother man into a mere instrument for the promotion of his own interest," who not only pursued private gain but did so "through the sacrifice of the rights of the other," and who habitually engaged in these acts "without restraint or correction" stood as the very embodiment of "selfishness." This was no mere self-centeredness. In the language of reformers it meant acting as an agent of unbounded appropriation. "Selfish" individuals hoped to absorb the world within themselves, using any means possible. They exhibited what one advocate said of slavery: "a hateful supremacy over every other consideration."[10]

Slavery, as described by reformers, was perfectly suited to the exaltation of self. It produced wealth based on the labors of others and required no expenditure of energy from oneself. Slaveholders neither engaged in nor honored labor; they expected that rewards would come effortlessly.[11] Slavery offered a life of pure self-indulgence, allowing masters the free and unrestricted reign of will and passion. Without the checks of conscience, heart, or obligation, slavery promoted habits of irresponsible power, cruel force, and immoral impulse. All of these problems continually built on one another: selfishness generated idleness and indulgence; base and artificial wants multiplied; the demands on slaves increased; and satisfied demand spawned new selfish desires. Slavery, as Phillips observed, followed a steadily downward course, "adding horror to horror, bloody statute to bloody statute, selfishness to selfishness, . . ."[12] In the closed and tightly interwoven domain of slavery, selfishness grew ever larger. The masters born into this world, bred in its self-serving habits, and guided by its "intrinsically and unchangeably selfish" legal relations were themselves selfish – not as a quirk of personality but as the predictable outcome of an order. As Charles C. Burleigh stated before the American Anti-Slavery Society, the administrators of slavery "must naturally and necessarily tend to become like the system which they administer."[13]

Slaveholders saw no need to control their behavior; they domineered as a matter of reflex; and they felt "contempt for all human rights, which [their] own selfishness [could] not appropriate." In other words, the slave power had no experience in self-government – and neither the preparation nor the capacity for "private virtue, or . . . true republicanism." Instead, they let their political imaginations run in the direction of selfishness. Political ideas concocted by minds such as these, Parker wrote, "must lead to a corresponding government; that will be unjust in its substance – for it will depend not on natural right, but on personal force; not on the constitution of the universe, but on the compact of men. . . . Its form will be despotism – the government of all by a part, for the sake of a part."[14] Tyrannical abuses of power, the essence of oppression, were merely "the workings of the selfish principle in man."[15] By attacking liberty, the slave power stayed in character.

The slaveholders' scorn for freedom may have seemed obvious when they denied the humanity and inalienable rights of slaves. But reformers sensed that some observers might still think it unfair to indict slaveholders so harshly as the "enemies" of freedom; for surely, even those who had aggressively and coldly acquired human merchandise would jealously protect their own right to claim and use that property. Some residual regard for freedom *had* to exist, even among despots.

Reformers disagreed, claiming that the circumstances of Southern law and custom – created by the slave power itself – demonstrated how far liberty had flown from the region. Slaveholders did not enjoy the right to dispose of their property freely; legislation restricted emancipation. They could not freely improve the value of their property; teaching slaves to read, for example, was a crime. Slaveholders could not freely discuss the slave system; the mere hint of disapproval, reformers argued, brought legal and extra-legal retaliation.[16]

One reform article suggested that the slaveholders' responses to these conditions revealed their true feelings about freedom. Slaveholders who voluntarily submitted to restrictions could not have had much love for liberty; by refusing to raise petitions, appeals, or suits, they willingly surrendered "the common republican means of getting tyrannical laws repealed." Slaveholders who involuntarily submitted probably had no love of liberty to begin with. And those who remained unaware of restrictions were so far removed from liberty, so drenched in despotism, that they suffered "a disregard of human rights; an inability even to comprehend them."[17]

James W. C. Pennington, a former bondsman aligned with the Tappans in the American and Foreign Anti-Slavery Society, offered his own thoughts on the slaveholder's constraints and suggested one other category of persons who held slaves: those who evaded restrictions. Even in their hearts, Pennington argued, the current of freedom did not flow. Slaveholders who circumvented formal codes only demonstrated the arbitrary approach they took to law and exposed their tyranny all the more.[18]

For Pennington and others, questions about the slaveholders' use of their own property provided convincing proof of slave-power tyranny. Slaveholders denied liberty to slaves, despised the exercise of liberty among most whites, and distrusted liberty even among themselves. But if slaveholders were not deeply committed to disposing of chattel as they wished, what did they desire? The answer was simple: having access to chattel. Once again the imperatives of the market took precedence over ethical or political principle. Slaveholders proved they were far more interested in the acquisition of property than in the rights of property; their passion burned for engrossment rather than entitlement.

In the eyes of reformers, the slave power built a world on the model of the market: it merchandised mankind, encoded accumulation, and systematized selfishness. Abolitionists held that these actions not only shaped the relation of master and slave but ordered the structure of the South as a whole.

The transformation of people into things altered the South's conception of "property." By amassing so much of this property, the slave power defined the region's conception of "wealth." But in its constant pursuit of *selfish* gain, the slave interest made certain that the distribution of wealth steadily narrowed. Abolitionists believed the slaveholders' hunger for land was so great that the slave power would "prevent the poorer class of people from acquiring real estates, or even a comfortable subsistence." The price of slaves continued to rise, "confin[ing] their possession almost exclusively to the rich." Labor stood in such low esteem that "industry [was] necessarily discouraged." And the masters' desire for "acquiescence of the major part of the white population" left education in a primitive state. An abolitionist tract by a former resident of the South summed up the condition of "the poor white man" by observing that "there is absolutely no sphere for him but to labor for the supply of his animal wants, despised and rejected."[19]

Their reading of Southern relations did not lead abolitionists to raise the question of slavery's profitability; they knew it paid. Instead, reformers raised the paradox of slavery's profitability: the chattel system profited a few but impoverished the many.[20] From the slave power's vantage point, such an arrangement "worked": it placed wealth and authority in their hands and directed more of those advantages to a smaller and smaller number. One result was a fitting social order for the slave power's calculating designs: an "aristocracy" which, by its nature and by its influence, modeled the South's distinctive market experiment.

On the surface, the aristocracy of the South appeared rather unremarkable – out of place in a republic, to be sure, but on the whole familiar in its features. The slave interest was powerful and privileged, small in number and dominant in wealth. It ruled over millions who were "comparatively poor and uneducated, without rank, without influence, sometimes brutalized and depraved, always in a state of vassalage."[21] But there the similarities with other elite orders – including that of the North – ended.

Phillips, Parker, and other abolitionists acknowledged that the North bore its own marks of concentrated wealth and covetous, material passion. Enormous power and influence lay in the hands of a relative few who claimed to speak and act in the name of the many. For reformers, the threats posed by a Northern aristocracy were certainly serious and wide-ranging; but they were *comparatively* less urgent than the dangers posed by the slave power. The Southern aristocracy not only controlled workers but owned them; it not only abused laborers but degraded the virtues of labor; it not only exploited the lower ranks of society but firmly closed the doors of opportunity and advancement. The slave interest, James Birney observed, did not even have the republican good sense to refrain from celebrating its own aristocratic character.[22]

All aristocracies exhibited the "tendency" to tyrannize and oppress labor, but the slave power did so in an extraordinary way: by subverting the self-evident truth that people were not "mere disposable property." The slave interest created "an aristocracy of the most oppressive and debasing nature, in which no trace is discernible of the equal rights of men." The aristocracy of the South defied both common sense and America's common past. In the view of Garrisonian Edmund Quincy, it remained in an elite world all its own. The South's "Aristocracy of Legrees" did not rest on "honest acres" or "former services"; it had "no claim on hereditary gratitude, no ancestral record of great historical events and governmental changes." Rather, it stood as an "arbitrary and tyrannical Aristocracy, which rests . . . on the ownership of human beings." The South bowed to the privileged who had no past; it respected those who had acquired, not achieved. The slave-power aristocracy represented the idealization of enthrallment over enlightenment. Perhaps for this reason, Parker insisted that it was in fact "not an Aristocracy – the rule of the best – but a Kakistocracy – the rule of the worst."[23]

Reformers believed that the slave-power aristocracy not only sprang from peculiar roots but showed traces of its origin in the influence it exercised, especially over the aristocratic elements of the North. Whatever prestige or control it exercised, the leadership of the North meekly or tamely or even fearfully submitted to the will and command of the slave-power aristocracy. As political abolitionist Rev. George Allen asked in an 1847 address, "In what sphere of influence is not its evil genius present . . . ? In what mart of commerce does she not win the love of gain? What wheel of frugal industry does not watch her humor to know when to whirl, and when to rust in idleness?"[24]

Reformers tried to explain the dominance of the Southern aristocracy in a number of ways. The slave power's commercial pressure seemed one likely cause: to keep Southern customers, the North vowed silence on slavery. Others raised financial concerns: a mountain of Southern debt reduced the North to a "wretched, conquered provinc[e]." Rev. Henry M. Dexter of Boston's Pine Street Church defined the issue as one of character: the master's exalted power and impaired morality made for just the right kind of "self-seeking, licentious, imperious, unscrupulous" individual who could "get the advantage of a comparatively cautious and conscientious Northern[er]."[25] But for many other reformers, the dominance of the Southern aristocracy arose from its informing purpose: the *single-minded* pursuit of the chattel principle. Phillips observed that the South's wealth, power, and prestige did not reside in a "scattered class"; "they know they are one solid column." Douglass also suggested that "while the North is divided and subdivided, the South is united; and it is her unity of action which must account for the success which has attended her." Because the North was not as true to liberty as the Southern aristocracy was to bondage, free peoples did the bidding of the slave power. Douglass noted the curious result: while Southerners formed "the slave-holding states," Northerners formed "the slavery-upholding states."[26]

In the workings of a plantation or the relations of society, the slave interest carried out its obsessive, unvarying devotion to property in humanity. But the slave power's peculiar effort to direct human experience along the lines of the market also found fulfillment in the politics of the nation, radically altering the organization and operation of government.

The first major political change achieved by the slave power involved two questions of "representation": *who* should perform the service and *what* they should represent. Douglass frequently noted that 150,000 to 300,000 slaveholders held the reins of political power in the South. They were its governors and legislators; they received the honors and emoluments of rule; they monopolized all offices except, Douglass said, for "Negro-whippers" – *that* they kept for Northerners. Referring to a political gathering in Kentucky, Douglass reminded an audience that nonslaveholders comprised 96 percent of the state's population: yet "at the recent State Convention . . . the slaveholding interest was so powerful, so all-pervading, that not a single delegate appeared in the Convention as a representative of the 700,000 people embraced in that non-slaveholding population." Slaveholders simply ruled "as though there was not a white man in the whole South besides themselves." Having legally obliterated the "being" of blacks by making them merchandise, slaveholders played off their wealth in human chattel to obliterate politically the white nonslaveholder, a person who became, in Douglass's words, "almost a cypher – literally a nonentity."[27]

Slaveholders stood as the representatives of the South because they rather thoroughly eliminated the competition. Careful design also helped. Using South Carolina as his example, Douglass noted that potential legislators had to meet a peculiar property requirement, owning at least ten slaves to be eligible for office. If they could not fulfill that requirement, another reformer added, they had to own more land. But the end result remained the same, because in order to make landownership profitable, one had to purchase human chattel. Simply put, all eligible Southern representatives were "interested in 'Slave property.'"[28]

The qualification rules established by Southern governments clarified who acted as a representative; the three-fifths rule established by the national government clarified what the deputy actually represented. Speaking to Ohioans in 1840, political abolitionist Joshua Leavitt speculated on the meaning of apportionment rules that counted the slave as three-fifths of a person. The formula granted no political power to bondspeople. Instead, Leavitt argued, it conceded extra power to slave owners, in their capacity as "possessors." The three-fifths rule, he concluded, was "mere property representation."

Leavitt warned of the formula's dangers: it gave slave states an edge in national power, left the North a "'conquered province'" with an unequal voice in government, and, as a result, challenged the very foundations of "true republicanism."[29] His comments also pointed to one other part of the slaveholders' "calculating" efforts. The slave power had reordered "material resources," from the conventional idea that encompassed property to one that included people; the slave power also reordered "representation," from the republican idea that encompassed people to one that included property.

With property protected in formal codes and represented in government halls, proponents of the chattel system successfully altered the legal and structural basis of politics. They brought the same change to the *process* of politics. Reformers claimed that the slave power rejected the twin principles of "genuine" republican politics: first, an unswerving devotion to freedom, which demanded that law serve the cause of liberty; and secondly, the maintenance of virtue among citizens, which demanded vigilance against tyranny and knowledge of civic duty.[30] In place of these commitments, the slave power offered a new set of guidelines emphasizing the pursuit of private gain and selfish advantage attained by any possible means. The behavior and standards of the marketplace defined the political process.

Francis Jackson, president of the Massachusetts Anti-Slavery Society, warned of the character that government had acquired through the slave power's "master hands" and the North's submissive accommodation: "Principles have yielded place to policies, and men have fought, not for eternal laws of Right, but for laws of political and financial economy." Wendell Phillips echoed Horace

Greeley's words as he declared that the supporters of this political system "'love liberty less than profit, dethrone conscience, and set up commerce in its stead.'" As a result, Theodore Parker argued, "officers ought to be sworn on the federal currency; they should make the sign of the dollar, ($) as their official symbolic cross; it is a State of commerce."[31]

Jackson, Phillips, and Parker all stressed Northern complicity in the transformation of the political process but strongly believed that the slave power held ultimate responsibility for inaugurating and guiding the new order. Jackson noted that future federal policy, like that of the past, was "sure to be moulded by the same master hands" of the slave interest. Phillips stated that the informing principles of the new politics lay intertwined in "the three-strand cable of the Slave Power, – the prejudice of race, the omnipotence of money, and the almost irresistible power of aristocracy." And Parker argued that while candidates of all sections had to woo money and majorities in order to succeed politically, "the particular body which sways the destinies of the nation, or its politics, is an army of Slaveholders, some three hundred thousand strong. They direct the money; they sway the majority; and are the controlling force in America."[32]

Having dispensed with pesky codes of principle and morality, those engaged in the "politics of peddlers" focused on the only issue they deemed important, the one concern they believed all problems represented: narrow, mean, and pecuniary questions of interest.[33] The Reverend John Weiss of Massachusetts noted that government overflowed with officials "whose faith is that every man has his price and that every measure is a marketable thing." Selling one's program and buying another's support were the daily activities on the American political exchange. And because, as Parker observed, the system operated under the belief that "'all dollars are equal, . . . [that] each has unalienable rights,'" every interest entered the government market on the same terms.[34]

In this way, reformers insisted, the slave power secured its hold on the nation – not only through its own outward aggression, but also through the way it was *perceived* by the altered political mind of America. Officeholders who paid scant attention to despotic power and moral decay did not see slavery as the scourge of republicanism. Typically, slavery entered political debate as a simple, uncomplicated question of "property." It became just one more legitimate, neutral interest, to be treated as any other.[35]

Still, as Weiss observed, the conventional wisdom of the political trade held that interests clash and that "conflicting interests of the national life admit no remedy." The solution was to rely, again, on what abolitionists saw as the method of the marketplace: on compromise. Rev. Henry M. Dexter described the process as "mean commercial bargaining – the 'I will do this for you, if you will do that for me,' theory of morals." Rather than troubling themselves over the question of "'What ought to be?,'" political leaders concerned themselves only with the question of "'What can be?'" Their compromises "facilitated" laws on slavery and shaped the whole course of the Republic's history. Dexter concluded that compromise "has been, perhaps, in every instance, the logic by which the South has prevailed against the North."[36]

Abolitionists condemned the process on several counts. First and foremost, compromise admitted no fixed principle. As he considered past agreements on the slave trade and present deals on slavery extension, the Reverend George B. Cheever asked if there was anything "that constitutes an absolute authority, not to be questioned for a moment?" All pronouncements, liberties, and Revolutionary doctrines failed to prevent the despotic encroachments of slavery. Revered historic maxims were routinely perverted in the service of supposed political benefits. In light of these conditions, Cheever insisted, some point of reference had to remain fixed: "There must be something of principle, or when there is nothing but interest, God himself will desert us forever."[37]

Having denied such established standards, public officials and party leaders transformed politics into a matter of bargaining. As a result, they not only rewarded selfishness and corruption but, more importantly, "basely bartered" moral rights for material advantage. Reflecting on the twenty-year extension of the slave trade, Dexter regretted "that the Fathers could not have seen that, by these compromises of what they knew and felt to be moral right, for what they imagined would be pecuniary profit and the immediate comfort of an adopted government, they were mixing clay with the iron with which they were shaping the feet of this young republic."[38]

Political bargaining endangered the Republic, fixed the bondsman's chains ever tighter, and allowed the slave interest not only to feel secure but to flourish. As Weiss stated, "Step by step the power of slavery has enlarged its limits, and magnified its constitutional privileges. It has succeeded in making the policy of the country one of deliberate compromise, till at last both the great parties acknowledge slavery to be a national interest and freedom a subordinate principle, whose development must only be consistent with the safety of its proud antagonist."[39]

The friends of liberty had nothing to show for all the deals cut with the slave power. Political parties, paid to be silent on freedom and vocal on bondage, allowed citizens of the North and slaves of the South to "become subsidized to this overshadowing oligarchy." The slave power had the ability to direct electoral majorities and define national policies. Candidates of all regions tried to curry favor with the power-making slave interest. And the highest office in the land was formed completely at the whim and will of proslavery forces. The South, Parker argued,

> always makes the Presidents. As the Catholic priest takes a bit of baker's bread, and says, "Bread, thou art, become a God!" and the dough is God, – so the South takes any man and transubstantiates him, – "Thou art a man! become a President!" And by political transubstantiation Polk and Pierce are Presidents, to be "lifted up," to be "exhibited," set on high and worshipped accordingly. . . . A new President is presently to be kneaded together, to be baked to the requisite hardness, transubstantiated, and then set up in 1856. Several old *Ephraims*, alas! cakes "not turned," begin to swell, and bubble, and crack, and break, hoping presently to be in condition to be transubstantiated. Some Northern dough is leavening itself to suit the Southern taste. Alas! "It is not in man that walketh to direct his steps." Many are leavened, but few *rise*.[40]

As a theologian, Parker may have intended his words to put a supernatural spin on the familiar image of the Northern "dough-face."[41] But as a reformer, he argued in the lecture as a whole that the slave interest's extraordinary control over American politics did not derive from a transmundane source. The reasons for its success were far more down-to-earth, in fact fundamentally and dangerously materialistic. The slave power's advance resulted from its ability to direct national wealth, to extend monetary power into government, and to corrupt the political process.

Even the language of politics took on a new face as a result of the slave power's influence. "Patriotism" proclaimed support for slavery, "Public Duty" involved the vigilant recapture of runaways, and "Republicanism" itself meant submission to the will of tyrants. The whole structure and process of politics took on the character that Francis Jackson associated with the party apparatus: "They smacked of the Shop rather than of the Senate, of the Counter more than of the Cabinet."[42]

Freedom gained nothing by succumbing to what Parker called "penny wisdom." Slaveholders and their allies would not remain content with their gains; the agents of tyranny were eager to make as well as break promises about America's future course. "To say," as Weiss warned, "that peace and settlement will result from successive bargainings with slavery, is to say that health results while elements of death prey on the vital powers." Security for the nation would be won only when freedom once more became "the great interest and central principle of this republic."[43]

An even more important lesson, abolitionists insisted, was that nothing *could* be gained by engaging in deals with the slave power. On certain matters, the political bargain was completely out of place. Reflecting on Henry Clay's 1850 resolutions, James Birney wrote in his diary that "a moral question – one on which human liberty is depending in any way – cannot be compromised or settled by Congress." Furthermore, on the matter of human chattel, the political bargain literally had no "place"; there was no "point" where the principles of liberty and slavery intersected. Freedom and enslavement were diametrically opposed. It was simply "impossible," Garrison argued, "to reconcile, under a republican government, the enemies and friends of absolute despotism." The search for a common ground left the political bargain-hunter high and dry, trapped in what one minister labeled "the vacuum of betweenity."[44]

By radically redirecting government's shape and course, Douglass wrote, the slave power provided history's clearest example "of what a few men can do in getting possession of political power." The slave interest believed it had to maintain its power and authority while stripping opponents of theirs. The slaveholders' commitment was, in William Goodell's view, the "key" that unlocked the mysteries of American politics. The slave power's intentions and aspirations were equally clear to reformers. Rev. Cheever warned that free people faced "the despotism of an oligarchy of the worst principles on which ever yet any oligarchy under heaven was grounded, the principles of property in human flesh." Their encroachment on liberty was "clinched, and clamped, and guarded," closing the doors to government and barring entrance to its halls. "It is a combination-lock of tyranny," explained by one central conviction: "Their slave-*properties* are *the* principles of the whole usurpation, and they mean to make them the principles of the nation."[45]

* * *

Reflecting on the philosophy of abolition in an 1853 speech, Phillips stated that the movement hoped "to alter public opinion" but recognized that it had choices in the way it could accomplish that goal: "Did we live in a market, our talk should be of dollars and cents, and we would seek to prove only that slavery was an unprofitable investment. . . . But we happen to live in the world – the world made up of thought and impulse, of self-conceit and self-interest, of weak men and wicked. To conquer, we must reach all." Though they made reference at times to the material benefits of abolition or the profitability of justice, reformers typically agitated their world through appeals they believed were substantively at odds with the slave power's.[46]

Abolitionists insisted that "the natural effects of slavery" represented a determined challenge to "true republicanism"; that self-professed "republican citizens" held an obligation to abolish slavery; and that antislavery advocates alone spoke for genuine republican principles.[47] Their very participation in the campaign, reformers argued, demonstrated an effort to transcend selfishness. Advocates believed that they worked for the liberty of others and not themselves; that they gave freely of their own time, money, and prestige to emancipate the four millions; and that they gained no material advantage for their efforts. Edmund Quincy declared it impossible for anyone "to attribute to us any self-seeking. . . . because we stand in an unmistakably unselfish and disinterested position."[48] Reformers also believed they stood in the moral and ethical position of history's distinguished republicans, invoking their memory and reenacting the "ancient and heroic virtues" of economy, temperance, frugality, industry, and concern for the common weal.[49] Such codes of character and conduct, so essential for the health of the republic, also sprang from the "honest, hard-handed, clear-headed, free laborers, and mechanics of the North," individuals who formed the "bone and muscle" of society, who stood opposite "purse-proud aristocrats and penniless profligates," contributing the industry which was "the hand-maid of virtue." Respect for labor itself served as one indication of republican commitment.[50]

Perhaps the clearest indication that abolitionists opposed both the slave power and its ordering of the world came from the movement's most familiar appeals: no compromise, because liberty and slavery stood as mutually exclusive forces; no compensation, since the slave was a brother and a sister rather than an article; and no sacrifice of principle to interest, as the truth of reform convictions was self-evident and absolute.[51]

The abolitionist argument on the political economy of slavery raises a number of broader suggestions about topics in the antebellum period. First, when examining the reformers' view of Northern capital and labor, it is important to recall that advocates commonly raised the subject in a comparative context, measuring the economic activity of the free states in relation to a society which, they believed, enshrined the dollar and dehumanized the worker. Abolitionists did not argue that Northern labor was completely free of restriction and injustice. But the stark contrasts that reformers saw between the Northern and Southern systems may have led them to overestimate the free workers' means of redress and to slight subtler forms of labor compulsion whose tools of constraint were not as obvious as the whip or the manacle.[52]

Secondly, in their portrayal of the slave power's market mentality, abolitionists clearly hoped to turn the tables on the proslavery argument. They argued that slaveholders were not devotees of refinement, morality, and paternal care but disciples of thieving and corrupting mammon. Ironically, the abolitionists' critique of a grasping, calculating, acquisitive culture bore a striking similarity to the proslavery attack on avaricious materialism.[53]

That points to a third issue: the shifts within the ideology of republicanism. Reformers conceived of human events in terms that would have been quite familiar to late eighteenth-century Patriots. Both saw the world as the scene of ongoing conflict between Power and Liberty in which corrupt tyrants hatched conspiratorial schemes to destroy freedom. Both believed that the vigilant defenders of freedom needed to uphold their constitution as well as their character in order to provide Liberty with strong structural and ethical bases of support. But abolitionists invoked a version of republicanism that might have troubled a patriot such as Jefferson. Reformers placed little confidence in the states as the key guarantors of liberty in the domestic sphere; the South, after all, seemed to have done a poor job of providing republican government for its people. Advocates placed little confidence in territorial expansion as a base for future security; the slave power not only transformed people into chattels but also converted the "empire for liberty" into an "empire for slavery."[54]

Abolitionists also drew upon a version of republicanism much more accommodated to a world of trade and manufacture than Jefferson's. Reformers did reject a market obsession that trampled on humanity, virtue, and natural rights; they had little confidence in individuals liberated from both constraint and duty; and they feared that the common good was not inevitably served by open and prosperous exchange. They believed, however, that modern economic activities were quite compatible with traditional agrarian pursuits and could actually serve important "republican" purposes. David Lee Child, for example, spoke of the moral and political strengths shown by "the yeoman *and* the mechanic," and the traits of industry, modesty, simplicity, and rugged good sense shared by both. Phillips noted that the backward, wasteful, and unproductive character of the Southern economy did not jeopardize the slave power's political order because "despotisms are cheap." He celebrated the commerce, production, and free labor of Massachusetts for the prosperity that they generated, because "free governments are a dear luxury, – the machinery is complicated and expensive." The costs of liberty were high, and someone had to foot the bill.[55]

6

DECLARATIONS OF
INDEPENDENCE

THE LANGUAGE OF LIBERTY & THE
IDENTITY OF THE REPUBLIC

ON JANUARY 30, 1845, a large audience in Boston's Faneuil Hall listened to a public appeal by the Great Anti-Texas Convention. The address was so long that it had to be delivered by two alternating speakers who bitterly attacked the plan underfoot to annex Texas to the United States. The scheme "to uphold the interests of slavery, extend its influence, and secure its permanent duration" was no ordinary matter of debate, the Convention insisted. The Texas question had to be understood in special terms, in a framework that matched the breadth and gravity of the choices before the nation. Why was annexation so serious and threatening? Why did the Texas controversy hold the potential for such extensive and dangerous transformation? The Convention's speakers had a clear and revealing answer: "This question transcends all the bounds of ordinary political topics. It is not a question how the United States shall be governed, but what shall hereafter constitute the United States: it is not a question as to what system of policy shall prevail in the country, but what shall the country itself be. It is a question which touches the identity of the republic."[1]

Abolitionists recognized the influence of slavery over the key political, economic, religious, and historical issues of their day. But they feared that the chattel system had done more than alter the structure, enterprise, soul, and memory of the nation. As orators from the Anti-Texas Convention suggested, slavery reached into another area of human experience, affecting the very self-conception that Americans held of themselves and of their nation. Advocates interpreted the suffering of blacks, the decay of the South, and the spread of tyranny as signs of a deepening crisis in national self-knowledge. Unless Americans resolved their inner crisis, the outer turmoil would remain. Because of this problem, abolitionists envisioned their effort, in part, as a cultural movement, hoping to establish on a firm and ennobling base the identity of the American people.[2] Advocates measured the success of their cause by its ability to abolish chattel slavery and by its capacity to establish national identity. That identity needed to conform to republican standards which abolitionists claimed to explain and exhibit.

At the center of America's cultural confusion lay the self-destructive effort to join republican liberty and chattel slavery. For reformers, there was no clearer indication that republican citizens stood at odds with their own informing principles. At the center of the solution to this problem lay more than an alteration in power and conduct; abolitionists also sought change in the very terms through which Americans articulated ideas of power and conduct. For reformers, the abolition movement required the reordering of language as it did the extension of liberty. The quest for both national self-knowledge and the containment of power was not merely a mechanical process but a verbal one as well. Reformers hoped to provide both a language and a literature fit for a republican society. Advocates saw their campaign, then, both as a warning of cultural confusion and as a performance of cultural possibilities.

The most alarming illustration of cultural confusion in America – the example abolitionists repeatedly cited over the course of their campaign – was the nation's attempt to build a harmonious way of life out of the discordant principles of liberty and slavery. In the reformers' view, a nation so long committed to such an irrational, dangerous, and destructive project clearly had grown away from its authentic roots and highest ideals. No people could establish an accord between freedom and enslavement; if any people should have recognized that fact, it was Americans.

Black abolitionist James W. C. Pennington only stated the common position of reformers when he proclaimed that "slavery is the antipode of liberty. No two things can be more directly opposed." Such incongruous elements, argued a convention of women abolitionists, could never long remain at peace with one another. In Lydia Maria Child's words, America confronted a "Siamese question" in which they were asked to "join two things, which have no affinity with each other, and which cannot permanently co-exist."[3]

The mutually exclusive character of freedom and slavery, Charles Follen noted, ought to have been particularly apparent to citizens of a republic whose own history grew out of the struggle between the "two hostile principles" of liberty and oppression. Americans attempted to realize what poet and political abolitionist John Greenleaf Whittier called "a moral impossibility," bringing together naturally irreconcilable forces, "the one based upon the pure principles of rational liberty; the other, under the name of freedom, reviv[ing] the ancient European system of barons and villains – nobles and serfs." The nation had long been engaged in an effort that was logically unsound, historically groundless, and culturally misplaced.[4]

One example of national chaos could be found in America's political order, or, more precisely, its radical disorder. The "strange compound" of freedom and enslavement, in political abolitionist Richard Hildreth's words, had worked itself into political, constitutional, and legal systems. Because "such hostile and repulsive elements" remained at apparent peace with one another for so long, the nation imagined that no conflict would ever arise. "But those who reason thus," Hildreth warned, "have not well considered the history of the American States." Unity could not possibly flow out of "that heterogeneous mixture."[5]

The antagonistic forces shaping politics, government, and law were so pervasive, advocates feared, that Americans could never resolve their cultural dilemma by adhering merely to the forms of nationhood. Yet, reformers asserted, this was where fellow citizens had mistakenly placed their trust.[6] Fidelity to the "Union," for example, could not solve the nation's predicament because the Union itself was an empty shell, having lost both its meaning and its authority. What authentic force of cohesion or fusion could possibly result from the combination of opposed principles, Frederick Douglass asked. "There is no such thing," he wrote, "as a perfect Union while we have both Liberty and Slavery." Hildreth expressed his skepticism in a different fashion, noting that Americans had transformed the Union into an entity to be feared rather than respected. "When the thing has changed its nature," he said, "what though it still retain its former name? Though it be called a Union, what is it but a base subjection, a miserable servitude?" Similarly, Theodore Parker maintained that balance could not proceed out of fundamental imbalance. The principles of liberty and slavery stood "in exact opposition to each other," capable only of uneven struggle rather than harmonious resolution. America found itself "poised" on the brink of disorder. "So long as these two ideas exist in the nation as two political forces there is no national unity of idea, of course, no unity of action. For there is no center of gravity common to freedom and slavery. They will not compose an equilibrious figure."[7]

There could not be, in other words, *a* nation, *a* people in the midst of such deep division. Although many reformers assumed that this underlying confusion projected a poorly defined identity, Douglass held that the opposite was true. The problem was not the complete absence of national character but the disturbing presence of an unflattering, shameful, and tragically appropriate identity. Douglass told a Rochester audience in 1848 of a cartoon he had seen in the British journal *Punch* which depicted "Brother Jonathan" (see p. xii). The illustrator drew a thin, shrivelled figure stretched out on chairs with his legs propped up on a bust of George Washington. Armed with a pistol, lash, and knives, Jonathan sat in the midst of warfare, slave auctions, brandings, and whippings, all proceeding with the approval of respectable society, under the banner of the Stars and Stripes, to the satisfied gaze of Satan himself. "Here I conceive to be a true picture of America," Douglass noted, "and I hesitate not to say but this description falls far short of the real facts and of the aspect we bear to the world around us." A people who draped themselves with the symbols of freedom while clinging to the levers of despotic power presented all too clear a picture to others. America, Douglass argued on other occasions, "stands prominently forth as a land of inconsistencies" and its "civilization abounds in strange and puzzling contradictions." Americans, as Douglass and other reformers believed, did hold an identity – but as a people of paradox.[8]

The attempt to incorporate slavery into a republican system demonstrated to reformers that the nation misunderstood or shunned its own informing principles. Rev. Samuel Johnson warned a Lynn, Massachusetts, congregation that they lived in "a time of inverted values," when those descended from "the good stock of Algernon Sidney, George Fox, and Harry Vane, have mainly dwindled into a herd of trading politicians" cutting deals with the malevolent slave power. William Goodell described the state of the nation in terms of "incompleteness" because of government's failure to achieve its primary task: securing the blessings of liberty for all – "a somewhat significant incompleteness," Goodell added. In an 1855 pamphlet, Boston pacifist and antislavery administrator Joshua Pollard Blanchard denounced those grown satisfied with a society whose "principles of the Revolution have not been realized." What passed for conventional political wisdom, he argued, suffered from "want of definition."[9]

It was the undefined state of the nation that so concerned abolitionists. Basic questions about freedom and fundamental commitments to liberty remained in an unresolved or amorphous condition. Douglass warned citizens: "We have been sitting at the feet of its Calhouns and its Taneys so long that we have ceased to comprehend the elements out of which the nation sprung into existence." Wendell Phillips sensed that Americans were not at all inclined to take on the meaning and challenge of their heritage. "We have never accepted, – as Americans," he reflected, "we have never accepted our own civilization. We have held back from the inference which we ought to have drawn from the admitted principles which underlie our life. We have all the timidity of the Old World, when we think of the people." The question William Lloyd Garrison asked early in the abolitionist campaign was raised in various ways by advocates over three decades of reform activity: "Must we now begin to inquire, for the first time, what are our duties and responsibilities as American citizens?"[10]

For reformers, questions about American obligation, national definition, and cultural authenticity were not abstract or aesthetic issues but pressing political concerns. A nation so uncertain of its purpose and so unaware of its conduct suffered from more than a lack of self-knowledge; it could scarcely comprehend the requirements of self-preservation either. A people who knew little about their best interests could do little against their worst threats. Tyranny took root not only in the schemes of rulers true to their own ambition, but also in the ignorance of citizens unaware of their own identity.

Advocates believed that one way to hasten America's cultural recovery was through the abolition of slavery, ending the senseless effort to harmonize liberty and enslavement. One other way to secure cultural cohesion lay in the very expression of the abolition message. The reformers' appeals were meant not only to *contain* the truth of the American condition but also to *convey* that truth in a manner entirely appropriate to the nation. Through their attention to the uses and creations of language, abolitionists believed that they had produced nothing less than a distinctive way of perceiving and describing reality, an American voice to announce the American identity.

For three decades, abolitionists reminded audiences of the simple point that language mattered in the work of republican reform. Their own cause stood as proof. Garrison called on his audience to remember what difference reformers made when they altered the call for gradual emancipation with a single term: "The whole antislavery battle in this country has turned upon the word IMMEDIATE – a word which has shaken the nation, from Maine to the Rocky Mountains, like a blast from the trump of the great archangel." That one word, Garrison argued, exposed the tyrannical nature of slavery and the fragile state of liberty. Opponents to reform simply wanted the term repudiated. "So important, so essential, so omnipotent does a little word sometimes become in the progress of human events, and the conflict of LIBERTY with DESPOTISM!"[11]

In the reformers' view, language also helped to account for the spread of the chattel system. The slave power's extraordinary influence depended not only on political clout, economic leverage, and social prestige but also on argumentative skill – or, more to the point, argumentative deception – in order to alter that "throne of a republic," "public opinion." As clergyman and political abolitionist George Allen observed, "slavery, itself a power, lays hold of greater power, alike by subtilty [sic] and by arrogant decision."[12]

Much of the slave power's success could be attributed to its deliberate verbal and logical distortions, laying over the national conscience a rhetorical gauze that, Douglass argued, "veiled the hideous and hell-black imp of Slavery." According to reformers, the slave power's words created "airy phanthoms" that perverted the "plainest precepts" and acted as "stage trick[s]" to divert attention from the crimes of slavery.[13] Such rhetorical chicanery even led proslavery advocates to rename the chattel system, replacing the harsh but precise word "slavery" with innocuous or dignified terms. In 1859, Phillips noted that what had once been known simply and honestly as "bondage" was now called the "patriarchal institution," the "domestic institution," the "peculiar institution," "economic subordination," "warranteeism," or "a different type of industry." "And so they have banished slavery into pet phrases and fancy flash-words. If, one hundred years hence, you should dig our Egyptian Hunkerism up from the grave into which it is rapidly sinking, we should need a commentator of the true German blood to find out what all these queer, odd, peculiar imaginative paraphrases meant in this middle of the nineteenth century."[14] Reliance on euphemisms disclosed a fear of even naming, much less justifying, the system of slavery. Unable to "pronounce" their central object, proslavery advocates tried to transform slavery verbally into an innocuous practice in much the same way as they politically accommodated its oppression into a republican form of government.

As far as reformers were concerned the slave power's indirect and deceptive language took the hard edge off the chattel system, offering the only possible way of talking about a system which proslavery forces themselves recognized as illegitimate. "There is not a man on earth," wrote Garrison, "who does not believe that slavery is a curse." The *Anti-Slavery Record* stated that slavery interests "feel constrained to give their assent" to abolition principles. The controversy over the chattel system came down to "A STRIFE BETWEEN PRINCIPLE ON THE ONE HAND, and NO PRINCIPLE

vailing abolitionist assumption: that the slaveholders' purposes and designs were made manifest not only by "their laws, their usages, and their entire treatment of their slaves," but also by "the whole vocabulary of slaveholders." As Henry David Thoreau suggested, their own words sentence-d them.[18]

Both the form and substance of the proslavery appeal betrayed political intentions as clearly as habits of coercion and cruelty. The slave power's purposeful corruption of speech was as threatening as any corruption of office and offered as clear an indication of tyranny's approach.[19] Abolitionists took to heart a lesson taught by their own analysis of American life: that oppressors not only enact but bespeak tyranny.

As the foes of freedom announced their true character through verbal guile, the friends of freedom had to adopt their own authentic voice, a point Angelina Grimké raised in an 1836 essay. Grimké wrote that abolitionists needed to respond to the "'lies,'" "sophistry," and "absurdity" of the proslavery argument through a particular form of address. Reformers had a responsibility to "come back to the good old doctrine of our forefathers who declared to the world, 'this self-evident truth that *all* men are created equal and that they have certain *inalienable* rights.'" Grimké examined both the firm commitments and the simple expression of the founders. Her message to contemporary reformers was clear. The times required rededication not only to particular ideals of human rights but also to the distinctive mode of public discussion through which those goals were first announced – to a self-evident, plain style.[20]

In their discussions of the plain style, reformers assumed a strict correspondence between appearance and reality: the character of one's words reflected the character of one's nature. Affected and overly elegant prose revealed elitism; obscurantism signaled disguise and dishonesty; refinement embodied "craftiness" of the most sinister sort. Philadelphia lawyer and abolitionist David Paul Brown reminded an audience that, "in the foppery and vanity of chosen expressions, in the fervour of poetical fancy, in the ardour of animated debate, when selfishness and success were the prime objects, the rights of thousands have been sacrificed to swell the triumph of a well-turned period." In comparison, homely, concrete, and unpretentious discourse announced a writer's sincerity and honesty. Rhetorical restraint indicated self-discipline. References to the commonplace demonstrated an author's interest in appealing to the masses rather than the few.[21]

According to reformers, the key elements of American republicanism embodied the plain style not as a question of taste but as a matter of principle. An essay in the *Liberator* observed that the Declaration of Independence outlined "great propositions, expressed in clear and exact phraseology. Observe – our fathers do not speak hypothetically; they use not the language of supposition; they declare their sentiments seemingly with all the certainty and authority of inspiration, and deem them so palpable as to scorn to argue the matter." The Declaration was a triumph of precepts and of presentation; both points deserved emulation. Frederick Douglass defended the Constitution on the same grounds in an 1852 address, praising the document's legal protections as well as its mode of stating those guarantees. Citing Vice-President George M. Dallas, Douglass noted: "The Constitution, in its words, is plain and intelligible, and is meant for the home-bred, unsophisticated understandings of our fellow citizens." The widespread knowledge of government that the Constitution provided allowed it to serve the people effectively. The same quality also ensured that issues of constitutionality were questions *for* the people, not for the few. Gerrit Smith noted the link between political and stylistic accessibility in an 1855 letter critical of Know-Nothing Party challenges to immigrant suffrage. Foreigners did not need a lengthy period of residence in the country to familiarize themselves with its republican institutions. "It is derogatory to these institutions to regard them as so artificial, complex, and abstruse," Smith insisted. "They are natural and obvious truths; and with the help of an honest heart, are readily learned." Antislavery and temperance reformer Alonzo Miner argued that America's glory rested not only on ideals of liberty but also on the clear expression of those ideals. The *terms* of freedom could tolerate no equivocation, just as the defense of freedom could endure no compromise. In America, the people's birthrights were set down – and must remain – in their "lowest algebraic formula." The "self-evident" principles designed to shape American life were intentionally simple, clear, and precise. They formed a model of political experience and of political expression.[22]

Abolitionists argued that a single set of standards held for the principles of a republican order, the operation of its structures, and the proper discussion of its core issues. At all three levels, clarity, precision, straightforwardness, and comprehensibility had to prevail. In order to control power, the nation had to state its goals and organization in an exact, uncomplicated, recognizable fashion. It also needed to maintain a broadly based, vigorous discussion of public issues. In what they said and in what they did, republican citizens had to invite inspection openly, delimit power clearly, and specify rights precisely. The greatest challenge to this order came from a slave power that conspired to undermine national ideals through a corrupt style of expression. Citizens had grown so confused over the basic terms of republicanism that they could no longer conceive of and describe its proper relations. The people set themselves up as the perfect targets for tyrants; they could be talked into anything. The recovery of exact, uncomplicated, and comprehensible public discussion offered a way out. At the heart of the antislavery argument lay an assumption that republican discourse required the same care and attention as republican institutions.

An advocate from Oswego, New York, James Brown, argued that this was precisely the issue that abolitionism addressed. In a series of essays on the chattel system, Brown acknowledged the link between politics and language. He warned of the slave power's "mystification" and "ingenuity" of argument, its suspicion of simplicity, its "fidgeting spirit of circumstance," and its "chamelion [sic] morality." He argued that abolitionists stood apart from their opponents both ideologically and stylistically. Brown believed his fellow reformers had taken up the project that he had set out for himself and that despots dared not attempt: "to study a clearness, simplicity and artlessness of style."[23]

Abolitionists embraced all three parts of Brown's project. First, advocates sought to clarify the complicated language and sinister redefinition of terms that tyrants worked so hard to achieve. "The first step in a moral reformation," proclaimed the *Anti-Slavery Record,* "is to restore to things their appropriate names," to end mischievous mislabeling, and to stop the endless "qualifications, exceptions, buts, and ifs" of oppressors. To speak truthfully about the problem of slavery was to speak starkly, deliberately, and pointedly, to avoid becoming in relation to language what abolitionists called those who wavered in politics: a "trimmer."[24] As Ohioan Charles Olcott observed, however, that very clarity left abolitionists under attack in their own day: "It is the right and proper *use* of language, by the abolitionists, in reference to slavery, and not their abuse of it, that enrages the enemies of righteousness in this country." The foes of freedom, Garrison wrote, found reformers guilty of "calling things by their right names." Perhaps, he continued, the charge had to be expected in an age which, as the martyred English republican Algernon Sidney said of his own time, " 'makes *truth* pass for *treason.'* "[25]

Republican heroes like Sidney demonstrated a second theme in abolitionist expression: "The times require great plainness of speech, and the most radical measures of reform."[26] Arguments that were simple, unambiguous, and understandable satisfied the requirements both of honesty and of republicanism. Reformers saw little sense in complicating abolition's "self-evident" truths, equivocating on their position by evasive language, or limiting their appeals through obscure references. Garrison reflected on the importance of simplicity in reform appeals as he toured Britain in 1846:

> My manner of expressing my thoughts and feelings is somewhat novel, and not always palatable, in this country, on account of its plainness and directness; but it will do more good, in the end, than a smoother mode. . . I am led to be more plain-spoken, because almost every one here deals in circumlocution, and to offend nobody seems to be the aim of the speaker. *If I chose,* I could be as smooth and politic as any one; but I do not so choose, and much prefer nature to art.[27]

Garrison's preference for "nature" points to a third theme in abolition arguments. Appeals that aimed for refinement and formality presumably had no place in the work of republican reform. Such works enhanced the reputation of their creators rather than furthering the cause of liberty. And by relying on manufactured effects or invented images, their authors distracted attention from the *natural* rights that abolitionists sought to defend.

The artlessness that Garrison and others hoped to achieve did not come easily. Advocates took pains to argue that, despite appearances, their expression did not take root in the imagination but in the actual world. Abolitionist and editor Seymour Boughton Treadwell offered an example as he explained his use of a conventional simile. Comparing Americans to master builders who constructed and maintained the "great temple" of republican government, he urged readers to secure the structure's foundations, provide its required supports, and protect the beauty of its finish. Having presented such a simple image, Treadwell still deemed it necessary to clarify his intentions: "While this idea is couched in a figure, may it be remembered that it is no fiction." Treadwell did not mean to distract his readers or distort his subject with ornamentation and special effects. His trope, in its root sense, did not involve a turn at all but plainly and soberly stated the facts of the case. Treadwell's caveat conveyed his uneasiness over what could be taken as a flight of fancy – which, for reformers sensitive to charges of falsehood and flamboyance, was probably a good issue to air. The author simply had no desire to speak figuratively.[28]

William Goodell paused in his account of the antislavery movement to reflect on another problem of language and reality. Historical reviews, he noted, often presented an unbelievable record of discontinuity in human behavior, portraying the world as the scene of stark, sudden contrasts. His own report of these wrenching upheavals defied "the ordinary vicissitudes of credible history." Goodell feared that readers would believe him "to have been writing fiction, and even the verity of the public documents cited, will scarcely escape suspicion." He insisted that the course of recent American events could only be described in terms of jarring narrative dissonance. However literary such a feature may have seemed, it was not an act of invention on the author's part but a manifestation of keen, realistic insight. The fictive tone provided assurance of the work's fundamental factuality. By focusing on abolitionism's jagged, uneven path, Goodell believed that he had not turned history into romantic fantasy but had instead empirically validated a romantic perspective on human experience. In this case, art imitated life.[29]

Garrison and Douglass also addressed the relation of word to world as they defended the "strong language" of their abolition appeals. Reformers had no choice but to engage in "hard" talk, Garrison explained: "I, for one, say in extenuation, that I have not been able to find a *soft* word in the English tongue to describe villany [sic], or identify the perpetrator of it." There were no terms in conventional usage to convey the enormity of slavery's crimes. "The whole scope of the English language," he argued, "is inadequate to describe the horrors and impieties of slavery, and the transcendant [sic] wickedness of those who sustain this bloody system."[30] Trying to respond to the slave power with limited linguistic resources, Garrison developed what critics condemned as his worst excess. He insisted, however, that his rough talk did not paint an extraordinary picture of slavery; the words remained faithful to the facts. In the middle of a Fourth of July address he asked, "Is the picture I have sketched overdrawn? Can the most lynx-eyed lawyer detect a single flaw in the indictment?" His prose, Garrison maintained, was not only in keeping with the vast problem of slavery but also fit the model established by republican forebears: "*The day is consecrated to declamation,* such as burst from the lips of James Otis, and Joseph Warren, and Patrick Henry."[31]

Douglass also defended the movement's alleged verbal excesses. He assumed that the language of reform usually came up short when confronting the true history of slavery and the republic. To make an accurate report on human chattel, one had to go to extremes: "In writing upon a system of such boundless and startling enormity, where the wildest fancy is over-matched by the terrible reality, it is not easy to steer clear of exaggeration in individual cases. Some extravagance may indeed be looked for and excused in treating of such a subject."[32] Considering the actual horrors and deprivations endured by the slave, Douglass believed that the charge of artifice ought to be leveled against restrained debate rather than intense discussion. "We have not contemplated his wrongs with too much excitement," he stated, "but with *unnatural* calmness and composure. For my part, I cannot speak as I feel on this subject. My language, though never so bitter, is less bitter than my experience."[33] For Douglass, the abolitionists' tone was appropriate, not affected, suited to a condition in which words failed them.

Garrison and Douglass insisted that "hard" talk did not violate the standards of the plain style. They held that their vocabulary was not fanciful; their addresses did not rely on invention, speculation, or distortion; their images of the chattel system were not imagined or manufactured. Rather, their language was a necessary and fitting form of expression for the movement and for the nation.

Perhaps even more important, abolition appeals did not simply provide America with a political critique or a blueprint for social reorganization. Reformers believed that their words also made a significant cultural contribution to the nation, offering, as Garrison said, "a new and stronger dialect."[34] Abolitionists sensed that their campaign liberated the language of America, freeing it from false constraints, ridding it of manipulative artifice, and releasing the possibilities of a native tongue. Advocates claimed that their cause had not only reclaimed the genuine meaning of republicanism but recovered its very terms as well.

* * *

Reformers sensed that their plain, self-evident appeals against slavery had developed a distinctive, republican language for the nation. But when reflecting on the tracts, essays, addresses, and books they produced, advocates maintained that the accomplishment of their cultural movement was far more extensive. For participants, the antislavery argument had created nothing less than an authentic American literature.[35]

One claim to such an achievement came from Wendell Phillips. Looking back over two decades of abolitionism, Phillips noted the "fullness of evidence," the "acute logic," the "masterly ability," and the "eloquent appeals" of reform advocates. Phillips hailed Richard Hildreth's essay on slavery and government as "a work which deserves a place by the side of the ablest political disquisitions of any age." Edmund Quincy's philosophical discussion of abolition made "a contribution of the highest value, and in a department where [he had] few rivals and no superior."[36] In Phillips's view, reformers had generated both a huge quantity of written material and the highest quality of critical analysis.

Refinements in learning and logic, however, served as only one part of a far greater accomplishment: the abolition argument also stood as the sign of American thought and expression coming into its own. Advocates believed that their appeals cut through the confused state of national identity and established a genuinely American style of argument. In an 1853 address on reform, Phillips stated that, up until the abolition movement,

> not only has our tone been but an echo of foreign culture, but the very topics discussed and the views maintained have been too often pale reflections of European politics and European philosophy. No matter what dress we assumed, the voice was ever "the voice of Jacob." At last we have stirred a question thoroughly American; the subject has been looked at from a point of view entirely American; and it is of such deep interest, that it has called out all the intellectual strength of the nation. For once, the nation speaks its own thoughts, in its own language, and the tone also is all its own.[37]

Phillips believed that abolitionism shook America because the movement hit home. By revealing an immediate crisis, by constructing arguments fit for the nation, and by speaking in an authentic and original tongue, reformers gave America a taste of itself. The jarring sensation set off was simply the shock of recognition. The American people came to understand themselves through a reform movement that actively created cultural identity. In Phillips's words, "this discussion has been one of the noblest contributions to a literature really American."[38]

Abolitionists held that the national literature they created arose from many sources. Frederick Douglass noted that "scholars, authors, orators" and "[t]he most brilliant of American poets volunteer in its service." John Greenleaf Whittier, James Russell Lowell, and William Cullen Bryant all stood with the cause according to Douglass; abolition's "auxiliaries are everywhere" among these leading lights.[39]

Valuable cultural and reform expression also issued from unexpected sources, sometimes in a manner that put the great names to shame. Thoreau, for example, celebrated John Brown as both a martyr and a national author. Thoreau explained to a Fourth of July rally in 1860 how the imprisoned Brown had written, "not a *History of the World,* like Raleigh, but an American book which I think will live longer than that." Brown's talent came from understanding what "literary gentlemen, editors, and critics" all missed: that a plain style and a native tongue convey wisdom. "The art of composition," Thoreau said, "is as simple as the discharge of a bullet from a rifle, and its masterpieces imply an infinitely greater force behind them. This unlettered man's speaking and writing are standard English. Some words and phrases deemed vulgarisms and Americanisms before, he has made standard American. . . . It suggests that the one great rule of composition . . . is, to *speak the truth.* This first, this second, this third; pebbles in your mouth or not."[40]

According to Thoreau, John Brown altered the course of American expression as he reordered the face of American politics. Brown's achievements in literature and national debate in the fall of 1859 were so captivating, Thoreau argued, that the death in November of a presumed literary giant, Washington Irving, "went almost unnoticed."[41]

Another individual like Brown who focused public attention on slavery through morally compelling and culturally distinct argument was Harriet Beecher Stowe. Though some within the reform movement questioned the treatment of colonization in *Uncle Tom's Cabin,* most hailed its author for her attack on slavery, her influence over the public mind, and her assistance to the abolition cause.[42] In the view of reformers, Stowe also assumed leadership in national literary ranks. The *Liberator* described her writing as the product of "an undoubted genius, in some respects of a higher order than any American predecessor or contemporary." For others, *Uncle Tom's Cabin* represented more than a milestone in American expression; Douglass proclaimed it "the *master book* of the nineteenth century."[43]

Abolitionists did not simply praise Stowe's cultural achievement; they also tried to account for the novel's success. Their explanations brought together the key cultural assumptions at work in the reform movement. The *Liberator* attributed the persuasiveness of the novel to Stowe's stylistic commitments. The striking feature of *Uncle Tom's Cabin* was not its complex melodramatic texture but writing of a very different stripe. The *Liberator* suggested that Stowe told a powerful and moving story without relying on special effects, needless embellishment, or other forms of artifice. The novel unfolded in a straightforward and sensible sequence. Incidents within the plot tugged at the reader's heart because of the self-evident tragedy of slavery. The story irresistibly led the reader to the conviction that abolition must take place. Quite simply, the truth hurt. No invention on the author's part was required to persuade readers of slavery's evil:

> One's heart throbs, and one's eyes are suffused with tears without a moment's notice, and without anything like effort or preparation on the writer's part. We are, on the contrary, soothed in our spontaneous emotions by the conviction of the writer's artlessness; and when once a gifted woman has satisfied her most captious reader that such is the case, she thenceforth leads him on with an air of loving and tender triumph, a willing captive to the last.[44]

The "captivation" of readers followed, in other words, from dramatic fact plainly told. Stowe related a compelling tale in an appropriate way by purposely avoiding ornamentation, manipulation, and the other kinds of deception associated with the slave power's verbal tyranny. *How* she wrote was as important as what she wrote.

For other reformers, the very substance of the novel helped explain its persuasiveness and influence. Phillips, commenting on the national literature of abolition, argued that Stowe's genius derived from both her gifted pen and her acute eye. Stowe recognized that audiences responded to experience that was immediate, to a body of events that grew out of the familiar rounds of a nation's life. No fictional import from the Old World and no work of fantasy could affect a reader like a homespun tale. Stowe dared to write of slavery, which was the issue authors and readers usually chose to avoid but the subject that most clearly defined America. By focusing on the chattel system as a national reality, Stowe accomplished two closely related goals: she forced audiences to come to terms with themselves, and she uncovered a proper and fitting subject for American self-expression. For Phillips, the comments of a visiting Swedish reformer provided a guide to the significance of Stowe's novel:

> Frederika Bremer only expressed the common sentiment of many of us, when she declared that "the fate of the negro was the romance of our history." Again and again, from my earliest knowledge of the cause, have I heard the opinion, that in the debateable land between Freedom and Slavery, in the thrilling incidents of the escape and sufferings of the fugitive, and the perils of his friends, the future Walter Scott of America would find the "border-land" of his romance, and the most touching incidents of his "sixty years since"; and that the literature of America would gather its freshest laurels from that field.[45]

Stowe structured *Uncle Tom's Cabin* around one simple and significant fact: in the outcome of struggles over slavery and black equality, America would find both its destiny and its voice. Stowe's novel demonstrated what Frederick Douglass had long held: that "the Negro is the test of American civilization." In black history, one found not only a fitting subject for American thought but the informing experience of national life. By comprehending the record of blacks, whites understood the state of their own rights, ideals, and identity. With no blacks "to clink their chains," a counterhistorical Douglass once suggested, "I do not know but the United States would rot in this tyranny."[46] Fortunately, the "flash from the heart-supplied intellect of Harriet Beecher Stowe" awakened the nation to its failures and its possibilities. Through works like *Uncle Tom's Cabin,* Douglass noted, America would become known for something other than tyranny and discord: "the present will be looked to by after coming generations, as the age of anti-slavery literature – when supply on the gallop could not keep pace with the ever growing demand – when a picture of a Negro on the cover was a help to the sale of the book." Thoreau proclaimed that the American artist, "no longer going to Rome for a subject," discovered in the great debate over slavery the essential materials from which truth and beauty would emerge.[47]

For Douglass, Thoreau, and others, *Uncle Tom's Cabin* clarified the emancipation appeal; in addition, Stowe's work crystallized the cultural principles of abolitionism. The novel announced the moral wickedness of the chattel system, exposed the contradictions between slavery and liberty, and expressed its message in an appropriate and authentic voice. Reformers praised Stowe's unadorned, plain style of writing, her choice of subject, and her contribution to a distinctly American literature. In its matter and manner, *Uncle Tom's Cabin* illuminated the crisis of the nation as it helped forge the identity of the nation.

* * *

From 1855 to 1856, Herman Melville composed "Benito Cereno," a complex moral tale of slave insurrection on the high seas. At the conclusion of the short story, the blindly optimistic American officer, Amasa Delano, approaches the Spanish Captain Cereno on whose fated vessel the uprising had occurred. Delano could not understand the despair on his friend's face so long after the incident had taken place. After a series of questions to Cereno, there is a final exchange of words:

> "You are saved," cried Captain Delano, more and more astonished and pained; "you are saved; what has cast such a shadow upon you?"
> "The negro."[48]

The issue which so troubled Cereno stood at the center of the abolition appeal. The question of black freedom and equality served as a touchstone for the American condition. Abolitionists hoped their response would serve as a base of both American liberty and American culture. "The fate of the negro," to use Frederika Bremer's words, rested in an ambiguous state, a sign to abolitionists not just of a racist culture but of an evasive culture as well, the sign of a people willing to let questions about their character, principles, and aspirations remain vague and ill-defined. Looking across society, advocates saw a divided, bewildered, and culturally uncertain people with little sense of who they were. The resolution that abolitionists hoped to bring to issues of emancipation and equality would, they believed, also answer the question of national identity.

CONCLUSION

THE REPUBLICAN EDGE

IN HIS MASTERFUL STUDY of events leading to the Civil War, David M. Potter reflects on one of the central disagreements between the North and the South: whether the Republic was a "unitary nation" or a "pluralistic league" – whether America was one, single political entity or a composite of many political units. "Perhaps," Potter writes, "the United States is the only nation in history which for seven decades acted politically and culturally as a nation, and grew steadily stronger in its nationhood, before decisively answering the question of whether it was a nation at all."[1]

Although Potter raises this point in the specific context of Southern separatism, his observation contains far broader implications. His study examines how a people engaged in continental expansion without a secure grounding in national explanation, how they took risks on the taken-for-granted, how they acted without knowing finally what they were about. Potter's argument suggests that a political body can travel only so far before confronting the consequences of self-evasion; at some point, the definition of underlying national principles and purposes has to take place.

Abolitionists believed that their campaign provided such an exercise. They not only conceived of their cause in the language of republicanism; they also concluded that the reform movement would determine if theirs was a republican society at all. Proponents maintained that the abolitionist argument drew out "those high-principled republicans, who wish fully to carry out the noble and the incontrovertible principle on which their own independence is based." Reformers sought to demonstrate that the contest between slavery and liberty was one "involving the very existence of the Republic"; that "slavery is inconsistent with the genius of re-

149

publicanism, and has a tendency to destroy those principles on which it is supported, as it lessens the sense of the equal rights of mankind, and habituates us to tyranny and oppression"; that the individual who could "regard the *chattelizing* of his fellow man as an *institution,* one of the things that *law* can *establish,* has stepped off from the platform of republicanism"; and that those committed to the abolition of slavery were "the only true republicans of America."[2] Advocates who expressed their efforts through the terms of republican thought held that abolition brought the nation to terms with its republican purposes.

Drawing on the vocabulary and values of republican ideology, reformers made sense of their world, perceived the dangers of the chattel system, and explained the urgency of abolition. Advocates called for the nation to recognize its own republican sources of tyranny; they alerted citizens to the threats posed by moral and political corruption; they envisioned a more inclusive notion of republican liberty. The abolitionists' argument took on prevailing custom and foresaw new political arrangements, threatening to end the slaveholders' political and economic clout while promising to alter the status of one-sixth the American people. In light of these positions, themes of confrontation and change appear to have dominated the republican discourse of reformers. They seem to have stood at odds with mainstream society, resisting its accepted norms, rejecting the present order, fixing their gaze on the future, pressing for continuous liberation, thinking the unthinkable. It is tempting to portray abolitionists as prospective, progressive, even modern in their fundamental temperament and expectations.

Yet the language through which advocates defied their existing order also served to delimit their conceptual boundaries. From their republican frame of reference, abolitionists envisioned and announced extraordinary transformations in the conduct of American life; but, as with any set of ideological constructs, they saw only so much and so far. The point is an obvious one but important to recall when examining advocates who released themselves from so many of the political and imaginative constraints of their time.[3] The abolitionists' informing assumptions not only arranged and explained the world but demarcated it. Reformers could not help but exclude, overlook, or rest unaware of a wide range of possibilities for the nation. However much advocates seemed to anticipate the principles of a later age of reform, their point of reference remained tied to an earlier age of history. However remarkable the abolitionists' perspective and program, much remained inconceivable to them. The reformers' republican beliefs spoke not only to emancipation but to definition and closure as well.

The abolitionists' ideas about their own identity, the character of reform, the question of race, and the nature of society illustrate how those receptive to extraordinary change ventured only so far in their formulas and forecasts. Advocates explained their role in terms of a compelling but uncompleted body of experience located in an earlier time. They spoke with a measure of generational validity about Founding Fathers and Mothers; reformers sought to recover the first principles of eighteenth-century republicanism that guided the struggle for national independence; they saw themselves as heirs obliged to accept and enact the historic cause of human liberty. In so much of the language and imagery used to describe abolition, advocates conceived of their identity retrospectively rather than prospectively, pointing to an unfulfilled mission based in the past rather than an unforeseen turning point located in the future. In other words, abolitionists did not see themselves as "ante-bellum" reformers. Theirs was a "post-Revolutionary" movement.

The advocates' republican identity clarified not only their sense of time but also their understanding of reform. Abolitionists insisted that their movement was not a work of invention or novelty, not an experiment in untested, unconventional, or iconoclastic ideas. Advocates believed their campaign was an act of renovation rather than innovation. They tried to reclaim, establish, and enlarge the Revolution's unrealized doctrines of freedom by completing a project revered in principle but flawed in practice. Abolitionists relied on a strategy of provocation through invocation, exhorting citizens to action by appealing to the familiar values of the republic, settling long-delayed national questions through long-established national commitments. As they worked toward that goal, the advocates' language of resolution and completion described reform in a particular way – as a process that focused on fulfillment rather than alteration, as a course of action that was defined, bounded, and closed rather than ongoing, processive, and open-ended. Abolitionists looked upon a splintered, fluid nation that had no clear sense of direction and no fixed republican meaning. They intended to take that aimless and divided entity and recover its cohesion and solidarity. As he described the fundamental task of abolition, Garrison wrote that he eagerly awaited the day when "what is now fragmentary, shall in due time be crystallized." He and other advocates hoped to reinstate a sense of purpose to a disoriented people, to bring order once again to a formless nation – literally, to re-form the world.[4]

Through the principles of republicanism, abolitionists set the boundaries of their identity and intentions. From the same ideological base, they also established a specific context for understanding slavery. Advocates viewed the chattel system as the embodiment of corruptive, conspiratorial, and passionate tyranny. Slavery presented an extreme form of the arbitrary authority that routinely plagued human affairs and threatened republican orders. By examining bondage in terms of power and its abuses, reformers focused their attention primarily on the *political* character of American slavery. The chattel system took on meaning and significance in relation to the continuing struggle of power and liberty. While sharpening the choices before the nation, the abolitionist argument may have ultimately dulled the appreciation of another point suggested by historian Carl N. Degler: that the peculiar institution "was not just American slavery" – or to use the reformers' idiom, American republican slavery – "but American *Negro* slavery." Slavery did, of course, represent a scheme of domination and subordination, but it also presented "a form of distinction between peoples of different color."[5] From Degler's perspective, political *and* racial forces were not only combined in the chattel system; they were intertwined and mutually reinforcing. What emerged from their interaction was a system for which the language of republicanism may not have satisfactorily accounted.

In similar fashion, the reformers' republican understanding of character and constitution illustrated their traditional, rather than innovative, conception of society. Abolitionists saw themselves in a political arena that was surely fearful but hardly alien. Advocates reduced its complexity to familiar terms: they judged self and society, person and nation, by the same set of standards and expectations. To essayist William Ingersoll Bowditch, the institutions of a country were nothing more than "the outward embodiments of the ideas and habits of the people. If these ideas and habits are bad, the institutions will be bad also." In the opinion of political abolitionist Seymour Boughton Treadwell, "national characteristic" was simply "made up of *individual* characteristic."[6]

Reformers judged the conduct of these larger entities according to readily comprehensible codes. Massachusetts minister George Allen warned Northerners not to think they would remain unsullied by Southern slavery because any contact with the region would leave its mark: "intimacy never leaves men as it finds them, and that which does not purify, corrupts." The reason for this was obvious to Allen: "the law of individuals is the law of communities, because the law of human nature." Wendell Phillips adopted much the same line of reasoning in outlining the standards of behavior for political systems and their citizens to follow: "government is only an association of individuals, and the same rules of morality which govern my conduct in relation to a thousand men, ought to regulate my conduct to any one." What was a state or party, asked a Massachusetts church conference report, "but the aggregation of individuals?" Furthermore, the committee argued,

> what are national acts or party acts but the aggregated acts of the individuals that compose the nation or make up the party? Wrong is wrong, whether committed by an individual, party or nation. Shall we not so decide? Or is the nation going back to the infidel philosophy of Hobbes or Mandeville, to contend that virtue and right are but subjects of legislative enactment, and that moral obligation follows only the behests of courts and the decrees of governments?

Reformers assumed that the same standards of responsibility imposed on individuals held for larger social and political groups.

The complex systems that men and women set in motion did not operate according to arcane, impenetrable laws but by a dynamic that continually referred back to familiar, personal experience. Advocates presumed that society did not have a life of its own distinct from that of its agents but, instead, mirrored their very condition.[7]

It followed that the remedy for social ills should correspond to the treatment given individual disorder: the moral rehabilitation of both self and society offered the surest path to recovery. A republic's greatest security lay in the vigilance, self-sacrifice, and civic duty of citizens. Refine these habits within individuals and society at large would be healed. Reformers proposed that the answer to social discord rested in a straightforward approach that focused on virtuous behavior. Unfortunately, the nation's leaders trusted to complex devices that promoted corrupt behavior. The self-serving parties and unprincipled compromise that promised to create social order only complicated simple truths and plunged the nation into deeper confusion.

Reformers charged that their *opponents* promoted dangerous innovation. The misguided strategy adopted by the foes of abolition caused three sets of problems. First, leaders who responded to the form and balance of the republic neglected its crucial moral component. No political construction or instrument, however precise in its calibration of structural force, could compensate for inattentiveness to individual character. No such machine could harmonize irreconcilable principles. As Garrisonian advocate Charles Lenox Remond reminded his readers, "human society is not like a piece of mechanism, which may be safely taken to pieces and put together again by the hands of ordinary artists, without reference to the will of its maker. Nature has made Freedom safe and Slavery dangerous, and both antagonists of each other. To connect them in indissoluble bonds must baffle the ingenuity of man."[8]

Secondly, intricate procedural and mechanical solutions placed yet another set of obstacles in the path of social recovery. "[I]nstead of relying on the simple lever of truth," Samuel J. May argued, the sponsors of such measures "waste much of their power in merely overcoming the friction of their own machinery." Rather than building marvels of elaborate political engineering, republican simplicity demanded a plain commitment to liberty and virtue.[9]

Thirdly, those adept at compromise and manipulation viewed the fragmentation of society as a given. Their purpose was not to overcome division but to manage it. They attempted what advocates deemed impossible: to use faction against faction, to accommodate any and all interests, and to create harmony out of disharmony. The nation's political leaders sought a balanced republic rather than a virtuous one. Abolitionists could not envision the functions of social conflict in such a political order. The rise of the slave power proved to them where ethical indifference, routine bargaining, and the cultivation of factions would inevitably lead. The nation had attempted what "authentic" republicanism proved impossible. The German emigré and reform organizer Charles Follen argued that the nation had to examine its political techniques, to recognize their novelty and hazards, and to reconcile what those procedures had sundered: "to embrace the whole sphere of human action, watching and opposing the slightest illiberal and anti-republican tendency."[10]

As they reflected on the composition of society, abolitionists did indeed break from their contemporaries and anticipate a new order: advocates dared to envision a community without slaves. But as they engaged in the analysis of society, abolitionists looked back to traditional categories of thought. Reformers conceived of "society" as an extension of the individual, understood in like terms, with similar expectations. Their arguments did not draw attention to a vast, interconnected social web or to the priority of collective experience or to a sense of society as something more than the sum of its parts. In this respect, abolitionists were not proto-progressives but reformers who maintained a highly personalized interpretation of society. However advanced their notions of liberty, advocates were not in the vanguard of social theory.

As they defined a sense of purpose, outlined the problem of power, and examined the behavior of the people, reformers revealed their debt and commitment to the principles of republican thought. The abolitionists' republican "edge" played itself out in two ways, however. Their republican critique offered a penetrating perspective on the nation. At the same time, it expressed the limits of the advocates' imagination. While their campaign for more extensive and inclusive freedom displays a strong affinity with modern reform, the abolitionists remain both temporally and conceptually distant from the present world.

NOTES

INTRODUCTION

1. Charles Follen et al., *Address to the People of the United States, by a Committee of the New-England Anti-Slavery Convention,* . . . (Boston: Garrison & Knapp, 1834), 12.

2. Ronald G. Walters, *The Antislavery Appeal: American Abolitionism after 1830* (Baltimore: Johns Hopkins University Press, 1978; New York: W. W. Norton, 1984), vii–viii, xi; Merton L. Dillon, *The Abolitionists: The Growth of a Dissenting Minority* (DeKalb: Northern Illinois University Press, 1974; New York: W. W. Norton & Company, 1979), 39–46. Abolitionists also viewed 1831 as a pivotal year. See: Maria Weston Chapman, *Right and Wrong in Massachusetts* (Boston: Dow & Jackson Anti-Slavery Press, 1839; reprint, New York: Negro Universities Press, 1969), 4–5; Moncure Conway, *Testimonies Concerning Slavery* (London: Chapman and Hall, 1864; reprint, New York: Arno, 1969), 79; and Gerrit Smith, "Address of the Anti-Slavery Convention of the State of New York, . . . to the Slaves in the United States of America," *Emancipator and Free American,* 11 February 1842.

3. William Ingersoll Bowditch, *The Anti-Slavery Reform, Its Principle and Method* (Boston: Robert F. Wallcut, 1850), 16; J[oshua] P[ollard] Blanchard, *Principles of the Revolution: Showing the Perversion of Them and the Consequent Failure of Their Accomplishment* (Boston: Damrell and Moore, 1855), 23; "Speech of Edmund Quincy," in *Proceedings of the American Anti-Slavery Society, at its Second Decade,* . . . (New York: American Anti-Slavery Society, 1854), 48–49. For examples of Parker's argument, see: "The State of the Nation" (1850), in *The Rights of Man in America,* ed. F. B. Sanborn (Boston: American Unitarian Association, 1911; reprint, New York: Negro Universities Press, 1969), 107; *The Nebraska Question. Some Thoughts on the New Assault upon Freedom in America* . . . , *Feb. 12, 1852* (Boston: Benjamin B. Mussey & Co., 1854), 11–14, 27–

28; and "The Aspect of Freedom in America. . . ." (5 July 1852), in *Additional Speeches, Addresses, and Occasional Sermons,* 2 vols., (Boston: Little, Brown, 1855), 1:112–13; Edward D. Barber, *An Oration, Delivered before the Addison County Anti-Slavery Society, on the Fourth of July, 1836* (Middlebury, Vt.: Knapp and Jewett, 1836), 13; Providence Anti-Slavery Society, "First Annual Report," in Massachusetts Anti-Slavery Society, *A Full Statement of the Reasons . . . Why There Should Be No Penal Laws Enacted, and No Condemnatory Resolutions Passed by the Legislature, Respecting Abolitionists and Anti-Slavery Societies* (Boston: Isaac Knapp, 1836), 37.

4. Henry Highland Garnet, "Speech Delivered at the Liberty Party Convention, Massachusetts, 1842," in Earl Ofari, *"Let Your Motto Be Resistance": The Life and Thought of Henry Highland Garnet* (Boston: Beacon Press, 1972), 143; "Speech of Wendell Phillips" (26 May 1858), *Liberator,* 11 June 1858.

5. See Bibliographic Essay, "Republicanism."

6. James T. Kloppenberg, "The Virtues of Liberalism: Christianity, Republicanism, and Ethics in Early American Political Discourse," *Journal of American History* 74 (June 1987): 9–33; Steven J. Ross, "The Transformation of Republican Ideology," *Journal of the Early Republic* 10 (Fall 1990): 324–25.

CHAPTER 1

1. Gerrit Smith, "Address of the Anti-Slavery Convention of the State of New York, . . . to the Slaves in the United States of America," *Emancipator and Free American,* 11 February 1842, and "Liberty Triumph in Smithfield," *Emancipator and Free American,* 30 March 1843; Lydia Maria Child, *Anti-Slavery Catechism,* 2d ed. (Newburyport; Charles Whipple, 1839), 25; *Proceedings of the Convention of Radical Political Abolitionists, Held at Syracuse, N. Y., June 26th, 27th, and 28th, 1855* (New York: Central Abolition Board, 1855), 7–8; Charles Follen et al., *Address to the People of the United States, by a Committee of the New-England Anti-Slavery Convention, . . .* (Boston: Garrison & Knapp, 1834), 5, 15; John Weiss, *Reform and Repeal, a Sermon Preached on Fast-Day, April 6, 1854, and Legal Anarchy, a Sermon Preached on June 4, 1854, after the Rendition of Anthony Burns* (Boston: Crosby, Nichols, and Company, 1854), 10–11; "Are Slaveholders Man-Stealers?" *Anti-Slavery Record* 3 (September

1837): 10; James McCune Smith, "An Address to the People of the United States," in *Proceedings of the Colored National Convention, Held in . . . Philadelphia, October 16th, 17th and 18th, 1855* (Salem, N.J.: The National Standard, 1856), 31; "Ernestine Rose: Her Address on the Anniversary of West Indian Emancipation," *Journal of Negro History* 34 (July 1949): 348.

2. Wendell Phillips, "The Boston Mob" (21 October 1855), in *Speeches, Lectures, and Letters* (Boston: Lee and Shepard, 1872), 213, 218, 225.

3. My approach to the study of ideology draws from: Bernard Bailyn, "The Central Themes of the Revolution: An Interpretation," in *Essays on the American Revolution,* ed. Stephen G. Kurtz and James H. Hutson (Chapel Hill: University of North Carolina Press, 1973), 10–15; Lance Banning, *The Jeffersonian Persuasion: Evolution of a Party Ideology* (Ithaca: Cornell University Press, 1978), 14–15; and Eric Foner, *Free Soil, Free Labor, Free Men: The Ideology of the Republican Party before the Civil War* (New York: Oxford University Press, 1980), 4–5. These scholars refer, in turn, to the arguments of Clifford Geertz, "Ideology as a Cultural System," in *Ideology and Discontent,* ed. David E. Apter (New York: Free Press, 1964), 47–76.

4. J. G. A. Pocock, "Languages and Their Implications: The Transformation of the Study of Political Thought," in *Politics, Language, and Time: Essays on Political Thought and History* (New York: Atheneum, 1971), 25–26.

5. Ibid., 36. For a demonstration of this approach, see Bernard Bailyn's analysis of "the logic or grammar of thought" of American Revolutionaries in *The Ideological Origins of the American Revolution* (Cambridge: The Belknap Press of Harvard University Press, 1967), ch. 2.

6. For a review of key studies in the field, see Bibliographic Essay, "Republicanism."

7. On the connotations of "slavery" for republicans, see: Bailyn, *Ideological Origins,* 232–46; and Kenneth S. Greenberg, "Revolutionary Ideology and the Proslavery Argument: The Abolition of Slavery in Antebellum South Carolina," *Journal of Southern History* 42 (August 1976): 366n.

8. On the material foundations of republican thought see: J. G. A. Pocock, "Machiavelli, Harrington, and English Political Ideologies in

the Eighteenth-Century," *William and Mary Quarterly,* 3d ser., 22 (October 1965): 549–83, and "Virtue and Commerce in the Eighteenth Century," *Journal of Interdisciplinary History* 3 (Summer 1972): 119–34; Drew R. McCoy, *The Elusive Republic: Political Economy in Jeffersonian America* (Chapel Hill: University of North Carolina Press, 1980); Edmund S. Morgan, "Slavery and Freedom: The American Paradox," *Journal of American History,* 59 (June 1972): 7–13; Robert E. Shalhope, *John Taylor of Caroline: Pastoral Republican* (Columbia, S.C.: University of South Carolina Press, 1980), 59–69. For an example of one individual's views of this issue, compare Thomas Jefferson's Query XIX in "Notes on the State of Virginia" and his letter to Benjamin Austin, 9 January 1816, both in *The Portable Thomas Jefferson,* ed., with an introduction by Merrill D. Peterson (New York: Viking, 1975), 216–17, 547–50.

9. Bailyn, *Ideological Origins,* 57–58. On the patterns of history, see also: Douglass G. Adair, "Experience Must be Our Only Guide: History, Democratic Theory, and the United States Constitution," in *The Reinterpretation of the American Revolution, 1763–1789,* ed. Jack P. Greene (New York: Harper & Row, 1968), 401–2.

10. Bailyn, *Ideological Origins,* 94–159; Gordon S. Wood, *The Creation of the American Republic, 1776–1787* (Chapel Hill: University of North Carolina Press, 1969), 39–41; Pauline Maier, *From Resistance to Revolution: Colonial Radicals and the Development of American Opposition to Britain, 1765–1776* (New York: Knopf, 1972), 183–97.

11. John Adams, "Novanglus: or, a History of the Dispute with America, from its Origin, in 1754, to the Present Time," in *The Works of John Adams, Second President of the United States,* ed. Charles Francis Adams, 10 vols. (Boston: Charles C. Little and James Brown, 1851), 4:14–15, 18, 23–25.

12. Ibid., 4:13, 124–25. See also Gordon S. Wood, "The Democratization of Mind in the American Revolution," in Library of Congress Symposia on the American Revolution, *Leadership in the American Revolution: Papers Presented at the Third Symposium, May 9 and 10, 1974* (Washington, D.C.: Library of Congress, 1974), 75–76. Morton White presents a study of the epistemological ground of Revolutionary thought in *The Philosophy of the American Revolution* (New York: Oxford University Press, 1978).

13. H. Trevor Colbourn, *The Lamp of Experience: Whig History and the Intellectual Origins of the American Revolution* (Chapel Hill: University of North Carolina Press, 1965), 122–23, 135, 187; Lester H. Cohen, *The Revolutionary Histories: Contemporary Narratives of the American Revolution* (Ithaca: Cornell University Press, 1980), 134–46.

14. Cohen, *Revolutionary Histories*, 198–205.

15. On the tension between resistance and restraint see Maier, *From Resistance to Revolution*, 27–48.

16. Pocock, "Languages and Their Implications," 18. For the diverse readings of republicanism in America, see Bibliographic Essay, "Republicanism."

17. Richard Hildreth and Frederick Douglass both recognized the closeness of proslavery and antislavery positions. See: Richard Hildreth, *Despotism in America: An Inquiry into the Nature, Results, and Legal Basis of the Slave-Holding System in the United States* (Boston: John P. Jewett & Co., 1854), 300–303; Frederick Douglass, "Eulogy on the late Hon. Wm. Jay . . . , May 12, 1859," in *The Life and Writings of Frederick Douglass,* ed. Philip S. Foner, 5 vols. (New York: International Publishers, 1950, 1975), 5:449.

18. "Sermon by Rev. Edwin M. Wheelock" [27 November 1859], in *Echoes of Harper's Ferry,* ed. James Redpath (Boston: Thayer and Eldridge, 1860; reprint, New York: Arno, 1969), 183.

19. David L[ee] Child, *The Despotism of Freedom; or the Tyranny and Cruelty of American Republican Slave-Masters* . . . (Boston: Boston Young Men's Anti-Slavery Association for the Diffusion of Truth, 1833), 14.

20. Nathaniel P. Rogers, *An Address Delivered before the Concord Female Anti-Slavery Society* . . . (Concord, N.H.: William White, 1838), 7. See also John G. Whittier, "Justice and Expediency; Slavery Considered with a View to its Rightful and Effectual Remedy, Abolition" (1833), in *Essays and Pamphlets on Antislavery* (Westport, Conn.: Negro Universities Press, 1970), 21.

21. George Bourne, *Slavery Illustrated in its Effects upon Woman and Domestic Society* (Boston: Isaac Knapp, 1837; reprint, Freeport, N.Y.: Books for Libraries Press, 1972), 45; Henry C. Wright, *The Natick Resolution; Or, Resistance to Slaveholders the Right and Duty of Southern Slaves and Northern Freeman* (Boston: Printed for the

Author, 1859), 30; "Hints on Anti-Abolition Mobs," *Anti-Slavery Record* 2 (July 1836): 2; Southern and Western Liberty Convention, *Address . . . to the People of the United States, . . .* (Cincinnati: Printed at the Gazette Office [1845]), 4; [Stephen S. Foster], *Revolution the Only Remedy for Slavery,* Anti-Slavery Tracts, old series, no. 7 (New York: American Anti-Slavery Society, 1855–1856), 5. See also Samuel Johnson, *The Crisis of Freedom, a Sermon, . . . June 11, 1854* (Boston: Crosby, Nichols & Co., 1854), who stated that "the essence of Slavery is the absolute subjugation of man" (18). On the abolitionists' conception of slavery as an oppressive power relation, see also Ronald G. Walters, *The Antislavery Appeal: American Abolitionism after 1830* (Baltimore: Johns Hopkins University Press, 1978; New York: W. W. Norton, 1984), 70–72. Walters grounds his discussion in the Revolution itself rather than in Revolutionary republicanism. In Chapter 5, he also discusses the sexual rather than civic meanings of "virtue" in the antislavery argument.

22. "Slavery a Sin [From the Declaration of Sentiments of the Ohio Anti-Slavery Convention]," *Anti-Slavery Record* 1 (July 1835): 75.

23. American Anti-Slavery Society, *Third Annual Report . . .* (New York: William S. Dorr, 1836), 5.

24. [Louisa J. Barker], *Influence of Slavery upon the White Population, by a Former Resident of the Slave South,* Anti-Slavery Tracts, old series, no. 9 (New York: American Anti-Slavery Society, 1855–1856), 9.

25. Douglass, "American Slavery Lecture No. VII . . . , Jan. 12th, 1851," in *Writings,* 5:178.

26. Theodore Parker, *The Effect of Slavery on the American People. A Sermon . . .* (Boston: William Kent, 1858), 12.

27. Douglass, "American Slavery Lecture No. VII . . . , Jan. 12th, 1851," in *Writings,* 5:178–79; John G. Palfrey, *Papers on the Slave Power, First Published in the "Boston Whig"* (Boston: Merrill, Cobb & Co., 1846), passim. See also Russell B. Nye, "The Slave Power Conspiracy: 1830–1860," in *Conspiracy: The Fear of Subversion in American History,* ed. Richard O. Curry and Thomas M. Brown (New York: Holt, Rinehart, and Winston, 1972), 78–86.

28. "How Can It Be Done?" *Anti-Slavery Record* 2 (September 1836): 10. See also: Rev. William Barnes, *American Slavery, A Ser-*

mon, Preached at Hampton, Connecticut, April 14th 1843, the Day of the Annual Public Fast (Hartford: Elihu Geer, 1843), 10.

29. Douglass, "American Slavery Lecture No. VII . . . , Jan. 12th, 1851," in *Writings*, 5:178.

30. Letter, Angelina Grimké to Anna R. Frost, 18 August [1839], Theodore D. Weld Papers, Manuscript Division, Library of Congress, Washington, D.C.; L[ydia] Maria Child, *The Right Way, the Safe Way, Proved by Emancipation in the British West Indies, and Elsewhere*, Anti-Slavery Tracts, new series, no. 6 (New York: American Anti-Slavery Society, 1860), 5; Rev. Dr. Wardlaw, "Slavery & Freedom," *Anti-Slavery Record* 1 (June 1835): 71.

31. *Resolutions Passed at the National Liberty Party Convention, at Albany, N. Yo., April 1, 1840, (Copied from the 'Friend of Man,' Utica, N.Y., Apr. 22, 1840.)*, Elizur Wright Papers, VI, Manuscript Division, Library of Congress, Washington, D.C.

32. Child, *Anti-Slavery Catechism*, 35.

33. Samuel J. May, "Speech to the Convention of Citizens of Onondaga County, in Syracuse, on the 14th of October, 1851, . . ." in *Legal and Moral Aspects of Slavery: Selected Essays* (New York: Negro Universities Press, 1969), 20; Henry Highland Garnet, "An Address to the Slaves of the United States of America, Buffalo, N.Y., 1843," in Earl Ofari, *"Let Your Motto Be Resistance": The Life and Thought of Henry Highland Garnet* (Boston: Beacon Press, 1972), 147; William Henry Furness, *Our American Institutions* . . . (Philadelphia: T. B. Pugh, 1863), 11.

34. For examples, see: American Anti-Slavery Society, *Second Annual Report* . . . (New York: William S. Dorr, 1835), 67; [Julius R. Ames], *"Liberty"* (New York: American Anti-Slavery Society, 1837), 51.

35. Thomas Wentworth Higginson, *Massachusetts in Mourning: A Sermon, Preached in Worcester, on Sunday, June 4, 1854* (Boston: James Munroe and Company, 1854), 9.

36. Harriet Beecher Stowe, *The Two Altars: Or, Two Pictures in One*, Anti-Slavery Tracts, old series, no. 13 (New York: American Anti-Slavery Society, 1852), 4.

37. "Speech of Wm. Lloyd Garrison," *Liberator*, 18 June 1858; "The Right Sort of Politics" (14 September 1843), in *The Influence of the Slave Power with Other Anti-Slavery Pamphlets* (Westport,

Conn.: Negro Universities Press, 1970), 2; Lydia Maria Child, ed., *The Patriarchal Institution, As Described by Members of Its Own Family* (New York: American Anti-Slavery Society, 1860), 4–8; Massachusetts Anti-Slavery Society, *A Full Statement of the Reasons . . . Why There Should Be No Penal Laws Enacted, and No Condemnatory Resolutions Passed by the Legislature, Respecting Abolitionists and Anti-Slavery Societies* (Boston: Isaac Knapp, 1836), 28; American Anti-Slavery Society, *Fourth Annual Report . . .* (New York: William S. Dorr, 1837), 60.

38. Charles Olcott, *Two Lectures on the Subjects of Slavery and Abolition. . . .* (Massillon, Ohio: Printed for the Author, 1838), 73.

39. Charles C. Burleigh, quoted in "Anti-Slavery Celebration of Independence Day . . . ," *Liberator,* 16 July 1858.

40. William Lloyd Garrison, "Anti-Slavery Celebration of the Fourth of July, 1856," *National Anti-Slavery Standard,* 12 July 1856; [William Lloyd Garrison et al.], "Disunion: Address of the American Anti-Slavery Society; and F. Jackson's Letter on the Pro-Slavery Character of the Constitution," *Anti-Slavery Examiner* 12 (1845): 19.

41. William Lloyd Garrison to Louis Kossuth, February 1852, in *The Letters of William Lloyd Garrison,* ed. Walter M. Merrill and Louis Ruchames, 6 vols. (Cambridge: The Belknap Press of Harvard University Press, 1971–1981), 4:119, 124, 126–27, 129–32; [Zebina Eastman], *Slavery a Falling Tower. A Lecture on Slavery the Cause of the Civil War in the United States, Delivered at the Arley Chapel, Bristol, June, 1862,* 2d ed. (Chicago: John R. Walsh [1862?]), 14–16; "Wendell Phillips's Lecture, Delivered at the Broadway Tabernacle, New York, . . . January 9th, 1855," *National Anti-Slavery Standard,* 20 January 1855. See also Gerrit Smith, "The Liberty Party," *American and Foreign Anti-Slavery Reporter* 2 (1 November 1842): 91. Reformers often reflected on monarchic Britain's 1833 abolition of slavery and republican America's continued expansion of the slave power: William Goodell, *Slavery and Anti-Slavery; A History of the Great Struggle in Both Hemispheres; . . .* (New York: William Harned, 1852; reprint, New York: Negro Universities Press, 1968), 52; Samuel J. May, "The American Revolution," in *The Liberty Bell* (Boston: National Anti-Slavery Bazaar. 1858), 66–67; Gerrit Smith to Wendell Phillips (20 February 1855), *Liberator,* 16 March 1855; L[ydia] M[aria] Child, *An Appeal in Favor of that Class of Americans Called*

African (Boston: Allen and Ticknor, 1833), 224. Angelina E. Grimké compared American Protestant republicans to Mexican Catholic republicans in the Texas controversy; see, "Appeal to the Christian Women of the South," *Anti-Slavery Examiner* 1 (September 1836): 24–25.

CHAPTER 2

1. For a different reading of the abolitionists' historical imagination, see David Brion Davis, "The Emergence of Immediatism in British and American Antislavery Thought," *Mississippi Valley Historical Review* 49 (September 1962): 209–30, and Lewis Perry, "'We Have Had Conversation in the World': The Abolitionists and Spontaneity," *Canadian Review of American Studies* 6 (Spring 1975): 3–26. Both focus on the reformers' desire to break the bonds of the past, to realize an unpremeditated, improvisational, *ex tempore* level of experience, and to achieve a release (or emancipation) from time. In later studies, however, Davis and Perry also explore the abolitionists' sense of development and continuity; see especially Davis's *Slavery and Human Progress* (New York: Oxford University Press, 1984) and Lewis Perry and Michael Fellman, eds., *Antislavery Reconsidered: New Perspectives on the Abolitionists* (Baton Rouge: Louisiana State University Press, 1979), viii–ix.

2. Moncure Conway, *Testimonies Concerning Slavery* (London: Chapman and Hall, 1864; reprint, New York: Arno, 1969), 79; "Mr. Webster's Speech on Bunker Hill, No. I," *Liberator,* 7 July 1843; Frederick Douglass, "First of August Address, at Canandaigua, New York, August 1, 1847," in *The Life and Writings of Frederick Douglass,* ed. Philip S. Foner, 5 vols. (New York: International Publishers, 1950, 1975), 5:55; Wendell Phillips, *The Philosophy of the Abolition Movement* (27 January 1853), Anti-Slavery Tracts, new series, no. 8 (New York: American Anti-Slavery Society, 1860), 16. See also: Phillips, "Public Opinion" (28 January 1852), "The Pilgrims" (21 December 1855), and "Harper's Ferry" (1 November 1859), in *Speeches, Lectures, and Letters* (Boston: Lee and Shepard, 1872), 36, 230–31, 278–79; William Goodell, *Slavery and Anti-Slavery; A History of the Great Struggle in Both Hemispheres; . . .* (New York: William Harned, 1852; reprint, New York: Negro Universities Press, 1968), 84, 221, 236; Douglass, "Visit to Philadelphia" (13 October 1848), in

Writings, 5:101; and Theodore Parker, "The Boston Kidnapping" (12 April 1852), in *The Slave Power,* ed. James K. Hosmer (Boston: American Unitarian Association, 1916; reprint, New York: Arno, 1969), 358, and "The Aspect of Freedom in America. . . ." (5 July 1852), in *Additional Speeches, Addresses, and Occasional Sermons,* 2 vols. (Boston: Little, Brown, 1855), 1:112.

3. Parker, "The Boston Kidnapping" (12 April 1852), in *Slave Power,* 316–22, 326.

4. Ibid., 324–38, 376–77.

5. William Lloyd Garrison to Pennsylvania Anti-Slavery Society, 20 October 1857, *The Letters of William Lloyd Garrison,* ed. Walter M. Merrill and Louis Ruchames, 6 vols. (Cambridge: The Belknap Press of Harvard University Press, 1971–1981), 4:491–96.

6. Parker, "The Destination of America" (1848) in *Slave Power,* 131, 144.

7. Ibid., 129.

8. John Weiss, *Reform and Repeal, a Sermon Preached on Fast-Day, April 6, 1854, and Legal Anarchy, a Sermon Preached on June 4, 1854, after the Rendition of Anthony Burns* (Boston: Crosby, Nichols, and Company, 1854), 8, 9, 10.

9. Rev. Frederick Frothingham, *Significance of the Struggle between Liberty and Slavery . . .* (New York: American Anti-Slavery Society, 1857), 8, 18; Wendell Phillips, "Crispus Attucks" (5 March 1858), in *Speeches, Lectures, and Letters, Second Series* (Boston: Lee and Shepard, 1891; reprint, New York: Arno, 1969), 75.

10. Adin Ballou, *The Voice of Duty. An Address Delivered at the Anti-Slavery Picnic at Westminster, Mass., July 4, 1843* (Milford, Mass.: Community Press, Hopedale, 1843), 3; "Independence Day," *Liberator,* 2 July 1858; "Mr. Webster's Address at Bunker Hill, No. II," *Liberator,* 14 July 1843.

11. "Mr. Webster's Speech on Bunker Hill, No. I."

12. Rev. John G. Richardson, *Obedience to Human Law Considered in the Light of Divine Truth. . .* (Lawrence, Mass.: Homer A. Cooke, 1852), 12–13; Dr. James McCune Smith, "Citizenship," *Douglass' Monthly* 2 (June 1859): 94n.

13. Douglass, "The Reproach and Shame of the American Government. . . , August 2, 1858," in *Writings,* 5:402; Rev. P. S. Cleland, *A*

Sermon, Delivered, Sabbath, July 4, 1841, in the Presbyterian Church, Greenwood, Indiana, . . . (n. p.: 1841), 10.

14. For an account of this meeting and a record of the speeches, see *Liberator,* 15 December 1837.

15. David M. Potter, *The Impending Crisis, 1848–1861,* comp. and ed. Don E. Fehrenbacher (New York: Harper & Row, 1976), 49–50. On the idea of indefinite temporizing, see: Elizur Wright and H. B. Stanton to [unspecified], 8 November 1838, Elizur Wright Papers, Manuscript Division, Library of Congress, Washington, D. C.; [James Freeman Clarke], *Secession, Concession, or Self-Possession: Which?* (Boston: Walker, Wise, and Company, 1861), 27; and Weiss, *Reform and Repeal,* 12.

16. "Mr. Webster's Speech on Bunker Hill, No. I"; Ballou, *Voice of Duty,* 3, 12; Edward D. Barber, *An Oration, Delivered before the Addison County Anti-Slavery Society, on the Fourth of July, 1836* (Middlebury, Vt.: Knapp and Jewett, 1836), 5.

17. The major source of the following discussion is H. Trevor Colbourn, *The Lamp of Experience: Whig History and the Intellectual Origins of the American Revolution* (Chapel Hill: University of North Carolina Press, 1965). See also: Herbert Butterfield, *The Whig Interpretation of History* (London: G. Bell and Sons, 1931), and *The Englishman and His History* (Cambridge: Cambridge University Press, 1944); Caroline Robbins, *The Eighteenth-Century Commonwealthman: Studies in the Transmission, Development, and Circumstances of English Liberal Thought from the Restoration of Charles II until the War with the Thirteen Colonies* (Cambridge: Harvard University Press, 1959), 42–47, 200–02, 289–95, 363–65; J. G. A. Pocock, *The Ancient Constitution and Feudal Law: English Historical Thought in the Seventeenth Century* (New York: Norton, 1967), 230–45; F. Smith Fussner, *The Historical Revolution: English Historical Writing and Thought, 1580–1640* (New York: Columbia University Press, 1962), 30, 271.

18. Colbourn, *Lamp of Experience,* 6–10, 188–93.

19. Ibid., 25–33, 194–98. Interpretive differences over the English or Continental origins of the Saxon spirit of liberty gave rise to a variety of myths about the Anglo-Saxon peoples. See Pocock, *Ancient Constitution,* 56–58, 64.

20. "Discourses on the First Decade of Titus Livius," in *Ma-*

chiavelli: The Chief Works and Others, trans. Allan Gilbert, 3 vols. (Durham, N.C.: Duke University Press, 1958–1965), 1:419.

21. Butterfield, *Englishman and His History,* 89. Compare the historical appeals David Donald finds among proslavery theorists. Their invocations of the past expressed an uncritical, sentimental nostalgia that inspired restoration, the simple return to the past, rather than a more complex effort to recover and surpass previous experience ("The Pro-Slavery Argument Reconsidered," *Journal of Southern History* 37 [February 1971]: 3.18). In contrast, abolitionists intended their historical appeals to incite rather than assuage.

22. Colbourn, *Lamp of Experience,* 191–92.

23. Phillips, "The Scholar in a Republic," in *Speeches, Second Series,* 332–33; James Freeman Clarke, *The Rendition of Anthony Burns, its Causes and Consequences, . . .,* 2d ed. (Boston: Crosby, Nichols & Co., and Prentiss & Sawyer 1854), 14; Samuel Johnson, *The Crisis of Freedom, a Sermon, . . . June 11, 1854* (Boston, Crosby, Nichols & Co., 1854), 13. For Phillips on Sidney, see "Idols," in *Speeches,* 248–49. For other examples of references to these figures see: Charles Olcott, *Two Lectures on the Subjects of Slavery and Abolition. . . .* (Massillon, Ohio: Printed for the Author, 1838), 82; David Paul Brown, *An Oration, . . . before the Anti-Slavery Society of New York, on the Fourth of July, 1834* (Philadelphia: T. K. Collins & Co., 1834), 4.

24. "Sidney" wrote five letters to the *Courier* (16 January–6 February 1837), all reprinted in the *Liberator.* Garrison replied to four of these during March. For Garrison's responses, see *Letters of Garrison,* 2:217–32, 234–51. A notice in the *Liberator,* 11 March 1837, identified naval captain Walter Colton (1797–1851), as the author of the "Sidney" letters. See *Letters of Garrison,* 2:222.

25. *Letters of Garrison,* 2:218, 219, 221, 224.

26. Olcott, *Lectures on Slavery,* 29, 31; Phillips, "The Scholar in a Republic," in *Speeches, Second Series,* 336; Theodore Parker, "The Relation of Slavery to a Republican Form of Government, . . ." *Liberator,* 11 June 1858. See also Parker's addresses on: "The Destination of America" (1848), 120–28; "The State of the Nation" (1850), "The Progress of America" (1854), "The Rights of Man in America" (1854), and "The Present Aspect of the Anti-Slavery Enterprise" (1856), in *The Rights of Man in America,* ed. F. B. Sanborn (Boston: American

Unitarian Association, 1911; reprint, New York: Negro Universities Press, 1969), 100–107, 196–213, 370–71, 394, 425–29. For references to Saxonism that carried a more critical tone, see: "Slavery, the Principal Cause of the Decline and Fall of Nations [from *The Philanthropist*]," *Emancipator and Free American,* 13 April 1843, which took Alfred the Great to task as a heroic but flawed Saxon leader; Conway, *Testimonies Concerning Slavery,* 10, which tied the cruelty of Southern masters back to the latent "ferocity" of the Saxon character; and Parker, "The Progress of America" (1854), in *Rights of Man,* 213, which charged that Southern descendants of the Anglo-Saxons cultivated dangerous traits of commercial ambition while Northerners developed beneficent moral and religious ideals.

27. Parker, "The Present Crisis in American Affairs" (1856), in *Rights of Man,* 434–35, and "Relation of Slavery to a Republican Form of Government"; Michael Fellman, "Theodore Parker and the Abolitionist Role in the 1850s," *Journal of American History* 61 (December 1974): 672, 676, 682, 684. James Brewer Stewart argues that the language of advocates such as Phillips and Parker offered "echoes of unconscious white superiority" by glorifying Anglo-Germanic and Teutonic-Puritan sources of American traditions. See *Holy Warriors: The Abolitionists and American Slavery* (New York: Hill & Wang, 1976), 127–28.

28. Henry Highland Garnet, "The Past and the Present Condition and the Destiny of the Colored Race, Troy, 1848," in Earl Ofari, *"Let Your Motto Be Resistance": The Life and Thought of Henry Highland Garnet* (Boston: Beacon Press, 1972), 166; Douglass, "The Claims of Our Common Cause, Address of the Colored Convention held in Rochester, July, 1853, . . ." in *Writings,* 2:256–57. Reginald Horsman emphasizes the changing implications of Saxon imagery over the course of the nineteenth century. Before the early 1800s, Saxon references were usually tied to discussions of good law, representative assemblies, trial by jury, and skillfulness in the arts of government. Saxonism clarified political principles rather than claims of racial superiority. From 1815 to 1850, however, usage changed, and Saxon references more often celebrated the destiny of a race than they did the quality of political ideas (*Race and Manifest Destiny: The Origins of American Racial Anglo-Saxonism* [Cambridge: Harvard University Press, 1981], 3–10, 24–61, 98–228). Reformers who drew on Saxon-

ism may have tried to recover its older associations *in the face of* growing racism, as a reminder of Saxonism's former connotations of liberty, rather than new suggestions of hierarchy and subordination. When dealing with social protestors such as the abolitionists who were attentive to the uses and degradation of political language, such a strategy is all the more possible.

29. Douglass, "First of August Address, at Canandaigua, New York, August 1, 1847," in *Writings*, 5:57.

30. Lydia Maria Child, "The Black Saxons," *Liberator*, 8 January 1841. For a different analysis of the story, examining racial rather than historical concerns, see Ronald G. Walters, *The Antislavery Appeal: American Abolitionism after 1830* (Baltimore: Johns Hopkins University Press, 1978; New York: W. W. Norton, 1984), 57–58.

31. Phillips, "Toussaint L'Ouverture" (1861) in *Speeches*, 468–69.

32. Ibid., 481, 491–92. See also Phillips's talk on "Harper's Ferry" (1 November 1859), in *Speeches*, 281.

33. James Brown, *American Slavery in its Moral and Political Aspects Comprehensively Examined, . . .* (Oswego, N.Y.: George Henry, 1840), 47; "Mr. Webster's Speech on Bunker Hill, No. I"; Parker, "The Boston Kidnapping" (12 April 1852), in *Slave Power*, 372; William C. Nell, *Services of Colored Americans in the Wars of 1776 and 1812* (Boston: Prentiss & Sawyer, 1851), 7; Douglass, "The Reproach and Shame of the American Government . . . , August 2, 1858," in *Writings*, 5:404.

34. Douglass, "The Meaning of July Fourth for the Negro . . . , July 5, 1852," in *Writings*, 2:184–85.

35. O. S. Freeman, *Letters on Slavery, Addressed to the Pro-Slavery Men of America . . .* (Boston: Bela Marsh, 1855), 51.

36. Ibid., 58, 65–66.

37. Ibid., 58–60, 66. William Goodell also noted that the South was "overrun with tories" during the Revolution. See Goodell, *Slavery and Anti-Slavery*, 71.

38. Theodore Parker, *The Effect of Slavery on the American People. A Sermon . . .* (Boston: William Kent, 1858), 3, and *The Nebraska Question. Some Thoughts on the New Assault upon Freedom in America . . . , Feb. 12, 1852* (Boston: Benjamin B. Mussey & Co., 1854), 13; Goodell, *Slavery and Anti-Slavery*, 319–21; Charles Follen, "The Cause of Freedom in Our Country," *Quarterly Anti-Slavery*

Magazine 2 (October 1836): 62, 69. See also Frothingham, *Significance of the Struggle,* esp. 6–8.

39. Frederick Douglass, *The Frederick Douglass Papers, Series One: Speeches, Debates, and Interviews,* ed. John W. Blassingame (New Haven: Yale University Press, 1979), 93, 134–37, 183–84, 254, 311, 343–44, 352.

40. Douglass, "Shooting a Negro" (24 February 1854), in *Writings,* 5:318; *Proceedings of the Colored National Convention, Held in Rochester, July 6th, 7th and 8th, 1853* (Rochester: Office of Frederick Douglass's Paper, 1853), 3; *Minutes of the State Convention, of the Colored Citizens of Ohio, Convened at Columbus, January 9th, 10th, 11th, and 12th, 1850* (Columbus: The Ohio Standard Office, 1850), 21; "Address," in *Minutes of the National Convention of Colored Citizens: Held at Buffalo, on the 15th, 16th, 17th, 18th, and 19th of August 1843, for the Purpose of Considering Their Moral and Political Condition as American Citizens* (New York: Piercy & Reed, 1843), 4–6.

41. Johnson, *Crisis of Freedom,* 9.

42. William Jackson, *Views of Slavery, in its Effects on the Wealth, Population, and Character of Nations* (Philadelphia: Merrihew and Gunn, 1838), 8–11; [Julius R. Ames], *"Liberty"* (New York: American Anti-Slavery Society, 1837), 51; American Anti-Slavery Society, *Second Annual Report . . .* (New York: William S. Dorr, 1835), 66–67; David L[ee] Child, *The Despotism of Freedom; or the Tyranny and Cruelty of American Republican Slave-Masters, . . .* (Boston: Boston Young Men's Anti-Slavery Association for the Diffusion of Truth, 1833), 37; Richard Hildreth, *Despotism in America: An Inquiry into the Nature, Results, and Legal Basis of the Slave-Holding System in the United States* (Boston: John P. Jewett & Co., 1854), 100, 103; Horace James, *Our Duties to the Slave . . .* (Boston: Richardson & Filmer, 1847), 9; John Quincy Adams, quoted in [William Lloyd Garrison et al.], "Disunion: Address of the American Anti-Slavery Society; and F. Jackson's Letter on the Pro-Slavery Character of the Constitution," *Anti-Slavery Examiner* 12 (1845): 12.

43. "Slavery in Rome" (reprinted from *North American Review* 39 [October 1834]: 413–43) and William Pinkney, "Speech in the Maryland House of Delegates, 1789," in [Ames], *"Liberty,"* 30–31, 51–54. The American Anti-Slavery Society also reaffirmed the critical role of

the "yeomanry" in republican government through references to ancient Greek slavery. See *Second Annual Report, 67.*

44. Anne Warren Weston, "The Come-Outers of the Sixteenth and Nineteenth Centuries," in *The Liberty Bell* (Boston: Massachusetts Anti-Slavery Fair, 1845), 91–99; Freeman, *Letters,* 56, 65; Child, *Despotism of Freedom,* 38–40n; Thomas Wentworth Higginson, *The New Revolution: A Speech before the American Anti-Slavery Society . . . May 12, 1857* (Boston: R. F. Wallcut, 1857), 8–9; Edmund H. Sears, *Revolution or Reform: A Discourse Occasioned by the Present Crisis, Preached at Wayland, Mass., Sunday, June 15, 1856* (Boston: Crosby, Nichols & Co., 1856), 11. The concluding quote is taken from David Paul Brown, *Address of the Members of the Philadelphia Anti-Slavery Society to Their Fellow Citizens* (Philadelphia: W. P. Gibbons, 1835), 18.

45. James Brown, *American Slavery,* 43; Frothingham, *Significance of the Struggle,* 12; Phillips, "Harper's Ferry" (1 November 1859), in *Speeches,* 274; William Lloyd Garrison to the *Liberator,* 11 May 1847, in *Letters of Garrison,* 3:478–79; Samuel J. May, *Liberty or Slavery, the Only Question . . .* (Syracuse: J. G. K. Truair, 1856) 16.

46. Parker, "The Boston Kidnapping" (12 April 1852), in *Slave Power,* 377–78.

47. Phillips, "The Boston Mob" (21 October 1855) and "Disunion" (20 January 1861), in *Speeches,* 227, 349; [Zebina Eastman], *Slavery a Falling Tower. A Lecture on Slavery the Cause of the Civil War in the United States, Delivered at the Arley Chapel, Bristol, June 1862,* 2d ed. (Chicago: John R. Walsh, [1862?]), 16. See also: Goodell, *Slavery and Anti-Slavery,* 71; Parker, "The Boston Kidnapping" (12 April 1852), in *Slave Power,* 330; [Garrison et al.], "Disunion: Address of the American Anti-Slavery Society," 3. The question of historical parallels occasionally arose in response to proslavery historical arguments. Parker, Follen, and the *Emancipator* all rebutted opponents who were comforted by similarities between America's slave system and that of other peoples. Such arguments held that bondage in Hebrew, Grecian, Roman, and Saxon societies demonstrated slavery's inevitability, its positive functions, and its legitimacy, even in a republic. Abolitionists responded not by questioning historical parallelism but by dismissing the particular connections that slavery's apologists made. Reformers insisted that an accurate reading of the past revealed

only ominous parallels: the denial of liberty to many, the confinement of freedom to a few, and the degradation of labor for all brought inevitable ruin. See: Parker, "Relation of Slavery to a Republican Form of Government"; Charles Follen et al., *Address to the People of the United States, by a Committee of the New-England Anti-Slavery Convention, . . .* (Boston: Garrison & Knapp, 1834), 13; "Slavery the Principal Cause of the Decline and Fall of Nations," *Emancipator and Free American,* 13 April 1843.

48. Lewis Tappan to Salmon P. Chase, 23 June 1852, Tappan Letterbooks, Lewis Tappan Papers, Manuscript Division, Library of Congress, Washington, D.C.; *Proceedings of the Colored National Convention in Rochester,* 1853, 4; Samuel Willard, *The Grand Issue: An Ethico-Political Tract* (Boston: John P. Jewett & Co., 1851), 13; George B. Cheever, D.D., "Address on the Subject of the Iniquity of the Extension of Slavery . . ." (30 October 1856), in *God against Slavery: And the Freedom and Duty of the Pulpit to Rebuke it, as a Sin against God* (New York: Joseph H. Ladd, 1857; reprint, Miami: Mnemosyne Publishing, 1969), 193; Douglass, "The Kansas-Nebraska Bill" (30 October 1854), in *Writings,* 2:324.

49. Freeman, *Letters,* 53; Cheever, "Iniquity of the Extension of Slavery," 220, 222; S[eymour] B[oughton] Treadwell, *American Liberties and American Slavery, Morally and Politically Illustrated* (Boston: Weeks, Jordon & Co., 1838), 175.

50. Phillips, "The Right of Petition" (28 March 1837), in *Speeches, Second Series,* 3.

51. Henry David Thoreau, "The Last Days of John Brown," in *Thoreau: The Major Essays,* ed. Jeffrey L. Duncan (New York: E. P. Dutton, 1972), 172; Phillips, "The Murder of Lovejoy" (8 December 1837), in *Speeches,* 10.

52. American Anti-Slavery Society, *Sixth Annual Report . . .* (New York: William S. Dorr, 1839), 115.

53. Moncure D. Conway, "Rudiments," in *The Liberty Bell* (Boston: National Anti-Slavery Bazaar, 1858), 188.

54. James Russell Lowell, "Shall We Ever Be Republican?" *National Anti-Slavery Standard,* 20 April 1848; Southern and Western Liberty Convention, *Address . . . to the People of the United States, . . .* (Cincinnati: Printed at the Gazette Office [1845]), 7.

55. Douglass, "American Slavery" (24 January 1854) and "The Re-

proach and Shame of the American Government . . . , August 2, 1858," in *Writings,* 5:310, 397–98.

56. Goodell, *Slavery and Anti-Slavery,* 103, 105.

57. William Lloyd Garrison, "To the Abolitionists of Massachusetts," 17 July 1839, *Letters of Garrison,* 2:498; S[tephen] S. Foster, "Whither are We Drifting?" *Liberator,* 25 June 1858; Goodell, *Slavery and Anti-Slavery,* 477. The same feelings moved Amos Phelps to decry the introduction of the "woman question" into antislavery activity. See Phelps to Elizur Wright, 2 August 1838, Wright Papers. Garrison also argued that loyalty to the original principles of the 1833 *Declaration of Sentiments* was the major issue at stake between abolitionists who chose political action and those who embraced moral suasion. See his reply to an essay by James G. Birney: "To the Editor of the *Emancipator,*" 31 May 1839, *Letters of Garrison,* 2:464–86.

58. Thoreau, "Last Days of John Brown," 172 [emphasis added].

59. "Speech of Wendell Phillips," *Liberator,* 11 June 1858.

60. *Declaration of Sentiments of the American Anti-Slavery Society* . . . (New York: William S. Dorr, [1833]), 1–2; Anti-Slavery Convention of American Women, *An Appeal to the Women of the Nominally Free States* . . . (New York: William S. Dorr, 1837), 26–27; "Ohio Liberty State Convention, June 8, 1842," *Emancipator and Free American,* 7 July 1842; Southern and Western Liberty Convention, *Address . . . to the People of the United States,* . . . , 3, 8; William W. Brown, "A Lecture Delivered before the Female Anti-Slavery Society of Salem . . . , Nov. 14, 1847," in *The Narrative of William W. Brown, a Fugitive Slave* (Reading, Mass.: Addison-Wesley, 1969), 96; "Anti-Slavery Celebration of Independence Day," *Liberator,* 10 July 1857; Douglass, "The Reproach and Shame of the American Government . . . , August 2, 1858," in *Writings,* 5:400.

61. Douglass, "The Reproach and Shame of the American Government . . . , August 2, 1858," in *Writings,* 5:401; Henry Highland Garnet, "Speech Delivered at the Liberty Party Convention, Massachusetts, 1842," in Ofari, *Life and Thought,* 143; New York City Anti-Slavery Society, *Address . . . to the People of the City of New-York* (New York: West and Trow, 1833), 25; Phillips, "The Pilgrims" (21 December 1855), in *Speeches,* 230–31.

62. Douglass, "The Reproach and Shame of the American Government . . . , August 2, 1858," in *Writings,* 5:403; Frothingham, *Signifi-*

cance of the Struggle, 7–8. Douglass referred to President James B. Buchanan, Senators Lewis Cass (D-Michigan), and Isaac Toucey (D-Connecticut), and Rep. Howell Cobb (D-Georgia) (ibid., 5:539, n. 51).

63. Southern and Western Liberty Convention, *Address . . . to the People of the United States, . . .,* 8; Phillips, "Harper's Ferry" (1 November 1859), in *Speeches,* 268; James G. Birney, "Correspondence between the Hon. F. H. Elmore, One of the South Carolina Delegation in Congress, and James G. Birney, One of the Secretaries of the American Anti-Slavery Society," *Anti-Slavery Examiner* 8 (1838): 34; Conway, *Testimonies Concerning Slavery,* 129.

64. Phillips, "The Boston Mob" (21 October 1855), in *Speeches,* 226–27; Frothingham, *Significance of the Struggle,* 15; "The First of August," *Liberator,* 31 July 1846; American and Foreign Anti-Slavery Society, *Thirteenth Annual Report . . .* (New York: American and Foreign Anti-Slavery Society, 1853), 3–4.

65. John Greenleaf Whittier, "'The Bill of Abominations,'" *Anti-Slavery Record* 2 (July 1836): 10–11; Phillips, "Disunion" (20 January 1861), in *Speeches,* 348; Willard, *The Grand Issue,* 14; Douglass, "The Meaning of July Fourth for the Negro . . . , July 5, 1852," in *Writings,* 2:184; Parker, "The Rights of Man in America" (1854), in *Rights of Man,* 391. On the Revolutionaries as early abolitionists, see: Rev. William Barnes, *American Slavery, A Sermon, Preached at Hampton, Connecticut, April 14th, 1843, the Day of the Annual Public Fast* (Hartford: Elihu Geer, 1843), 16; Executive Committee of the Ohio Anti-Slavery Society, *Narrative of the Late Riotous Proceedings against the Liberty of the Press, in Cincinnati, . . .* (Cincinnati: [Ohio Anti-Slavery Society], 1836), 5–6.

66. Parker, *The Nebraska Question,* 71; Thoreau, "A Plea for Captain John Brown" (30 October 1859), in *The Major Essays,* 147, 158; speech of E. H. Heywood, in "Anti-Slavery Celebration of Independence Day, at the Framingham Grove, July 5, 1858," *Liberator,* 16 July 1858; "Resolution" [n.d.], Item 87, Massachusetts Anti-Slavery Society Papers, New York Historical Society, New York, N.Y.

67. "New-England Anti-Slavery Society" (1834), quoted in [Ames], *"Liberty,"* 108; Barber, *Oration before the Addison County Anti-Slavery Society,* 11. See also: Lowell, "Shall We Ever be Republicans?" 186, and "Fourth of July in Charleston," in *National Anti-Slavery*

Standard, 26 July 1849; Rev. James A. Thome, "The Anti-Slavery Movement: Its Past and Present, Delivered before the Church Anti-Slavery Society, at its Anniversary, May 6, 1861, in the Church of the Puritans, New York," newspaper clipping, Tappan Papers.

68. Garrison to Phillips, 1861, in "New Light on Wendell Phillips: The Community of Reform, 1840–1880," ed. Irving H. Bartlett, *Perspectives in American History* 12 (1979): 219.

69. David Paul Brown, *Address of the Members of the Philadelphia Anti-Slavery Society,* 18.

70. Child, *Despotism of Freedom,* 41.

71. Parker, "The Rights of Man in America" (1854), in *Rights of Man,* 334–40; Thomas Wentworth Higginson, *Massachusetts in Mourning: A Sermon, Preached in Worcester, on Sunday, June 4, 1854* (Boston: James Munroe and Company, 1854), 8–9. On the politics of time, see: J. G. A. Pocock, *The Machiavellian Moment: Florentine Political Thought and the Atlantic Republican Tradition* (Princeton: Princeton University Press, 1975), 3, 9, 27, 51, 84–85, 190, 320, 328–29.

72. "How Can It Be Done?" *Anti-Slavery Record* 2 (September 1836): 11.

CHAPTER 3

1. William Goodell, *Slavery and Anti-Slavery; A History of the Great Struggle in Both Hemispheres; . . .* (New York: William Harned, 1852; reprint, New York: Negro Universities Press, 1968), 387–88; Dwight Lowell Dumond, *Antislavery Origins of the Civil War in the United States* (Ann Arbor: University of Michigan Press, 1939), 35; Bertram Wyatt-Brown, *Lewis Tappan and the Evangelical War against Slavery* (Cleveland: Case-Western Reserve University Press, 1969), 287.

2. Gilbert Hobbs Barnes, *The Anti-Slavery Impulse, 1830–1844* (New York: D. Appleton-Century, 1933); Whitney R. Cross, *The Burned-Over District: The Social and Intellectual History of Enthusiastic Religion in Western New York, 1800–1850* (Ithaca: Cornell University Press, 1950); David Brion Davis, "The Emergence of Immediatism in British and American Antislavery Thought," *Mississippi Valley Historical Review* 49 (September 1962): 209–230, *The Problem of Slavery in Western Culture* (Ithaca: Cornell University Press,

1966), *The Problem of Slavery in the Age of Revolution, 1770–1823* (Ithaca: Cornell University Press, 1975), and *Slavery and Human Progress* (New York: Oxford University Press, 1984); Clifford S. Griffin, *Their Brothers' Keepers: Moral Stewardship in the United States, 1800–1865* (New Brunswick: Rutgers University Press, 1960); Anne C. Loveland, "Evangelicalism and 'Immediate Emancipation' in American Antislavery Thought," *Journal of Southern History* 32 (May 1966): 172–88; Lewis Perry, *Radical Abolitionism: Anarchy and the Government of God in Antislavery Thought* (Ithaca: Cornell University Press, 1973); Timothy L. Smith, *Revivalism and Social Reform: American Protestantism on the Eve of the Civil War* (Nashville: Abingdon, 1957); Richard S. Taylor, "Beyond Immediate Emancipation: Jonathan Blanchard, Abolitionism, and the Emergence of American Fundamentalism," *Civil War History* 27 (September 1981): 260–74; John L. Thomas, "Romantic Reform in America, 1815–1865," *American Quarterly* 17 (Winter 1965): 656–81.

3. Charles C. Cole, Jr., *The Social Ideas of the Northern Evangelists, 1826–1860* (New York: Columbia University Press, 1954); Charles Foster, *An Errand of Mercy: The Evangelical United Front, 1790–1837* (Chapel Hill: University of North Carolina Press, 1960); Carol V. R. George, "Widening the Circle: The Black Church and the Abolitionist Crusade, 1830–1860," in *Antislavery Reconsidered: New Perspectives on the Abolitionists,* ed. Lewis Perry and Michael Fellman (Baton Rouge: Louisiana State University Press, 1979), 75–95; John R. McKivigan, *The War against Proslavery Religion: Abolitionism and the Northern Churches, 1830–1865* (Ithaca: Cornell University Press, 1984); J. F. Maclear, "The Evangelical Alliance and the Antislavery Crusade," *Huntington Library Quarterly* 42 (Spring 1979): 141–64; Donald G. Mathews, *Slavery and Methodism: A Chapter in American Morality, 1780–1845* (Princeton: Princeton University Press, 1965); Wyatt-Brown, *Lewis Tappan.*

4. Lois W. Banner, "Religion and Reform in the Early Republic: The Role of Youth," *American Quarterly* 23 (December 1971): 677–95; Lawrence J. Friedman, *Gregarious Saints: Self and Community in American Abolitionism, 1830–1870* (Cambridge: Cambridge University Press, 1982); Donald M. Scott, "Abolition as a Sacred Vocation," in *Antislavery Reconsidered,* 51–74; Bertram Wyatt-Brown, "Conscience and Career: Young Abolitionists and Missionaries," in *Anti-*

Slavery, Religion, and Reform: Essays in Memory of Roger Anstey, ed. Christine Bolt and Seymour Drescher (Folkestone, Kent: Wm. Dawson & Sons, 1980), 183–203.

5. On the links between Christian and republican principles, see: James D. Essig, *The Bonds of Wickedness: American Evangelicals against Slavery, 1770–1808* (Philadelphia: Temple University Press, 1982), ch. 4; Paul Goodman, "Moral Purpose and Republican Politics in Antebellum America, 1830–1860," *Maryland Historian* 20 (Fall–Winter 1989): 5–39; Nathan O. Hatch, *The Democratization of American Christianity* (New Haven: Yale University Press, 1989), 69–77, 186–89, and "In Pursuit of Religious Freedom: Church, State, and People in the New Republic," in *The American Revolution: Its Character and Limits,* ed. Jack P. Greene (New York: New York University Press, 1987), 388–406; Duncan J. MacLeod, *Slavery, Race and the American Revolution* (Cambridge: Cambridge University Press, 1974), esp. 18–28; and Donald G. Mathews, "Religion and Slavery: The Case of the American South," in *Anti-Slavery, Religion, and Reform,* 212–20.

6. James Thome to Theodore Dwight Weld, 9 February 1836, in *The Letters of Theodore Dwight Weld, Angelina Grimké Weld, and Sarah Grimké, 1822–1844,* ed. Gilbert H. Barnes and Dwight L. Dumond, 2 vols. (New York: D. Appleton-Century, 1934; reprint, Gloucester, Mass.: Peter Smith, 1965), 1:257; James McCune Smith, "An Address to the People of the United States," *Proceedings of the Colored National Convention, Held in . . . Philadelphia, October 16th, 17th and 18th, 1855* (Salem, N.J.: The National Standard Office, 1856), 30; Sarah Grimké to Gerrit Smith, 12 January 1837, *Weld-Grimké Letters,* 1:357; Maria Weston Chapman, *Right and Wrong in Massachusetts* (Boston: Dow & Jackson Anti-Slavery Press, 1839; reprint, New York: Negro Universities Press, 1969), 6; New York City Anti-Slavery Society, *Address . . . to the People of the City of New-York* (New York: West and Trow, 1833), 11; Angelina E. Grimké, "Appeal to the Christian Women of the South," *Anti-Slavery Examiner* 1 (September 1836): 19–20; American Anti-Slavery Society, *Fourth Annual Report, . . .* (New York: William S. Dorr, 1837), 15–16; Rev. Arthur B. Bradford to Lewis Tappan, 1 July 1852, Lewis Tappan Letterbooks, Lewis Tappan Papers, Manuscript Division, Library of Congress, Washington, D.C.

7. William Lloyd Garrison, *An Address Delivered in Marlboro Chapel, Boston, July 4, 1838* (Boston: Isaac Knapp, 1838), 3; Frederick Douglass, "The Meaning of July Fourth for the Negro . . . , July 5, 1852," in *The Life and Writings of Frederick Douglass*, ed. Philip S. Foner, 5 vols. (New York: International Publishers, 1950, 1975), 2:199–200. Another abolitionist located the reason for slave suicides in the desire "to get beyond the reach of this American republicanism and American christianity." See S[eymour] B[oughton] Treadwell, *American Liberties and American Slavery, Morally and Politically Illustrated* (Boston: Weeks, Jordon & Co., 1838), 252.

8. Treadwell, *American Liberties*, 378, 417–18; Wendell Phillips, "The Lesson of the Hour," in *Disunion, Two Discourses at Music Hall, on January 20th, and February 17th, 1861* (Boston: Robert F. Wallcut, 1861), 15.

9. Enoch Mack, "The Revolution Unfinished, or American Independence Begun," in *Trumpets of Glory: Fourth of July Orations, 1786–1861*, ed. Henry A. Hawken (Granby, Conn.: The Salmon Brook Historical Society, 1976), 172; Garrison, *Address Delivered in Marlboro Chapel*, 34. See Isaiah 61:1 and Luke 4:18.

10. William Henry Furness, *Two Discourses Occasioned by the Approaching Anniversary of the Declaration of Independence, . . .* (Philadelphia: John Pennington, 1843), 4–5.

11. Religious Anti-Slavery Convention, *The Declaration and Pledge against Slavery, Adopted by the Religious Anti-Slavery Convention, Held at the Marlboro' Chapel, Boston, February 26, 1846* (Boston: Devereux & Seaman Printers, 1846), 6, 7; "Motives for Anti-Slavery Effort," *The Liberty Almanac for 1850* (New York: American and Foreign Anti-Slavery Society, 1850), 38; William Lloyd Garrison to Elizabeth Pease, 20 June 1849, in *The Letters of William Lloyd Garrison*, ed. Walter M. Merrill and Louis Ruchames, 6 vols. (Cambridge: The Belknap Press of Harvard University Press, 1971–1981), 3:633. See also Garrison's essay on "The American Union" in *The Liberty Bell* (Boston: Massachusetts Anti-Slavery Fair, 1845), 231.

12. Rev. Charles Beecher, *The God of the Bible against Slavery*, Anti-Slavery Tracts, old series, no. 17 (New York 1855–56), 2, 3, 6.

13. Anti-Slavery Convention of American Women, *An Appeal to the Women of the Nominally Free States, . . .* (New York: William S. Dorr, 1837), 68; "Shall the Ministers of Religion Interfere in Politics"

(reprinted from the *Religious Monitor* [Philadelphia], which reprinted the article from the *Public Ledger* [Philadelphia]), *American and Foreign Anti-Slavery Reporter,* 1 (April 1841): 148; John Weiss, *Reform and Repeal, a Sermon Preached on Fast-Day, April 6, 1854, and Legal Anarchy, a Sermon on June 4, 1854, after the Rendition of Anthony Burns* (Boston: Crosby, Nichols & Co., 1854), 14; James Brown, *American Slavery in its Moral and Political Aspects Comprehensively Examined,* . . . (Oswego, N.Y.: George Henry, 1840), 28, 48; Theodore Parker, "The Rights of Man in America" (1854), in *The Rights of Man in America,* ed. F. B. Sanborn (Boston: American Unitarian Association, 1911; reprint, New York: Negro Universities Press, 1969), 396; Harriet Beecher Stowe, *Uncle Tom's Cabin* (1852), in *Three Novels* (New York: The Library of America, 1982), 502. On the "Liberal Orthodoxy" of Stowe, see Marie Caskey, *Chariot of Fire: Religion and the Beecher Family* (New Haven: Yale University Press, 1978), 161, 178, 184, 198–99, 241.

14. Charles Olcott, *Two Lectures on the Subjects of Slavery and Abolition.* . . . (Massillon, Ohio: Printed for the Author, 1838), 27.

15. [George Bourne], *A Condensed Anti-Slavery Bible Argument; By a Citizen of Virginia* (New York: S.W. Benedict, 1845), 89–90; Religious Anti-Slavery Convention, *Declaration and Pledge,* 2.

16. [Bourne], *Condensed Anti-Slavery Bible Argument,* 74; newspaper clipping, Journals and Notebooks, Tappan Papers.

17. Olcott, *Lectures on Slavery,* 20–21. See also Douglass, "Speeches Delivered at the Fifteenth Annual Meeting of the American Anti-Slavery Society, May, 1849," in *Writings,* 5:131–132. On proslavery readings of the Bible see: Larry E. Tise, *Proslavery: A History of the Defense of Slavery in America, 1701–1840* (Athens, Ga.: University of Georgia Press, 1987); Mathews, *Slavery and Methodism;* and Jack P. Maddex, Jr., "Proslavery Millennialism: Social Eschatology in Antebellum Southern Calvinism," *American Quarterly* 31 (Spring 1979): 46–62, and '"The Southern Apostasy' Revisited: The Significance of Proslavery Christianity," *Marxist Perspectives* 2 (Fall 1979): 132–41.

18. Mary Elizabeth Robbins, "Freedom," in *The Liberty Bell* (Boston: American Anti-Slavery Society, 1839), 51–52.

19. Daniel Foster, *An Address on Slavery, Delivered in Danvers, Mass.* (Boston: Bela Marsh, 1849), 25; H. P. Cutting, *The Crisis—Slav-*

ery or Freedom: A Discourse Preached in Williston and Hinesburgh, on Sundays, June 25th, and July 2d, 1854 (Burlington, Vt.: Sml. B. Nichols, 1854), 17; Lewis Tappan to Mrs. Bigelow, 14 January 1844, Tappan Letterbooks; George B. Cheever, *The Guilt of Slavery and the Crime of Slaveholding, Demonstrated from the Hebrew and Greek Scriptures* (Boston: John P. Jewett & Co., 1860; reprint, New York: Negro Universities Press, 1969), vi, 235–36. See also Cheever's sermon on *The Salvation of the Country Secured by Immediate Emancipation . . .* (New York: John A. Gray, 1861).

20. Cutting, *The Crisis,* 18; William Lloyd Garrison to Louis Kossuth, February 1852, *Letters of Garrison,* 4:160 [emphasis added].

21. William H. Furness, *An Address Delivered before a Meeting of the Members and Friends of the Pennsylvania Anti-Slavery Society . . .* (Philadelphia: Merrihew & Thompson, 1850), 16.

22. Douglass, "Speeches Delivered at the Fifteenth Annual Meeting of the American Anti-Slavery Society, May, 1849," in *Writings,* 5:130.

23. Samuel May, Jr., letter to the editor, *National Anti-Slavery Standard,* 18 October 1849; Religious Anti-Slavery Convention, *Declaration and Pledge,* 7; Weiss, *Reform and Repeal,* 15, 16; Foster, *Address on Slavery,* 9.

24. Lewis Tappan to Benjamin Tappan, 18 January 1845, Tappan Letterbooks [emphasis added]. Revelation 18:4 states: "And I heard another voice from heaven, saying, Come out of her, my people, that ye be not partakers of her sins, and that ye receive not of her plagues."

25. On nonresistant and disunionist factions in abolition, see: Lewis Perry, *Radical Abolitionism: Anarchy and the Government of God in Antislavery Thought* (Ithaca: Cornell University Press, 1973); Aileen S. Kraditor, *Means and Ends in American Abolitionism: Garrison and His Critics on Strategy and Tactics, 1834–1850* (New York: Pantheon, 1969), 206–7.

26. Letter, John Humphrey Noyes to William Lloyd Garrison, 22 March 1837, in Lorman Ratner, *Pre-Civil War Reform: The Variety of Principles and Programs* (Englewood Cliffs, N.J.: Prentice-Hall, 1967), 36–37.

27. [William Lloyd Garrison et al.], "Disunion: Address of the American Anti-Slavery Society; and F. Jackson's Letter on the Pro-Slavery Character of the Constitution," *Anti-Slavery Examiner* 12 (1845): 4, 19.

28. "Speech of Charles C. Burleigh," in *Proceedings of the American Anti-Slavery Society, at its Second Decade, . . .* (New York: American Anti-Slavery Society, 1854), 68.

29. Rev. W. H. Furness, "The Outrage at Washington" (25 May 1856), *National Anti-Slavery Standard,* 31 May 1856.

30. Rev. J[onathan] Blanchard and N[athan] L[ewis] Rice, *A Debate on Slavery, Held in the City of Cincinnati on the First, Second, Third, and Sixth Days of October 1845, upon the Question: Is Slave-Holding in Itself Sinful, and the Relation Between Master and Slave, a Sinful Relation?* (Cincinnati: Wm. H. Moore & Co., 1846; reprint, New York: Negro Universities Press, 1969), 237, 362–64; Rev. Charles E. Hodges, *Disunion Our Wisdom and Our Duty,* Anti-Slavery Tracts, old series, no. 11 (New York 1855–56), 4; *Declaration of Sentiments of the American Anti-Slavery Society, Adopted at the Formation of Said Society, in Philadelphia, on the 4th Day of December, 1833* (New York: William S. Dorr, n. d.), 2.

On slavery and sin, see Davis, *Problem of Slavery in Western Culture* and *Problem of Slavery in the Age of Revolution*; Donald G. Mathews, "Orange Scott: The Methodist Evangelist as Revolutionary," in *The Antislavery Vanguard: New Essays on the Abolitionists,* ed. Martin Duberman (Princeton: Princeton University Press, 1965), 71–101; Loveland, "Evangelicalism and 'Immediate Emancipation'," 172–88; and Scott, "Abolition as a Sacred Vocation," 51–74.

31. John G. Fee, *An Anti-Slavery Manual, Being an Examination, in the Light of the Bible, and of Facts, into the Moral and Social Wrongs of American Slavery, with a Remedy for the Evil* (Maysville, Ky.: The Herald Office, 1848), 126–28; Henry Highland Garnet, "An Address to the Slaves of the United States of America" (1843), in *Slavery Attacked: The Abolitionist Crusade,* ed. John L. Thomas (Englewood Cliffs, N.J.: Prentice-Hall, 1965), 100; Douglass, "Lecture on Slavery, No. 2" (8 December 1850), in *Writings,* 2:141; David Root, *A Fast Sermon on Slavery* (Dover, N.H.: The Enquirer Office, 1835), 6, 8, and *A Tract for the Times and for the Churches* (Boston: A. J. Wright [1845]), 12, 15.

32. James T. Dickinson, "An Anti-Slavery Sermon, Delivered at Norwich, July 4, 1834," 2d ed., in *Legal and Moral Aspects of Slavery: Selected Essays* (New York: Negro Universities Press, 1969), 1; John G. Fee, *The Sinfulness of Slavery Shown by Appeals to Reason*

and Scripture (New York: John A. Gray, 1851), 23; Rev. J[onathan] Blanchard, *Sermon on Slaveholding: Preached by Appointment, before the Synod of Cincinnati, at Their Late Stated Meeting at Mount Pleasant, Ohio, October 20th, 1841* (Cincinnati: n. p., 1842), 7. See also: Root, *Tract for the Times*, 15; Garnet, "Address to Slaves," 100; "Mr. Blanchard's Sixth Speech," in Blanchard and Rice, *Debate on Slavery*, 149; and William Lloyd Garrison to Theobald Mathew, 5 October 1849, in *Letters of Garrison*, 3:670–71.

33. William Henry Brisbane, *Slaveholding Examined in the Light of the Holy Bible* (New York: American and Foreign Anti-Slavery Society [1847?]), 158, 165; Root, *Tract for the Times*, 12, 15. See also Amos A. Phelps, *Letters to Professor Stowe and Dr. Bacon, on God's Real Method with Great Social Wrongs, in Which the Bible is Vindicated from Grossly Erroneous Interpretations* (New York: William Harned, 1848), 29.

34. "Letter from Mr. Birney," *Anti-Slavery Record* 2 (June 1836): 8; *Proceedings of the Convention of Radical Political Abolitionists, Held at Syracuse, N.Y., June 26th, 27th, and 28th, 1855* (New York: Central Abolition Board, 1855), 36; Rev. William W. Patton, *Thoughts for Christians, Suggested by the Case of Passmore Williamson: A Discourse Preached in the Fourth Congregational Church, Hartford, Conn., . . . October 7, 1855* (Hartford: Montague & Co., 1855), 18.

35. Edmund H. Sears, *Revolution or Reform: A Discourse Occasioned by the Present Crisis, Preached at Wayland, Mass., Sunday, June 15, 1856* (Boston: Crosby, Nichols & Co., 1856), 12.

36. "Shall the Ministers of Religion Interfere in Politics," 148.

37. Olcott, *Lectures on Slavery*, 125.

38. Wendell Phillips, "The Puritan Principle and John Brown" (18 December 1859), *Speeches, Lectures, and Letters, Second Series* (Boston: Lee and Shepard, 1891; reprint, New York: Arno, 1969), 293, 297, 299.

39. Sears, *Revolution or Reform*, 11. For other examples of the abolitionist perception of Puritanism, see: Lewis Tappan to the Members of the Congregation of the Church of the Pilgrim, 19 December 1853, Tappan Letterbooks; Rev. David Root, *The Abolition Cause Eventually Triumphant . . .* (Andover: Gould and Newman, 1836), 15; Lydia Maria Child, *Kansas Emigrants* [partial manuscript], Lydia Maria Child Papers, Manuscripts and Archives Divi-

sion, New York Public Library, New York, N.Y.; Theodore Parker, "The Boston Kidnapping" (12 April 1852), in *The Slave Power,* ed. James K. Hosmer (Boston: American Unitarian Association, 1916; reprint, New York: Arno, 1969), 323–24; Henry Highland Garnet, "Speech Delivered at the Seventh Anniversary of the American Anti-Slavery Society, 1840," in Earl Ofari, *"Let Your Motto be Resistance": The Life and Thought of Henry Highland Garnet* (Boston: Beacon Press, 1972), 128.

40. Theodore Parker, "The Aspect of Freedom in America. . . ." (5 July 1852), in *Additional Speeches, Addresses, and Occasional Sermons,* 2 vols. (Boston: Little, Brown, 1855), 1:109–110.

41. Thomas T. Stone, "The Second Reformation," in *The Liberty Bell* (Boston: National Anti-Slavery Bazaar, 1851), 120, 121, 122.

42. "Fragments" folder, 104 [n. d.], Elizabeth Cady Stanton Papers, Manuscript Division, Library of Congress, Washington, D.C.; Henry Clapp, Jr., "Modern Christianity," in *The Liberty Bell* (1845), 181.

43. Anne Warren Weston, "The Come-Outers of the Sixteenth and Nineteenth Centuries," in *The Liberty Bell* (1845), 99.

44. Olcott, *Lectures on Slavery,* 102; Goodell, *Slavery and Anti-Slavery,* 387. On the Union Church movement, see: McKivigan, *War against Proslavery Religion,* 95–96, 147–49, 159; Friedman, *Gregarious Saints,* 108–9.

45. Weiss, *Reform and Repeal,* 15; Goodell, *Slavery and Anti-Slavery,* 591–92.

46. Moncure Conway invoked II Corinthians 3:17 in his essay "Rudiments," in *The Liberty Bell* (Boston: National Anti-Slavery Bazaar, 1858), 198.

CHAPTER 4

1. American Anti-Slavery Society, *Second Annual Report . . .* (New York: William S. Dorr, 1835), 66–67.

2. Scholarly studies tend to focus on the abolitionists' political disagreements, emphasizing schisms within the movement rather than the common ideological base from which those differences emerged. See: Gilbert Hobbs Barnes, *The Anti-Slavery Impulse, 1830–1844* (New York: D. Appleton-Century, 1933); Dwight Lowell Dumond, *Antislavery: The Crusade for Freedom in America* (Ann Arbor: University of Michigan Press, 1961); Louis Filler, *The Crusade Against*

Slavery, 1830–1860 (New York: Harper & Row, 1960); Lawrence J. Friedman, *Gregarious Saints: Self and Community in American Abolitionism, 1830–1870* (Cambridge: Cambridge University Press, 1982); Aileen S. Kraditor, *Means and Ends in American Abolitionism: Garrison and His Critics on Strategy and Tactics, 1834–1850* (New York: Pantheon, 1969); Lewis Perry, *Radical Abolitionism: Anarchy and the Government of God in Antislavery Thought* (Ithaca: Cornell University Press, 1973).

3. Theodore Dwight Weld, ed., *American Slavery As It Is: Testimony of a Thousand Witnesses* (New York: American Anti-Slavery Society, 1839), 115, 116, 117, 118, 120.

4. William Jay to Amos A. Phelps, 3 July 1846, Tappan Letterbooks, Lewis Tappan Papers, Manuscript Division, Library of Congress, Washington, D.C.; "Centralization," *National Anti-Slavery Standard,* 5 August 1864; Charles Olcott, *Two Lectures on the Subjects of Slavery and Abolition. . . .* (Massillon, Ohio: Printed for the Author, 1838), 33. See also William Henry Furness, *Two Discourses Occasioned by the Approaching Anniversary of the Declaration of Independence, . . .* (Philadelphia: John Pennington, 1843), 4–5, and *Our American Institutions . . .* (Philadelphia: T. B. Pugh, 1863), 6–7, which, twenty years after the 1843 discourse, raised the same analysis of human nature's susceptibility to the charms of power.

5. Weld, ed., *American Slavery,* 116; O. S. Freeman, *Letters on Slavery, Addressed to the Pro-Slavery Men of America . . .* (Boston: Bela Marsh, 1855), 65; "Centralization"; Moncure D. Conway to Wendell Phillips, 21 April 1865, in "New Light on Wendell Phillips: The Community of Reform, 1840–1880," ed. Irving H. Bartlett, *Perspectives in American History* 12 (1979): 224–25.

6. David L[ee] Child, *The Despotism of Freedom; or the Tyranny and Cruelty of American Republican Slave-Masters . . .* (Boston: Boston Young Men's Anti-Slavery Association for the Diffusion of Truth, 1833), 41, 47; Samuel J. May, "Speech to the Convention of Citizens of Onondaga County, in Syracuse, on the 14th of October, 1851, . . ." in *Legal and Moral Aspects of Slavery: Selected Essays* (New York: Negro Universities Press, 1969), 7; Furness, *Our American Institutions,* 18–19.

7. Furness, *Our American Institutions,* 7.

8. Rev. A[lonzo] A[mes] Miner, *An Oration Delivered before the*

Municipal Authorities of the City of Boston, . . . July 4, 1855 (Boston: Moore & Crosby, 1855), 11–23; Edmund H. Sears, *Revolution or Reform: A Discourse Occasioned by the Present Crisis, Preached at Wayland, Mass., Sunday, June 15, 1856* (Boston: Crosby, Nichols & Co., 1856), 15; May, "Speech to the Citizens of Onondaga County," 11; Maria Weston Chapman, *"How Can I Help to Abolish Slavery?" or Counsels to the Newly Converted,* Anti-Slavery Tracts, old series, no. 14 (New York: American Anti-Slavery Society, 1855–1856), 4; Adin Ballou, *The Voice of Duty. An Address Delivered at the Anti-Slavery Picnic at Westminster, Mass., July 4, 1843* (Milford, Mass.: Community Press, Hopedale, 1843), 3–4. See also David Paul Brown, *An Oration, . . . before the Anti-Slavery Society of New York, on the Fourth of July, 1834* (Philadelphia: T. K. Collins & Co., 1834), 3, and *Address of the Members of the Philadelphia Anti-Slavery Society to Their Fellow Citizens* (Philadelphia: W. P. Gibbons, 1835), 18.

9. "Letter of Gerrit Smith to Rev. James Smylie of the State of Mississippi" (28 October 1836), *Anti-Slavery Examiner* 3 (1837): 34; Charles Follen, "The Cause of Freedom in Our Country," *Quarterly Anti-Slavery Magazine* 2 (October 1836): 65.

10. Follen, "Cause of Freedom," 65–69; "Revolutions and Republics," *Liberator,* 28 July 1848; David Paul Brown, *Address of the Members of the Philadelphia Anti-Slavery Society,* 9.

11. *The Portable Thomas Jefferson,* ed., with an introduction by Merrill D. Peterson (New York: Viking, 1975), 214–15.

12. Samuel J. May, *A Discourse on Slavery in the United States, Delivered in Brooklyn, July 3, 1831* (Boston: Garrison & Knapp, 1832), 10, 15–16; Samuel Willard, *The Grand Issue: An Ethico-Political Tract* (Boston: John P. Jewett & Co., 1851), 13–14; William Goodell, *Slavery and Anti-Slavery; A History of the Great Struggle in Both Hemispheres; . . .* (New York: William Harned, 1852; reprint, New York: Negro Universities Press, 1968), 236–37n.

13. John G. Fee, *An Anti-Slavery Manual, Being an Examination, in the Light of the Bible, and of Facts, into the Moral and Social Wrongs of American Slavery, with a Remedy for the Evil* (Maysville, Ky.: The Herald Office, 1848), 148; Olcott, *Lectures on Slavery,* 26–27; Lydia Maria Child, *Anti-Slavery Catechism,* 2d ed. (Newburyport: Charles Whipple, 1839), 14–15.

14. William Claggett, *An Address, Delivered before the Portsmouth*

Anti-Slavery Society, on the Fourth of July, A.D., 1839, . . . (Portsmouth, N.H.: C. W. Brewster, 1839), 10. See also Olcott, *Lectures on Slavery,* 96.

15. David Paul Brown, *Address of the Members of the Philadelphia Anti-Slavery Society,* 18; Sears, *Revolution or Reform,* 9–10; Frederick Douglass, "The Meaning of July Fourth for the Negro . . . , July 5, 1852," in *The Life and Writings of Frederick Douglass,* ed. Philip S. Foner, 5 vols. (New York: International Publishers, 1950, 1975), 2:201; L[ydia] Maria Child, *The Right Way, the Safe Way, Proved by Emancipation in the British West Indies, and Elsewhere,* Anti-Slavery Tracts, new series, no. 6 (New York: American Anti-Slavery Society, 1860), 5; Henry M. Dexter, *Our National Condition, and its Remedy. A Sermon Preached in the Pine Street Church, Boston, on Sunday, June 22, 1856* (Boston: John P. Jewett, 1856), 39–40; William Jay to Lewis Tappan, 27 May 1851, Tappan Letterbooks.

16. James Gillespie Birney, *The American Churches: the Bulwarks of American Slavery* (Newburyport: Charles Whipple, 1842; reprint, New York: Arno, 1969), 15–18, 26, 35; [George Bourne], *A Condensed Anti-Slavery Bible Argument; By a Citizen of Virginia* (New York: S. W. Benedict, 1845), 90.

17. "The Liberty Party – The Mexican War – Col. Cilley," *Liberator,* 12 March 1847; Samuel Johnson, *The Crisis of Freedom, A Sermon, . . . June 11, 1854* (Boston: Crosby, Nichols & Co., 1854), 19.

18. S[eymour] B[oughton] Treadwell, *American Liberties and American Slavery, Morally and Politically Illustrated* (Boston: Weeks, Jordon & Co., 1838), 178; "Speech of Hon. Wm. Claggett: In the Convention of the Liberty Party, at Concord, June 3, 1842," *Emancipator and Free American,* 7 July 1842; Austin Steward, *Twenty-Two Years a Slave and Forty Years a Freeman* (Rochester: William Alling, 1857; reprint, Reading, Mass.: Addison-Wesley, 1969), 80.

19. Olcott, *Lectures on Slavery,* 116.

20. Edward D. Barber, *An Oration, Delivered before the Addison County Anti-Slavery Society, on the Fourth of July, 1836* (Middlebury, Vt.: Knapp and Jewett, 1836), 6, 11–12.

21. On Wendell Phillips and republican agitation, see James Brewer Stewart, *Wendell Phillips: Liberty's Hero* (Baton Rouge: Louisiana State University Press, 1986), 34, 73, 136, 160–62, 285, 325–29. The discussion that follows owes a great deal to Stewart's analysis. I pro-

pose that many other abolitionists shared with Phillips an understanding of the agitator's place in a republican crisis. For a different interpretation, see Ronald G. Walters, *The Antislavery Appeal: American Abolitionism after 1830* (Baltimore: Johns Hopkins University Press, 1978; New York: W. W. Norton, 1984), who argues that abolitionists failed "to create a well-defined conception of agitation" and instead pursued a "diversity of forms and styles" in tackling the slavery question (22).

22. Wendell Phillips, "Public Opinion" (28 January 1852), in *Speeches, Lectures, and Letters* (Boston: Lee and Shepard, 1872), 43, 50–54 (citation, 53).

23. Theodore Parker, "The State of the Nation" (1850), in *The Rights of Man in America*, ed. F. B. Sanborn (Boston: American Unitarian Association, 1911; reprint, New York: Negro Universities Press, 1969), 124–28; George B. Cheever, D. D., "A Discourse on the Divinely-Appointed Freedom of the Pulpit, the Senate, and the Press, for the Preservation of Freedom to Mankind, . . . June, 1856," in *God against Slavery: And the Freedom and Duty of the Pulpit to Rebuke it, as a Sin against God* (New York: Joseph H. Ladd, 1857; reprint, Miami: Mnemosyne Publishing, 1969), 248, 256.

24. "Centralization"; Sears, *Revolution or Reform*, 15; Charles Follen et al., *Address to the People of the United States, by a Committee of the New-England Anti-Slavery Convention*, . . . (Boston: Garrison & Knapp, 1834), 12; Olcott, *Lectures on Slavery*, 83. See also William Lloyd Garrison et al., "Address to the Friends of Freedom and Emancipation in the United States," *Liberator*, 31 May 1844. Such announcements recall the theme of "ordered resistance" found in the radical whig political tradition invoked by colonial radicals. See Pauline Maier, *From Resistance to Revolution: Colonial Radicals and the Development of American Opposition to Britain, 1765–1776* (New York: Knopf, 1972), 31–76.

25. Douglass, "The Meaning of July Fourth for the Negro . . . , July 5, 1852," in *Writings*, 2:186; William Lloyd Garrison, *An Address Delivered in Marlboro Chapel, Boston, July 4, 1838* (Boston: Isaac Knapp, 1838), 5; Phillips, "Public Opinion" (28 January 1852), in *Speeches*, 54; Cheever, "Divinely-Appointed Freedom," in *God Against Slavery*, 255–56; C[harles] K[ing] Whipple, "Treason! Treason!! Treason!!!" in *Liberty Chimes* (Providence: Ladies' Anti-Slavery

Society, 1845), 46–47. See also: Thomas T. Stone, "The Second Reformation," in *The Liberty Bell* (Boston: National Anti-Slavery Bazaar, 1851), 120–21; Executive Committee of the Ohio Anti-Slavery Society, *Narrative of the Late Riotous Proceedings against the Liberty of the Press, in Cincinnati, . . .* (Cincinnati: [Ohio Anti-Slavery Society], 1836), 6–7.

26. "Speech of Hon. Thomas Morris of Ohio, in Reply to the Speech of the Hon. Henry Clay, in Senate, February 9, 1839," *Anti-Slavery Examiner* 10 (1839): 23–24; "Politics [from the *Herald of Freedom*]," *Liberator,* 12 July 1839; Barber, *Oration before the Addison County Anti-Slavery Society,* 11. Morris's base of political support among his fellow Democrats, already weakened by his mounting criticisms of slavery, collapsed after this speech. The Liberty Party named him its vice-presidential candidate in 1844. Morris died later that same year.

27. Barber, *Oration before the Addison County Anti-Slavery Society,* 13.

28. Phillips, "Public Opinion" (28 January 1852), in *Speeches,* 48, 50.

29. "Public Opinion," *American Anti-Slavery Almanac for 1842* (New York: S. W. Benedict, 1842), no pagination; Rev. Samuel J. May, "The Jerry Rescue Celebration: Annual Address" (1 October 1860), *Douglass' Monthly* 3 (December 1860): 379; Lucy Stone, "Why Do We Rejoice Today?" (1 August 1846), Speech, Article, and Book File, Lucy Stone (Mrs. Henry B. Blackwell) Papers, Manuscript Division, Library of Congress, Washington, D.C. See also: broadside, American Anti-Slavery Society, *An Appeal to Abolitionists.* (11 October 1837), Massachusetts Anti-Slavery Society Papers, New York Historical Society, New York, N.Y.; "Letter of Gerrit Smith to Rev. James Smylie," 49–50.

30. Goodell, *Slavery and Anti-Slavery,* 126–27, 129n.

31. Phillips, "Harper's Ferry" (1 November 1859), in *Speeches,* 264.

32. Goodell, *Slavery and Anti-Slavery,* 126.

33. American Anti-Slavery Society, *Declaration of Sentiments of the American Anti-Slavery Society . . .* (New York: William S. Dorr, [1833]), 2, 4. See: Walters, *Antislavery Appeal,* 7–18; Richard H. Sewell, *Ballots for Freedom: Antislavery Politics in the United States, 1837–1860* (New York: Oxford University Press, 1976), 3–23; James

B. Stewart, "The Aims and Impact of Garrisonian Abolitionism, 1840–1860" *Civil War History* 15 (September 1969): 197–209.

34. Sewell, *Ballots for Freedom*, 24–106; Merton L. Dillon, *The Abolitionists: The Growth of a Dissenting Minority* (DeKalb, Ill.: Northern Illinois University Press, 1974), 121–36; James Brewer Stewart, *Holy Warriors: The Abolitionists and American Slavery* (New York: Hill & Wang, 1976), 93–96.

35. Key studies of antislavery politics include: Sewell, *Ballots for Freedom;* and the wide-ranging essays in Alan M. Kraut, ed., *Crusaders and Compromisers: Essays on the Relationship of the Antislavery Struggle to the Antebellum Party System* (Westport, Conn.: Greenwood Press, 1983). See also: Goodell, *Slavery and Anti-Slavery,* 468–86; Kraditor, *Means and Ends in American Abolitionism,* 118–77; J. B. Stewart, *Holy Warriors,* 74–123; Dillon, *The Abolitionists,* 141–73. My purpose is not to offer a detailed history of the party organizations but to focus on the terms through which abolitionists perceived and expressed the party controversy.

36. Bernard Bailyn, *The Ideological Origins of the American Revolution* (Cambridge: The Belknap Press of Harvard University Press, 1967), 150–59; Lance Banning, *The Jeffersonian Persuasion: Evolution of a Party Ideology* (Ithaca: Cornell University Press, 1978), 205–6; Richard Buel, Jr., *Securing the Revolution: Ideology in American Politics, 1789–1815* (Ithaca: Cornell University Press, 1972), 3–7, 91–92; Ralph Ketcham, *Presidents above Party: The First American Presidency, 1789–1829* (Chapel Hill: University of North Carolina Press, 1984), 124–65, 188–214; Gordon S. Wood, *The Creation of the American Republic, 1776–1787* (Chapel Hill: University of North Carolina Press, 1969), 57–61, 402–3. For discussions of antipartyism in nineteenth-century debates, see: John Ashworth, *'Agrarians' & 'Aristocrats': Party Political Ideology in the United States, 1837–1846* (Cambridge: Cambridge University Press, 1987), 205–18; Ronald P. Formisano, "Political Character, Antipartyism and the Second Party System," *American Quarterly* 21 (Winter 1969): 683–709; Ronald P. Formisano, "Deferential-Participant Politics: The Early Republic's Political Culture, 1789–1840," *American Political Science Quarterly* 68 (June 1974): 473–87; Paul Kleppner, "Partisanship and Ethnoreligious Conflict: The Third Electoral System, 1853–1892," in Paul Kleppner et al., *The Evolution of American Electoral Systems*

(Westport, Conn.: Greenwood Press, 1981), 113–46; Edward L. Mayo, "Republicanism, Antipartyism, and Jacksonian Party Politics: A View from the Nation's Capital," *American Quarterly* 31 (Spring 1979): 3–20; Sewell, *Ballots for Freedom*, 43–45, 72–73; William G. Shade, "Political Pluralism and Party Development: The Creation of a Modern Party System, 1815–1852," in Kleppner et al., *American Electoral Systems*, 77–111; Michael Wallace, "Changing Concepts of Party in the United States: New York, 1815–1828," *American Historical Review* 74 (December 1968): 453–91; Harry L. Watson, *Liberty and Power: The Politics of Jacksonian America* (New York: Noonday Press, 1990), 47–48, 67–70, 86–88, 172–73.

37. John Weiss, *Conscience the Best Policy: A Fast Day Sermon, Preached on April 6, 1848* (New Bedford: Henry Tilden, 1848), 7; "Pro-Slavery Republicanism," *National Anti-Slavery Standard*, 25 June 1840; Rev. John G. Richardson, *Obedience to Human Law Considered in the Light of Divine Truth. . .* (Lawrence, Mass.: Homer A. Cooke, 1852), 6; "Politics [from the *Herald of Freedom*]"; "A Touch of Republicanism," *National Anti-Slavery Standard*, 28 January 1841; Francis Jackson et al., "Address to the Anti-Slavery Electors of Massachusetts," *Liberator*, 25 October 1839.

38. Executive Committee of the Michigan Anti-Slavery Society, "The Proposal for a Third Party," *Liberator*, 15 November 1839; Nathaniel Peabody Rogers, "Power" (15 December 1843), in *A Collection from the Newspaper Writings of Nathaniel Peabody Rogers* (Concord, N.H.: John R. French, 1847), 264; "Abolition and Politics," *National Anti-Slavery Standard*, 13 August 1840.

39. "Political Action," *National Anti-Slavery Standard*, 19 November 1840; Lewis Tappan to Benjamin Tappan, 26 October 1839, Tappan Letterbooks; "Address of the Western Reserve Anti-Slavery Convention – to the Citizens of the Western Reserve, on the Subject of Political Action," *Liberator*, 1 November 1839; S[amuel] J. May, "The Liberty Bell is Not of the Liberty Party," in *The Liberty Bell* (Boston: Massachusetts Anti-Slavery Fair, 1845), 161–62. From 1838 to 1848, Lewis Tappan's opinions on a third party shifted from strong opposition to privately expressed support to publicly expressed support. On the civic identity of republican citizens, see J. G. A. Pocock, *The Machiavellian Moment: Florentine Political Thought and the Atlantic Republican Tradition* (Princeton: Princeton University Press, 1975).

40. Chapman, *"How Can I Help to Abolish Slavery?"*, 3.

41. Rev. William Barnes, *American Slavery, A Sermon, Preached at Hampton, Connecticut, April 14th, 1843, the Day of Annual Public Fast* (Hartford: Elihu Geer, 1843), 20–21; Olcott, *Lectures on Slavery*, 110; William Lloyd Garrison, "A Farce in One Act," *Liberator*, 21 June 1839; Massachusetts Anti-Slavery Society, *Seventh Annual Report*... (Boston: Isaac Knapp, 1839; reprint, Westport, Conn.: Negro Universities Press, 1970), 6–7. The Massachusetts Anti-Slavery Society Board also suggested that "State anti-slavery societies, having special jurisdiction over their own appropriate territorial limits, may be regarded as important, if not indispensable, checks and balances to the action of each, and to the integrity of the cause." See Massachusetts Anti-Slavery Society, *Seventh Annual Report*, 8. See also, "Annual Meeting of the National Society," *Liberator*, 22 May 1840.

42. "Political Action [from the *Herald of Freedom*]," *Liberator*, 29 November 1839.

43. Lewis C. Gunn, letter to the editor, *Liberator*, 22 November 1839; Quintius, "Independent Political Action [from the *Rochester Freeman*]," *Liberator*, 3 January 1840.

44. Wendell Phillips, quoted in "Anti-Slavery Celebration of Independence Day," *Liberator*, 10 July 1857; William I. Bowditch, *God or Our Country, Review of the Rev. Dr. Putnam's Discourse, Delivered on Fast Day, Entitled God and Our Country* (Boston: I. R. Butts, 1847), 8.

45. Bowditch, *God or Our Country*, 12; "Political Action [for the *Emancipator*]," *Liberator*, 3 April 1840.

46. [William Lloyd Garrison], "Letters of Messrs. Morris, Delavan, and Sedgwick," *Liberator*, 16 August 1839; Phillips, "Anti-Slavery Celebration."

47. Jackson et al., "Address to the Anti-Slavery Electors."

48. "The Genesis of the Republicans," *National Anti-Slavery Standard*, 15 November 1856.

49. On the "political antipolitics" of Liberty Party supporters, see: J. B. Stewart, *Holy Warriors*, 97; Alan M. Kraut, "Partisanship and Principles: The Liberty Party in Antebellum Political Culture," in *Crusaders and Compromisers*, 71–99.

50. "Abolition and Politics [from the *Liberator*]," *Emancipator*, 2 April 1840; Lewis Tappan to Benjamin Tappan, 25 February 1847 and

11 September 1844, and Lewis Tappan to John Beaumont, 30 January 1844, Tappan Letterbooks; "Slavery – Anti-Slavery – Moral Suasion – Political Action," *Emancipator and Free American,* 18 August 1842; Gerrit Smith, "The Liberty Party," *American and Foreign Anti-Slavery Reporter* 2 (1 November 1842): 90–92, and broadside, Gerrit Smith to Messrs. E. S. Bailey of Brookfield, A. Raymond of Easton, and F. Rice of Cazenovia, 10 April 1846, Gerrit Smith Papers, New York Public Library, New York, N.Y.; Samuel E. Sewall to Elizur Wright, 9 September 1840, Elizur Wright Papers, Manuscript Division, Library of Congress, Washington, D.C.

51. Watson, *Liberty and Power,* 67–70.

52. Southern and Western Liberty Convention, *Address . . . to the People of the United States, . . . ,* (Cincinnati: Printed at the Gazette Office [1845], 8–9; "Ohio Liberty State Convention, June 8, 1842," *Emancipator and Free American,* 7 July 1842; Gerrit Smith, "Address of the Anti-Slavery Convention of the State of New York, . . . to the Slaves in the United States of America," *Emancipator and Free American,* 11 February 1842, and "Liberty Triumph in Smithfield," *Emancipator and Free American,* 30 March 1843; Joshua Leavitt, C. L. Knapp, Henry Gibbons, "Address of the National Convention of Abolitionists Held at Albany, July 31, 1839," *Emancipator,* 15 August 1839.

53. *Proceedings of the Convention of Radical Political Abolitionists, Held at Syracuse, N.Y., June 26th, 27th, and 28th, 1855* (New York: Central Abolition Board, 1855), 15–22; Lewis Tappan to Benjamin Tappan, 14 October 1844, Tappan Letterbooks; L. P. Noble, "Address of the Liberty State Convention, Held at Peterboro', Jan. 19, 20, 1842, to the Electors of the State of New York," *Emancipator and Free American,* 11 March 1842; "The Right Sort of Politics" (14 September 1843), in *The Influence of the Slave Power with Other Anti-Slavery Pamphlets* (Westport, Conn.: Negro Universities Press, 1970), 4; American and Foreign Anti-Slavery Society, *[Eleventh] Annual Report . . .* (New York: American and Foreign Anti-Slavery Society, 1851), 105–6; Follen et al., *Address to the People,* 9–10; J[oshua] P[ollard] Blanchard, *Principles of the Revolution: Showing the Perversion of Them and the Consequent Failure of Their Accomplishment* (Boston: Damrell and Moore, 1855), 4.

These discussions overlapped with abolitionist debates over the proslavery or antislavery character of the Constitution. Although the two sides' theories were "all marred by inconsistencies" (J. B. Stewart, *Holy Warriors*, 98), both measured the Constitution against the principles of the Declaration, both recognized the limited achievement of republican freedoms in the Revolutionary period, and both censured the habits of political compromise at work in the new republic. Party sponsors also maintained their opposition to concentrated power within either the national government or a specific party. Their fear of centralization, shared by party opponents, reflected one more aspect of the reformers' republican habits of thought. On the abolitionists' readings of the Constitution, see: Paul Finkelman, *An Imperfect Union: Slavery, Federalism, and Comity* (Chapel Hill: University of North Carolina Press, 1981), 107–11, 155–78, 340–43; Harold M. Hyman and William M. Wiecek, *Equal Justice Under Law: Constitutional Development 1835–1875* (New York: Harper & Row, 1982), 86–114, 140–42; Staughton Lynd, "The Abolitionist Critique of the United States Constitution," in *The Antislavery Vanguard: New Essays on the Abolitionists*, ed. Martin Duberman (Princeton: Princeton University Press, 1965), 209–39; William M. Wiecek, "Latimer: Lawyers, Abolitionists, and the Problem of Unjust Laws," in *Antislavery Reconsidered: New Perspectives on the Abolitionists*, ed. Lewis Perry and Michael Fellman (Baton Rouge: Louisiana State University Press, 1979), 219–37; William M. Wiecek, *The Sources of Antislavery Constitutionalism in America, 1760–1848* (Ithaca: Cornell University Press, 1977).

54. "Independent Nominations," *Emancipator*, 13 February 1840; Lewis Tappan to Benjamin Tappan, 26 October 1844, Tappan Letterbooks; "Don't Throw Away Your Vote" (28 September 1843), in *The Influence of the Slave Power*, 1; Southern and Western Liberty Convention, *Address . . . to the People of the United States, . . .*, 10.

55. Southern and Western Liberty Convention, *Address . . . to the People of the United States, . . .* , 12; Noble, "Address of the Liberty State Convention to the Electors"; "Resolutions Passed at the National Liberty Party Convention, at Albany, New York, April 1, 1840," *Friend of Man*, 22 April 1840.

56. "Ohio Liberty State Convention"; "Resolutions Passed at the National Liberty Party Convention"; Executive Committee of the American and Foreign Anti-Slavery Society, *Address to the Friends of Liberty* (New York: American and Foreign Anti-Slavery Society, 1848), 5.

57. Handbill, letter of Gerrit Smith to Wendell Phillips, 20 February 1855, Gerrit Smith Papers; "National Anti-Slavery Convention," *Liberator,* 16 August 1839.

58. "Abolition and Politics [from the *Liberator*]."

59. Lewis Tappan to S. M. Gates, 21 October 1843, Tappan Letterbooks. See also Lewis Tappan to John Beaumont, 30 January 1844, Tappan Letterbooks.

60. "District Nominations," *Emancipator,* 21 November 1839.

61. "Abolition and Politics [from the *Liberator*]."

62. Letter to the editor, *Emancipator,* 21 November 1839.

CHAPTER 5

1. Daniel Foster, *An Address on Slavery, Delivered in Danvers, Mass.* (Boston: Bela Marsh, 1849), 7 [emphasis added]. Though Foster referred to the "extension" of slavery in this part of the speech, he went on to urge "the *immediate overthrow* of American Slavery," 9 [emphasis added].

2. For general discussions of abolitionist political economy, see: Ronald G. Walters, *The Antislavery Appeal: American Abolitionism after 1830* (Baltimore: Johns Hopkins University Press, 1978; New York: W. W. Norton, 1984), ch. 7; and Allen Kaufman, *Capitalism, Slavery, and Republican Values: Antebellum Political Economists, 1819–1848* (Austin: University of Texas Press, 1982). On the subject of class relations, see: Aileen S. Kraditor, *Means and Ends in American Abolitionism: Garrison and His Critics on Strategy and Tactics, 1834–1850* (New York: Pantheon, 1969), 242–55; and James Brewer Stewart, *Wendell Phillips: Liberty's Hero* (Baton Rouge: Louisiana State University Press, 1986), ch. 6. On questions of labor, see: Eric Foner, "Abolitionism and the Labor Movement in Antebellum America," in *Anti-Slavery, Religion, and Reform: Essays in Memory of Roger Anstey,* ed. Christine Bolt and Seymour Drescher (Folkestone, Kent: Wm. Dawson & Sons, 1980), 254–71; Jonathan A. Glickstein, "'Poverty is not Slavery': American Abolitionists and the Competitive Labor Market," in *Antislavery Reconsidered: New Perspectives on the Abolitionists,* ed. Lewis Perry and Michael Fellman (Baton Rouge: Louisiana State University Press, 1979), 195–218; and Betty Fladeland, *Abolitionists and Working-Class Problems in the Age of Industrialization* (Baton Rouge: Louisiana State University Press, 1984). On

utilitarianism and political liberalism, see Louis S. Gerteis, *Morality & Utility in American Antislavery Reform* (Chapel Hill: University of North Carolina Press, 1987).

3. Drew R. McCoy, *The Elusive Republic: Political Economy in Jeffersonian America* (Chapel Hill: University of North Carolina Press, 1980), 5–11, 40–45; Ralph Lerner, *The Thinking Revolutionary: Principle and Practice in the New Republic* (Ithaca: Cornell University Press, 1987), ch. 6; James T. Kloppenberg, "The Virtues of Liberalism: Christianity, Republicanism, and Ethics in Early American Political Discourse," *Journal of American History* 74 (June 1987): 9–33; J. Budziszewski, "A Whig View of Slavery, Development, and the World Market," *Slavery and Abolition* 4 (December 1983): 199–213.

4. George B. Cheever, *God against Slavery: And the Freedom and Duty of the Pulpit to Rebuke it, as a Sin against God* (New York: Joseph H. Ladd, 1857; reprint, Miami: Mnemosyne Publishing, 1969), 25; Thomas Jefferson, "Notes on the State of Virginia," in *The Portable Thomas Jefferson*, ed., with an introduction by Merrill D. Peterson (New York: Viking, 1975), 214–15; Theodore Dwight Weld, ed., *American Slavery As It Is: Testimony of a Thousand Witnesses* (New York: American Anti-Slavery Society, 1839), 117; Lydia Maria Child, *Anti-Slavery Catechism*, 2d ed. (Newburyport: Charles Whipple, 1839), 14–15.

5. Wendell Phillips, "Disunion" (20 January 1861), in *Speeches, Lectures, and Letters* (Boston: Lee and Shepard, 1872), 344–45; Theodore Parker, "The Aspect of Freedom in America. . . ." (5 July 1852), in *Additional Speeches, Addresses, and Occasional Sermons*, 2 vols. (Boston: Little, Brown, 1855), 1:112–13.

6. Sarah Grimké to Gerrit Smith, 12 January 1837, in *The Letters of Theodore Dwight Weld, Angelina Grimké Weld, and Sarah Grimké, 1822–1844*, ed. Gilbert H. Barnes and Dwight L. Dumond, 2 vols. (New York: D. Appleton-Century, 1934; reprint, Gloucester, Mass.: Peter Smith, 1965), 1:357; Charles Follen, "The Cause of Freedom in Our Country," *Quarterly Anti-Slavery Magazine* 2 (October 1836): 63.

7. "Speech of Rev. O. B. Frothingham, of Jersey City, at the Annual Meeting of the American Anti-Slavery Society, New York, May 8, 1856," *National Anti-Slavery Standard*, 24 May 1856. See also: William Goodell, *Slavery and Anti-Slavery; A History of the Great Strug-*

gle in Both Hemispheres; . . . (New York: William Harned, 1852; reprint, New York: Negro Universities Press, 1968), 125–26; Theodore Parker, *The Nebraska Question. Some Thoughts on the New Assault upon Freedom in America . . . , Feb. 12, 1852* (Boston: Benjamin B. Mussey & Co., 1854), 28–30.

8. "Declaration of Sentiments, on Behalf of the Illinois State Anti-Slavery Society, Formed Oct. 28, 1837, at Alton," *Emancipator,* 8 March 1838; "Are Slaveholders Man-Stealers?" *Anti-Slavery Record* 3 (September 1837): 6 [emphasis added]; Frederick Douglass, "American Slavery" (18 March 1846), in *The Life and Writings of Frederick Douglass,* ed. Philip S. Foner, 5 vols. (New York: International Publishers, 1950, 1975), 5:28. For an analysis of one reformer's commentary on the language of nineteenth-century economics, see Leonard N. Neufeldt, "Thoreau's Enterprise of Self-Culture in a Culture of Enterprise," *American Quarterly* 39 (Summer 1987): 231–51.

9. John Rankin, *Letters on American Slavery, . . .* (Newburyport: Chas. Whipple, 1837), 24–25, 50–54; "Southern Notions of Rights and Liberty," *Anti-Slavery Record* 3 (1837): 160–61; Rev. J[onathan] Blanchard, *Sermon on Slaveholding: Preached by Appointment, before the Synod of Cincinnati, at Their Late Stated Meeting at Mount Pleasant, Ohio, October 20th, 1841* (Cincinnati: n. p., 1842), 4–5; Douglass, "Address at Abbey Church, Arbroath, Scotland, February 13, 1846," in *Writings,* 5:22–27; Lydia Maria Child, ed., *The Patriarchal Institution, As Described by Members of Its Own Family* (New York: American Anti-Slavery Society, 1860), 4–8; O. S. Freeman, *Letters on Slavery, Addressed to the Pro-Slavery Men of America; . . .* (Boston: Bela Marsh, 1855), 61–74.

10. American Anti-Slavery Society, *Sixth Annual Report. . .* (New York: William S. Dorr, 1839), 97; "Speech of Charles Burleigh," in *Proceedings of the American Anti-Slavery Society, at its Second Decade, . . .* (New York: American Anti-Slavery Society, 1854), 63; [Louisa J. Barker], *Influence of Slavery upon the White Population, by a Former Resident of the Slave South,* Anti-Slavery Tracts, old series, no. 9 (New York: American Anti-Slavery Society, 1855–1856), 2, 3.

11. [Barker], *Influence of Slavery,* 5; "American and Foreign Anti-Slavery Society Addresses the Non-Slaveholders of the South" (1843), in *The Antislavery Argument,* ed. William H. Pease and Jane H. Pease (Indianapolis: Bobbs-Merrill, 1965), 156, 158; L[ydia] Maria Child,

The Right Way, the Safe Way, Proved by Emancipation in the British West Indies, and Elsewhere, Anti-Slavery Tracts, new series, no. 6 (New York: American Anti-Slavery Society, 1862), 5.

12. [Barker], *Influence of Slavery,* 1–3, 6–7; Henry M. Dexter, *Our National Condition, and its Remedy. A Sermon Preached in the Pine Street Church, Boston, on Sunday, June 22, 1856* (Boston: John P. Jewett, 1856), 34–40; Rankin, *Letters,* 68–69; "Speech of Wendell Phillips," in *Proceedings of the American Anti-Slavery Society, at its Second Decade,* 74.

13. [Barker], *Influence of Slavery,* 1–2; Rev. Charles Beecher, *The God of the Bible against Slavery,* Anti-Slavery Tracts, old series, no. 17 (New York: American Anti-Slavery Society, 1855–1856), 6; "Illinois State Anti-Slavery Society"; "Speech of Charles Burleigh," 63.

14. Dexter, *Our National Condition,* 36, 39; Charles Follen et al., *Address to the People of the United States, by a Committee of the New-England Anti-Slavery Convention, . . .* (Boston: Garrison & Knapp, 1834), 5; Theodore Parker, "The Rights of Man in America" (1854), in *The Rights of Man in America,* ed. F. B. Sanborn (Boston: American Unitarian Association, 1911; reprint, New York: Negro Universities Press, 1969), 365.

15. Follen, "Cause of Freedom," 70.

16. Richard Hildreth, "Slavery as it Affects the Liberty of the Privileged Class," *National Anti-Slavery Standard,* 30 July 1840; "Southern Notions of Rights and Liberty," 160–61.

17. "Southern Notions of Rights and Liberty," 160–61.

18. James W. C. Pennington, "The Fugitive Blacksmith," in *Five Slave Narratives: A Compendium,* ed. William Loren Katz (New York: Arno and New York Times, 1968), 59.

19. Rankin, *Letters,* 70–71; "American and Foreign Anti-Slavery Society Addresses the Non-Slaveholders of the South," 149, 155, 156, 158; [Barker], *Influence of Slavery,* 5.

20. For other examples of the abolition argument on profits and poverty see: Goodell, *Slavery and Anti-Slavery,* 132–34; Parker, "An Anti-Slavery Address" (1854), in *Rights of Man,* 173, 179; Joshua Leavitt, "Warns of a Slave-Power Conspiracy (1840)," in *Slavery Attacked: The Abolitionist Crusade,* ed. John L. Thomas (Englewood Cliffs: Prentice-Hall, 1965), 74–75.

21. Edmund H. Sears, *Revolution or Reform: A Discourse Occa-*

sioned by the Present Crisis, Preached at Wayland, Mass., Sunday,
June 15, 1856 (Boston: Crosby, Nichols & Co., 1856), 13; "American
and Foreign Anti-Slavery Society Addresses the Non-Slaveholders of
the South," 151.

22. Wendell Phillips, *The Philosophy of the Abolition Movement*
(27 January 1853), Anti-Slavery Tracts, new series, no. 8 (New York:
American Anti-Slavery Society, 1860), 38; Parker, *The Nebraska
Question*, 28–30, and "The Destination of America" (1848) and "The
Boston Kidnapping" (12 April 1852), in *The Slave Power*, ed. James K.
Hosmer (Boston: American Unitarian Association, 1916; reprint,
New York: Arno, 1969), 153–55, 371; Foster, *Address on Slavery*, 30–
40; Elizur Wright, Jr., "Report," in American Anti-Slavery Society,
Fourth Annual Report . . . (New York: William S. Dorr, 1837), 60;
James G. Birney, "Correspondence between the Hon. F. H. Elmore,
One of the South Carolina Delegation in Congress, and James G. Bir-
ney, One of the Secretaries of the American Anti-Slavery Society,"
Anti-Slavery Examiner 8 (1838): 33n.

23. "How Can It Be Done?" *Anti-Slavery Record* 2 (September
1836): 10–11; J[oshua] P[ollard] Blanchard, *Principles of the Revolu-
tion: Showing the Perversion of Them and the Consequent Failure of
Their Accomplishment* (Boston: Damrell and Moore, 1855), 10;
"Speech of Edmund Quincy," in *Proceedings of the American Anti-
Slavery Society, at its Second Decade, . . . ,* 49; Theodore Parker, "The
Relation of Slavery to a Republican Form of Government, . . ." *Liber-
ator*, 11 June 1858. See also: speech by James Henry Hammond (1 Feb-
ruary 1836), quoted in Birney, "Correspondence between the Hon.
F. H. Elmore," 33n; Cheever, *God Against Slavery*, 223; William
Claggett, *An Address, Delivered before the Portsmouth Anti-Slavery
Society, on the Fourth of July, A. D., 1839, . . .* (Portsmouth, N.H.: C.
W. Brewster, 1839), 9–10; Parker, "The Rights of Man in America"
(1854), in *Rights of Man*, 347–48.

24. [Rev. George Allen], *Resistance to Slavery Every Man's Duty: A
Report on Slavery, Read to the Worcester Central Association, March
2, 1847* (Boston: Wm. Crosby & H. P. Nichols, 1847), 26.

25. Sears, *Revolution or Reform*, 13–14; Alvan Stewart, "The
Cause of the Hard Times" (1843), in *The Influence of the Slave Power
with Other Anti-Slavery Pamphlets* (Westport, Conn.: Negro Universities Press, 1970), 1–4; "Southern Paymasters," *American Anti-Slav-*

ery Almanac for 1842 (New York: S. W. Benedict, 1842), no pagination; Dexter, *Our National Condition,* 39–40.

26. "Speech of Phillips," in *Proceedings of the American Anti-Slavery Society, at its Second Decade,* 85; Douglass, "American Slavery Lecture No. VII . . . , Jan. 12, 1851," in *Writings,* 5:178–79, and "American Slavery, American Religion, and the Free Church of Scotland" (22 May 1846), in *The Frederick Douglass Papers, Series One: Speeches, Debates, and Interviews,* ed. John W. Blassingame (New Haven: Yale University Press, 1979), 1:271. See also: Parker, "An Anti-Slavery Address" (1854), in *Rights of Man,* 180, 194; Rev. Frederick Frothingham, *Significance of the Struggle between Liberty and Slavery . . .* (New York: American Anti-Slavery Society, 1857), 10.

27. Douglass, "American Slavery Lecture No. VII . . . , Jan. 12th, 1851," "Speech Delivered at the Mass Free Democratic Convention . . . , Oct. 14th, 1852," and "Speech Delivered at Convention of Colored Citizens . . . , September 4, 1855," in *Writings,* 5:178, 250, 358–59.

28. Douglass, "Speech Delivered at Convention of Colored Citizens . . . , September 4, 1855," in *Writings,* 5:358; [George W. Carleton?], *The Suppressed Book about Slavery! . . .* (New York: Carleton, 1864), 21. On eligibility requirements, Douglass noted: "What is *law* in South Carolina, is *custom* in nearly all the slave states of this Union" ("Speech Delivered at the Mass Free Democratic Convention . . . , Oct. 14th, 1852," in *Writings,* 5:250).

29. Leavitt, "Warns of a Slave-Power Conspiracy," 70. See also: Dexter, *Our National Condition,* 20–21; *The Liberty Almanac for 1850* (New York: American and Foreign Anti-Slavery Society, 1850), 32.

30. Dexter, *Our National Condition,* 44; Douglass, "The Kansas-Nebraska Bill" (30 October 1854), in *Writings,* 2:324; "Politics (from *Herald of Freedom),*" *Liberator,* 12 July 1839; Edward D. Barber, *An Oration, Delivered before the Addison County Anti-Slavery Society, on the Fourth of July, 1836* (Middlebury, Vt.: Knapp and Jewett, 1836), 6; "Speech of Hon. Wm. Claggett: In the Convention of the Liberty Party, at Concord, June 3, 1842," *Emancipator and Free American,* 7 July 1842; S[eymour] B[oughton] Treadwell, *American Liberties and American Slavery, Morally and Politically Illustrated* (Boston: Weeks, Jordon & Co., 1838), 179, 349.

31. Francis Jackson, "Report," in *Twenty-First Annual Report Presented to the Massachusetts Anti-Slavery Society . . .* (Boston: Prentiss & Sawyer, 1853), 71, 73; Phillips, "Disunion" (20 January 1861), in *Speeches,* 357, 363; Parker, *The Nebraska Question,* 30, 37, and "The Boston Kidnapping" (12 April 1852), in *Slave Power,* 323.

32. Jackson, "Report," 71; Phillips, "Disunion" (20 January 1861), in *Speeches,* 363; Parker, *The Nebraska Question,* 37.

33. Theodore Parker, "A Sermon of Merchants," in *Speeches, Addresses, and Occasional Sermons,* 3 vols. (Boston: Ticknor & Fields, 1861), 1:260; "Speech of Rev. O. B. Frothingham."

34. John Weiss, *Reform and Repeal, a Sermon Preached on Fast-Day, April 6, 1854, and Legal Anarchy, a Sermon Preached on June 4, 1854, after the Rendition of Anthony Burns* (Boston: Crosby, Nichols, and Company, 1854), 7; Parker, "A Sermon of Merchants," in *Speeches, Addresses, and Occasional Sermons,* 1:268.

35. Frothingham, *Significance of the Struggle,* 8.

36. Weiss, *Reform and Repeal,* 7; Dexter, *Our National Condition,* 27, 33. Parker, in *The Nebraska Question,* 41–54, catalogued past compromises and anticipated future political deals.

37. Cheever, *God Against Slavery,* 214, 217.

38. Dexter, *Our National Condition,* 22.

39. Cheever, "Address on the Subject of the Iniquity of the Extension of Slavery, . . ." (30 October 1856), in *God Against Slavery,* 214, 217; Dexter, *Our National Condition,* 22; *Encroachments of the Slave Power upon the Rights of the North. By a Northern Man* (Boston: Bela Marsh, 1848), 5; "Speech of Rev. O. B. Frothingham"; Weiss, *Reform and Repeal,* 12.

40. Sears, *Revolution or Reform,* 14; Parker, *The Nebraska Question,* 54–55.

41. An abolitionist etymology of the term may be found in Weld, ed. *American Slavery As It Is,* 114n; and Goodell, *Slavery and Anti-Slavery,* 384n. Both Weld and Goodell trace the term to John Randolph's description of timid "doe"- faces.

42. Parker, *The Nebraska Question,* 54–55; Sears, *Revolution or Reform,* 14; Jackson, "Report," 70.

43. Weiss, *Reform and Repeal,* 13.

44. Parker, "The Boston Kidnapping" (12 April 1852), in *Slave Power,* 371; James G. Birney, Diary, 15 February 1850, James G. Bir-

ney Papers, Manuscript Division, Library of Congress, Washington, D.C.; William Lloyd Garrison, resolution presented to Worcester County Anti-Slavery Society (11 March 1845), in "No Union with Slaveholders; Progress of the Revolution," *Liberator,* 21 March 1845; Rev. J[onathan] Blanchard and N[athan] L[ewis] Rice, *A Debate on Slavery, Held in the City of Cincinnati on the First, Second, Third, and Sixth Days of October 1845, upon the Question: Is Slave-Holding in Itself Sinful, and the Relation Between Master and Slave, a Sinful Relation?* (Cincinnati: Wm. H. Moore & Co., 1846; reprint, New York: Negro Universities Press, 1969), 357.

45. Douglass, "American Slavery Lecture No. VII . . . , Jan. 12th, 1851," in *Writings,* 5:178; Goodell, *Slavery and Anti-Slavery,* 321; Cheever, "Address," in *God Against Slavery,* 223, 228.

46. Phillips, *Philosophy of Abolition,* 12. For examples of reform appeals to economic interest, see: G. W. W. to Charles C. Burleigh, " 'Selfishness' Defended," *National Anti-Slavery Standard,* 10 September 1840; Charles C. Burleigh, *Slavery and the North,* Anti-Slavery Tracts, old series, no. 10 (New York: American Anti-Slavery Society, 1855–1856), 9–10; and Salmon P. Chase to Wendell Phillips (1 May 1866), in "New Light on Wendell Phillips: The Community of Reform, 1840–1880," ed. Irving H. Bartlett, *Perspectives in American History* 12 (1979): 156.

47. Follen et al., *Address to the People of the United States,* 15; *Proceedings of the Convention of Radical Political Abolitionists, Held at Syracuse, N. Y., June 26th, 27th, and 28th, 1855* (New York: Central Abolition Board, 1855), 7–8; Gerrit Smith, "Address of the Anti-Slavery Convention of the State of New York, . . . to the Slaves in the United States of America," *Emancipator and Free American,* 11 February 1842.

48. "Speech of Edmund Quincy," 100–101. See also: J[ohn] I. Gaines, speech on the anniversary of British West Indies emancipation (1 August 1849), *North Star,* 7 September 1849; Wendell Phillips, "Sims Anniversary" (12 April 1852), in *Speeches,* 82–83; Jackson, "Report," 69; Anti-Slavery Convention of American Women, *An Appeal to the Women of the Nominally Free States . . .* (New York: William S. Dorr, 1837), 26–27; Sarah Grimké and Angelina Grimké to "Clarkson," ca. 1 March 1837, *Weld-Grimké Letters,* 1:370–72; Ger-

rit Smith, "Abstinence from the Products of Slave Labor," *Anti-Slavery Record* 1 (Appendix 1835): 172.

49. Parker, "The Boston Kidnapping" (12 April 1852), in *Slave Power*, 376–77; Sears, *Revolution or Reform*, 15; Anti-Slavery Convention of American Women, *Appeal*, 5–6; Wendell Phillips, "The Question of Labor," *Liberator*, 9 July 1847; Claggett, *Address Delivered before the Portsmouth Anti-Slavery Society*, 3, 10; "Proceedings," *Minutes of the National Convention of Colored Citizens: Held at Buffalo, on the 15th, 16th, 17th, 18th, and 19th of August 1843, for the Purpose of Considering Their Moral and Political Condition as American Citizens* (New York: Piercy & Reed, 1843), 4–7.

50. Elizur Wright, Jr., "Third Annual Report," in American Anti-Slavery Society, *Third Annual Report . . .* (New York: William S. Dorr, 1836), 81–82; Claggett, *Address Delivered before the Portsmouth Anti-Slavery Society*, 11–12; Charles Olcott, *Two Lectures on the Subjects of Slavery and Abolition. . . .* (Massillon, Ohio: Printed for the Author, 1838), 72; Alvan Stewart, "The Cause of the Hard Times," 1; and "American and Foreign Anti-Slavery Society Addresses the Non-Slaveholders of the South," 158–59.

51. For examples, see: Garrison's statement of purposes in the first edition of the *Liberator* (1 January 1831); and American Anti-Slavery Society, *Declaration of Sentiments of the American Anti-Slavery Society . . .* (New York: William S. Dorr, [1833]).

See also: William Ingersoll Bowditch, *The Anti-Slavery Reform, Its Principle and Method* (Boston: Robert F. Wallcut, 1850), 14–17; Phillips, *Philosophy of the Abolition Movement*; and Douglass, "The True Issue" (January 1859) and "The Meaning of July Fourth for the Negro. . . , July 5, 1852," in *Writings*, 2:191, 441.

52. See: Phillips, "Question of Labor"; [Edmund Quincy], "Chattel Slavery and Wages Slavery," *Liberator*, 1 October 1847.

53. Drew Gilpin Faust, "A Southern Stewardship: The Intellectual and the Proslavery Argument," *American Quarterly* 31 (Spring 1979): 72–73.

54. McCoy, *The Elusive Republic*, ch. 8; Goodell, *Slavery and Anti-Slavery*, chs. 21–28.

55. Parker, "The Rights of Man in America" (1854), in *Rights of Man*, 363; Burleigh, *Slavery and the North*, 1–3; Weiss, *Reform and Repeal*, 9–11; David L[ee] Child, *The Despotism of Freedom; or the*

Tyranny and Cruelty of American Republican Slave-Masters . . . (Boston: Boston Young Men's Anti-Slavery Association for the Diffusion of Truth, 1833), 38–40n [emphasis added]; Phillips, "Disunion" (20 January 1861), in *Speeches,* 367.

CHAPTER 6

1. [Charles Allen and Stephen C. Phillips?], "Address to the People of the U. States, . . . by the Great Anti-Texas Convention," *Liberator,* 7 February 1845.

2. On reform and culture, see Ronald G. Walters, *The Antislavery Appeal: American Abolitionism after 1830* (Baltimore: Johns Hopkins University Press, 1978; New York: W. W. Norton, 1984, 129–45). Rather than focusing on the abolitionists' literary and imaginative expression, Walters examines the sense of national identity advocates conveyed through their views of the Union. He notes the advocates' "peculiar" unionism which insisted on adherence to moral over formal structures in political association.

3. J. W. C. Pennington, *Covenants Involving Moral Wrong are not Obligatory upon Man . . .* (Hartford: John C. Wells, 1842), 12; Anti-Slavery Convention of American Women, *An Appeal to the Women of the Nominally Free States . . .* (New York: William S. Dorr, 1837), 9; L[ydia] M[aria] Child, *An Appeal in Favor of that Class of Americans Called Africans* (Boston: Allen and Ticknor, 1833), 228.

4. Charles Follen, "The Cause of Freedom in Our Country," *Quarterly Anti-Slavery Magazine* 2 (October 1836): 62; John G. Whittier, "Justice and Expediency; Slavery Considered with a View to its Rightful and Effectual Remedy, Abolition" (1833), in *Essays and Pamphlets on Antislavery* (Westport, Conn.: Negro Universities Press, 1970), 21. See also: David L[ee] Child, *The Despotism of Freedom; or the Tyranny and Cruelty of American Republican Slave-Masters . . .* (Boston: Boston Young Men's Anti-Slavery Association for the Diffusion of Truth, 1833), 14; William H. Furness, *An Address Delivered before a Meeting of the Members and Friends of the Pennsylvania Anti-Slavery Society . . .* (Philadelphia: Merrihew & Thompson, 1850), 8.

5. Richard Hildreth, *Despotism in America: An Inquiry into the Nature, Results, and Legal Basis of the Slave-Holding System in the United States* (Boston: John P. Jewett & Co., 1854), 9, 10.

6. See John M. Murrin, "A Roof Without Walls: The Dilemma of

American National Identity," in *Beyond Confederation: Origins of the Constitution and American National Identity,* ed. Richard Beeman, Stephen Botein, and Edward C. Carter II (Chapel Hill: University of North Carolina Press, 1987), 333–48, which argues that the form of America's national government served as a substitute for national identity in the early republic: "American nationalism is distinct because, for nearly its first century, it was narrowly and peculiarly constitutional" (346–47).

7. Frederick Douglass, "The Danger of the Republican Movement" (28 May 1856), in *The Life and Writings of Frederick Douglass,* ed. Philip S. Foner, 5 vols. (New York: International Publishers, 1950, 1975), 5:389; Hildreth, *Despotism in America,* 28; Theodore Parker, "The Rights of Man in America" (1854), in *The Rights of Man in America,* ed. F. B. Sanborn (Boston: American Unitarian Association, 1911; reprint, New York: Negro Universities Press, 1969), 367–68.

8. Douglass, "Speech at American Anti-Slavery Society, May, 1848," "Speech Delivered in the Court House, at Chatham, Canada, C. W. August 3rd, 1854," and "American Civilization" (October 1859), in *Writings,* 5:80, 334, 456. The paradoxical character of America stands as one of the prominent themes in Hildreth's *Despotism in America.*

9. Samuel Johnson, *The Crisis of Freedom, a Sermon, . . . June 11, 1854* (Boston: Crosby, Nichols & Co., 1854), 13; William Goodell, *Slavery and Anti-Slavery; A History of the Great Struggle in Both Hemispheres; . . .* (New York: William Harned, 1852; reprint, New York: Negro Universities Press, 1968), 588n; J[oshua] P[ollard] Blanchard, *Principles of the Revolution: Showing the Perversion of Them and the Consequent Failure of Their Accomplishment* (Boston: Damrell and Moore, 1855), 13, 18.

10. Douglass, "The Reproach and Shame of the American Government . . . , August 2, 1858," in *Writings,* 5:402; Wendell Phillips, "Harper's Ferry" (1 November 1859), in *Speeches, Lectures, and Letters* (Boston: Lee and Shepard, 1872), 263–64; "The Liberator and Slavery," *Liberator,* 7 January 1832.

11. William Lloyd Garrison, "Address Delivered at South Scituate, Mass., before the Old Colony (Plymouth Colony) Anti-Slavery Society, July 4th, 1839," *Liberator,* 19 July 1839.

12. "Public Opinion," *Anti-Slavery Almanac for 1842* (New York:

S. W. Benedict, 1842), no pagination; [Rev. George Allen], *Resistance to Slavery Every Man's Duty: A Report on Slavery, Read to the Worcester Central Association, March 2, 1847* (Boston: Wm. Crosby & H. P. Nichols, 1847), 26.

13. Douglass, "The Reproach and Shame of the American Government . . . , August 2, 1858," in *Writings*, 5:406; Enoch Mack, "The Revolution Unfinished, or American Independence Begun," in *Trumpets of Glory: Fourth of July Orations, 1786–1861*, ed. Henry A. Hawken (Granby, Conn.: The Salmon Brook Historical Society, 1976), 180; James Birney to Lewis Tappan, 4 February 1836, Tappan Letterbooks, Lewis Tappan Papers, Manuscript Division, Library of Congress, Washington, D.C.; Theodore Parker, "The Boston Kidnapping" (12 April 1852), in *The Slave Power*, ed. James K. Hosmer (Boston: American Unitarian Association, 1916; reprint, New York: Arno, 1969), 346. See also: "Are Slaveholders Man-Stealers?" *Anti-Slavery Record* 3 (September 1837): 2–3; [Louisa J. Barker], *Influence of Slavery upon the White Population, by a Former Resident of the Slave South,* Anti-Slavery Tracts, old series, no. 9 (New York: American Anti-Slavery Society, 1855–1856), 11.

14. Phillips, "Harper's Ferry" (1 November 1859), in *Speeches,* 269. Phillips took all of this as a sign of abolition's progress: "The first evidence that a sinner, convicted of sin, and too blind or too lazy to reform, the first evidence he gives that his nature has been touched, is, that he becomes a hypocrite; he has the grace to pretend to be something" (268).

15. William Lloyd Garrison to Louis Kossuth, February 1852, *The Letters of William Lloyd Garrison,* ed. Walter M. Merrill and Louis Ruchames, 6 vols. (Cambridge: The Belknap Press of Harvard University Press, 1971–1981), 4:157; "No Principle at Strife with Principle; or, Ciphers in Battle Array with Whole Numbers," *Anti-Slavery Record* 3 (May 1837): 7, 8. See also: "Resolution" [n. d.], Item 87, Massachusetts Anti-Slavery Society Papers, New York Historical Society, New York, N.Y.; David Paul Brown, *An Oration, . . . before the Anti-Slavery Society of New York, on the Fourth of July, 1834* (Philadelphia: T. K. Collins & Co., 1834), 8; Angelina E. Grimké, "Appeal to the Christian Women of the South," *Anti-Slavery Examiner* 1 (September 1836): 24.

16. Edward D. Barber, *An Oration, Delivered before the Addison*

County Anti-Slavery Society, on the Fourth of July, 1836 (Middlebury, Vt.: Knapp and Jewett, 1836), 13.

17. Wendell Phillips, *The Philosophy of the Abolition Movement* (27 January 1853), Anti-Slavery Tracts, new series, no. 8 (New York: American Anti-Slavery Society, 1860), 10; William Lloyd Garrison to the Abolitionists of Massachusetts, 17 July 1839, *Letters of Garrison*, 2:501–2.

18. Theodore Dwight Weld, ed., *American Slavery As It Is: Testimony of a Thousand Witnesses* (New York: American Anti-Slavery Society, 1839), 110; Henry David Thoreau, "Slavery in Massachusetts" (4 July 1854), *Liberator*, 21 July 1854. See also Phillips, *Philosophy of the Abolition Movement*, 10. Thoreau made his comments at an Independence Day meeting organized in Framingham, Massachusetts, under the auspices of the American Anti-Slavery Society.

19. David Paul Brown, *Oration before the Anti-Slavery Society of New York*, 6.

20. Angelina Grimké, "Appeal to the Christian Women," 2.

21. David Paul Brown, *Oration before the Anti-Slavery Society of New York*, 6. For discussions of the plain style and self-evident argument in relation to the Founders and Revolutionary republicanism, see: Gordon S. Wood, "The Democratization of Mind in the American Revolution," in Library of Congress Symposia on the American Revolution, *Leadership in the American Revolution: Papers Presented at the Third Symposium, May 9 and 10, 1974* (Washington, D.C.: Library of Congress, 1974), 63–89; Morton White, *The Philosophy of the American Revolution* (New York: Oxford University Press, 1978), chs. 1–3; Lester H. Cohen, *The Revolutionary Histories: Contemporary Narratives of the American Revolution* (Ithaca: Cornell University Press, 1980), ch. 6.

22. "The Declaration of American Independence," *Liberator*, 5 September 1835; Douglass, "The Meaning of July Fourth for the Negro. . . , July 5, 1852," in *Writings*, 2:202; "Gerrit Smith to Wendell Phillips" (20 February 1855), *Liberator*, 16 March 1855; Rev. Alonzo Miner, *Oration Delivered before the Municipal Authorities of the City of Boston, . . . July 4, 1855* (Boston: Moore & Crosby, 1855), 12, 15.

23. James Brown, *American Slavery in its Moral and Political As-*

pects Comprehensively Examined, . . . (Oswego, N.Y.: George Henry, 1840), 21–25, 38, 39, 41.

24. "Are Slaveholders Man-Stealers?" *Anti-Slavery Record* 3 (September 1837): 1; Johnson, *Crisis of Freedom,* 19; Wendell Phillips, quoted in Carlos Martyn, *Wendell Phillips: The Agitator* (New York: Funk & Wagnalls, 1890), 436. See also William Lloyd Garrison to Elihu Burrit, 16 July 1845, *Letters of Garrison,* 2:298.

25. Charles Olcott, *Two Lectures on the Subjects of Slavery and Abolition.* . . . (Massillon, Ohio: Printed for the Author, 1838), 106; William Lloyd Garrison to the Editor of the Boston *Courier,* 4 March 1837, *Letters of Garrison,* 2:218.

26. William Lloyd Garrison to Henry C. Wright, 1 November 1845, *Letters of Garrison,* 3:323. See also Elizur Wright, Jr., "Defines Immediate Emancipation (1833)," in *Slavery Attacked: The Abolitionist Crusade,* ed. John L. Thomas (Englewood Cliffs, N.J.: Prentice-Hall, 1965), 15.

27. William Lloyd Garrison to Helen E. Garrison, 17 September 1846, *Letters of Garrison,* 3:412.

28. S[eymour] B[oughton] Treadwell, *American Liberties and American Slavery, Morally and Politically Illustrated* (Boston: Weeks, Jordon & Co., 1838), 174, 179–80.

29. Goodell, *Slavery and Anti-Slavery,* 119. He noted that one *could* discern the moral causes of these occurrences, which constituted "the most essential ingredient of true history" (119).

30. Garrison, "Address Delivered at South Scituate."

31. William Lloyd Garrison, *An Address Delivered in Marlboro Chapel, Boston, July 4, 1838,* (Boston: Isaac Knapp, 1838), 5.

32. Douglass, "Eulogy on the Late Hon. Wm. Jay . . . , May 12, 1859," in *Writings,* 5:448. Douglass raised this issue to make a point about Jay's work in abolition: "such extravagance will be looked for in vain in the writings of Judge Jay on slavery." Jay's verbal habits were, in Douglass's view, the exception rather than the rule in antislavery reform.

33. Frederick Douglass, "Speech before the American & Foreign Anti-Slavery Society," in American and Foreign Anti-Slavery Society, *Thirteenth Annual Report* . . . (New York: American and Foreign Anti-Slavery Society, 1853), 184 [emphasis added].

34. Garrison, "Address Delivered at South Scituate."

35. On the search for distinctively American forms of expression in the antebellum period, see: Kenneth Cmiel, *Democratic Eloquence: The Fight over Popular Speech in Nineteenth-Century America* (New York: William Morrow and Company, 1990); Lester H. Cohen, "Creating a Usable Future: The Revolutionary Historians and the National Past," in *The American Revolution: Its Character and Limits,* ed. Jack P. Greene (New York: New York University Press, 1987), 309–30; Joseph J. Ellis, *After the Revolution: Profiles of Early American Culture* (New York: W. W. Norton, 1979); Nathan O. Hatch, *The Democratization of American Christianity* (New Haven: Yale University Press, 1989); Myra Jehlen, *American Incarnation: The Individual, the Nation, and the Continent* (Cambridge: Harvard University Press, 1986); David Simpson, *The Politics of American English, 1776–1850* (New York: Oxford University Press, 1986); Larzer Ziff, *Literary Democracy: The Declaration of Cultural Independence in America* (New York: Viking, 1981).

36. Phillips, *Philosophy of the Abolition Movement,* 18, 19, 20.

37. Ibid., 24–25.

38. Ibid., 24.

39. Douglass, "The Anti-Slavery Movement" (January 1855), in *Writings,* 2:356.

40. Henry David Thoreau, "The Last Days of John Brown," in *Thoreau: The Major Essays,* ed. Jeffrey L. Duncan (New York: E. P. Dutton, 1972), 174, 175.

41. Ibid., 175.

42. James Brewer Stewart, *Holy Warriors: The Abolitionists and American Slavery* (New York: Hill and Wang, 1976), 160–62; Robert B. Stepto, "Sharing the Thunder: The Literary Exchanges of Harriet Beecher Stowe, Henry Bibb, and Frederick Douglass," in *New Essays on Uncle Tom's Cabin,* ed. Eric J. Sundquist (Cambridge: Cambridge University Press, 1986), 135–53.

43. "Mrs. Stowe as a Writer," *Liberator,* 4 November 1853; Douglass, "A Day and a Night in *Uncle Tom's Cabin*" (4 March 1853), in *Writings,* 2:227.

44. "Mrs. Stowe as a Writer." See also Jane Tompkins, *The Cultural Work of American Fiction, 1790–1860* (New York: Oxford University Press, 1985), 122–46, on the sense of "reality" that antebellum au-

diences perceived in the novel's attention to the human spiritual condition.

45. Phillips, *Philosophy of the Abolition Movement,* 29–30.

46. Douglass, "Our Recent Western Tour" (25 March 1859) and "Speech at American Anti-Slavery Society, May 1848," in *Writings,* 5:422, 83.

47. Douglass, "The Anti-Slavery Movement" (January 1855), in *Writings,* 2:356; Henry David Thoreau, "A Plea for Captain John Brown" (30 October 1859), in *Major Essays,* 169.

48. Herman Melville, "Benito Cereno" (1855–56), in *Herman Melville: Selected Tales and Poems,* ed. Richard Chase (New York: Holt, Rinehart, and Winston, Inc., 1950), 90.

CONCLUSION

1. David M. Potter, *The Impending Crisis, 1848–1861,* comp. and ed. Don E. Fehrenbacher (New York: Harper & Row, 1976), 479.

2. B[enjamin] Godwin, "England and America," in *The Liberty Bell* (Boston: Massachusetts Anti-Slavery Society, 1841), 14; Rev. Frederick Frothingham, *Significance of the Struggle between Liberty and Slavery* . . . (New York: American Anti-Slavery Society, 1857), 18; [Wendell Phillips], "The Constitution a Pro-Slavery Compact: Or Selections from the Madison Papers &c.," *Anti-Slavery Examiner* 11 (1844): 37; American Anti-Slavery Society, *Sixth Annual Report* . . . (New York: William S. Dorr, 1839), 97; George Thompson, quoted in W. Farmer, "The Great Reception," *Liberator,* 22 August 1851.

3. Rather than focusing on the reformers' conceptual limits, several works emphasize how vigorously abolitionists took on their own world and how clearly advocates speak to modern times. See: "Introduction," *The Antislavery Vanguard: New Essays on the Abolitionists,* ed. Martin Duberman (Princeton: Princeton University Press, 1965), x; Aileen S. Kraditor, *Means and Ends in American Abolitionism: Garrison and His Critics on Strategy and Tactics, 1834–1850* (New York: Pantheon, 1969), 20; Herbert Aptheker, *Abolitionism: A Revolutionary Movement* (Boston: Twayne Publishers, 1989), xi.

4. William Lloyd Garrison et al., "Address to the Friends of Freedom and Emancipation in the United States," *Liberator,* 31 May 1844. Daniel Walker Howe finds other examples of this reform tendency in the "evangelical organizing process" and the Whig Party's American

system. Both "represented an imposition of system and direction on a formless society" ("The Evangelical Movement and Political Culture in the North During the Second Party System," *Journal of American History* 77 [March 1991]: 1223).

5. Carl N. Degler, "The Irony of American Slavery," in *Perspectives and Irony in American Slavery*, ed. Harry P. Owens (Jackson, Miss.: University Press of Mississippi, 1976), 25.

6. William I. Bowditch, *God or Our Country, Review of the Rev. Dr. Putnam's Discourse, Delivered on Fast Day, Entitled God and Our Country* (Boston: I. R. Butts, 1847), 7–8; S[eymour] B[oughton] Treadwell, *American Liberties and American Slavery, Morally and Politically Illustrated* (Boston: Weeks, Jordon & Co., 1838), 179.

7. [Rev. George Allen], *Resistance to Slavery Every Man's Duty: A Report on Slavery, Read to the Worcester Central Association, March 2, 1847* (Boston: Wm. Crosby & H. P. Nichols, 1847), 28; [Wendell Phillips], "Can Abolitionists Vote or Take Office under the United States Constitution?" *Anti-Slavery Examiner* 13 (1845): 23; South Middlesex Conference of Churches, *The Political Duties of Christians: A Report, Adopted at the Spring Meeting . . . , April 18, 1848* (Boston: Andrews & Prentiss, 1848), 10. Other examples of this style of social and political analysis appear in: Rev. John G. Richardson, *Obedience to Human Law Considered in the Light of Divine Truth* . . . (Lawrence, Mass.: Homer A. Cooke, 1852), 15; James Brown, *American Slavery in Its Moral and Political Aspects Comprehensively Examined,* . . . (Oswego, N.Y.: George Henry, 1840), 21; and, incorporated in a pacifist argument, "Declaration of Sentiments Adopted by the Peace Convention Held in Boston, September 18, 19 & 20, 1838," *Liberator,* 28 September 1838.

8. Charles Lenox Remond, "The New Age of Anti-Slavery," in *The Liberty Bell* (Boston: Massachusetts Anti-Slavery Fair, 1845), 189.

9. S[amuel] J. May, "The Liberty Bell is Not of the Liberty Party," in *The Liberty Bell* (Boston: Massachusetts Anti-Slavery Fair, 1845) 161, 162.

10. Charles Follen, "The Cause of Freedom in Our Country," *Quarterly Anti-Slavery Magazine* 2 (October 1836): 72–73.

BIBLIOGRAPHICAL ESSAY

The notes provide a comprehensive listing of the source materials used in this book. What follows is a selective guide to the literature on two topics: abolitionism and republicanism.

ABOLITIONISM

The primary sources I examined fall into a number of general categories. The key manuscript collections used in this book were: the Lydia Maria Child Papers, Manuscripts and Archives Division, New York Public Library, New York, N.Y.; the Massachusetts Anti-Slavery Society Papers, New York Historical Society, New York, N.Y.; the Gerrit Smith Papers, New York Public Library, New York, N.Y.; the Elizabeth Cady Stanton Papers, the Lucy Stone (Mrs. Henry B. Blackwell) Papers, the Lewis Tappan Papers, the Theodore D. Weld Papers, and the Elizur Wright Papers, all in the Manuscript Division, Library of Congress, Washington, D.C.

The major newspapers used in this book were the *Emancipator* (also entitled the *Emancipator and Free American*) (New York and Boston, 1833–1850), the *Liberator* (Boston, 1831–1865), and the *National Anti-Slavery Standard* (New York, 1840–1870). Key periodicals included: the *American and Foreign Anti-Slavery Reporter* (New York), the *Anti-Slavery Examiner* (New York), the *Anti-Slavery Record* (New York), the *Anti-Slavery Reporter* (New York), *Douglass' Monthly* (Rochester, N.Y.), and the *Quarterly Anti-Slavery Magazine* (New York).

The pamphlet literature of the abolition campaign provided one of the most important bodies of material for this study. The Library of Congress houses a particularly extensive collection of abolition publications that I used in my research. And the Oberlin College Library "Collection of Anti-Slavery Propaganda," available on microcard, provided another valuable resource. For an informative and wide-ranging guide to antislavery writings, see Dwight Lowell Dumond, *A*

Bibliographic Essay

Bibliography of Antislavery in America (Ann Arbor: The University of Michigan Press, 1961).

A number of editorial projects have made the public and private writings of the abolitionists readily available. Among the most important sources for this study were: Gilbert H. Barnes and Dwight L. Dumond, eds., *The Letters of Theodore Dwight Weld, Angelina Grimké Weld, and Sarah Grimké, 1822–1844*, 2 vols. (New York: D. Appleton-Century, 1934; reprint, Gloucester, Mass.: Peter Smith, 1965); John W. Blassingame, ed., *The Frederick Douglass Papers*, 3 vols. (New Haven: Yale University Press, 1979–1985); Dwight L. Dumond, ed., *Letters of James Gillespie Birney, 1831–1857*, 2 vols. (New York: D. Appleton-Century, 1938); Philip S. Foner, ed., *The Life and Writings of Frederick Douglass*, 5 vols. (New York: International Publishers, 1950, 1975); Milton Meltzer and Patricia G. Holland, eds., *Lydia Maria Child: Selected Letters, 1817–1880* (Amherst: University of Massachusetts Press, 1982); Walter M. Merrill and Louis Ruchames, eds., *The Letters of William Lloyd Garrison*, 6 vols. (Cambridge: The Belknap Press of Harvard University Press, 1971–1981); C. Peter Ripley, ed., *The Black Abolitionist Papers*, 5 vols. (Chapel Hill: University of North Carolina Press, 1985–1992). Nineteenth- and early twentieth-century collections of works by Wendell Phillips and Theodore Parker were also quite helpful, though the writings are in need of editorial attention.

Other useful sources for this study were the annual reports of the American Anti-Slavery Society and the American and Foreign Anti-Slavery Society, the *Anti-Slavery Tracts* of the American Anti-Slavery Society, and annuals such as the *Liberty Bell*, published by abolitionist groups in Boston. I also drew heavily on the essays, speeches, letters, and pamphlets reprinted by Arno Press and Negro Universities Press in the late 1960s and early 1970s. Examples include: James Gillespie Birney, *The American Churches: the Bulwarks of American Slavery* (Newburyport: Charles Whipple, 1842; reprint, New York: Arno, 1969); Maria Weston Chapman, *Right and Wrong in Massachusetts* (Boston: Dow & Jackson Anti-Slavery Press, 1839; reprint, New York: Negro Universities Press, 1969); Moncure D. Conway, *Testimonies Concerning Slavery* (London: Chapman and Hall, 1864; reprint, New York: Arno, 1969); Massachusetts Anti-Slavery Society,

Seventh Annual Report ... (Boston: Isaac Knapp, 1839; reprint, Westport, Conn.: Negro Universities Press, 1970).

In the secondary literature, the works of several intellectual historians informed the present study. David Brion Davis explores the complex debates over slavery and antislavery in a number of books: *The Problem of Slavery in Western Culture* (Ithaca: Cornell University Press, 1966); *The Problem of Slavery in the Age of Revolution, 1770–1823* (Ithaca: Cornell University Press, 1975); and *Slavery and Human Progress* (New York: Oxford University Press, 1984). In *The Antislavery Appeal: American Abolitionism after 1830* (Baltimore: Johns Hopkins University Press, 1978; New York: W. W. Norton, 1984), Ronald G. Walters deals with American abolition as a coherent "structure of perception" that helped unite reformers and define their efforts (xiii). And James Brewer Stewart's *Wendell Phillips: Liberty's Hero* (Baton Rouge: Louisiana State University Press, 1986) demonstrates how a reformer's republican understanding of virtue, freedom, and order influenced both his private life and public activity.

Surveys of the abolition movement that proved especially helpful were: Herbert Aptheker, *Abolitionism: A Revolutionary Movement* (Boston: Twayne Publishers, 1989); Merton L. Dillon, *The Abolitionists: The Growth of a Dissenting Minority* (DeKalb, Ill.: Northern Illinois University Press, 1974); James Brewer Stewart, *Holy Warriors: The Abolitionists and American Slavery* (New York: Hill & Wang, 1976); and Walters, *Antislavery Appeal*, mentioned above.

A number of outstanding monographs guided my thinking on the abolition campaign: Robert H. Abzug, *Passionate Liberator: Theodore Dwight Weld and the Dilemma of Reform* (New York: Oxford University Press, 1980); Anthony J. Barker, *Captain Charles Stuart: Anglo-American Abolitionist* (Baton Rouge: Louisiana State University Press, 1986); R. J. M. Blackett, *Building an Antislavery Wall: Black Americans in the Atlantic Abolitionist Movement, 1830–1860* (Baton Rouge: Louisiana State University Press, 1983; Ithaca: Cornell University Press, 1989); Hugh Davis, *Joshua Leavitt: Evangelical Abolitionist* (Baton Rouge: Louisiana State University Press, 1990); Betty Fladeland, *Abolitionists and Working-Class Problems in the Age of Industrialization* (Baton Rouge: Louisiana State University Press, 1984); Lawrence J. Friedman, *Gregarious Saints: Self and Community in American Abolitionism, 1830–1870* (Cambridge: Cambridge

University Press, 1982); Louis S. Gerteis, *Morality & Utility in American Antislavery Reform* (Chapel Hill: University of North Carolina Press, 1987); Lawrence B. Goodheart, *Abolitionist, Actuary, Atheist: Elizur Wright and the Reform Impulse* (Kent: Kent State University Press, 1990); Allen Kaufman, *Capitalism, Slavery, and Republican Values: Antebellum Political Economists, 1819–1848* (Austin: University of Texas Press, 1982); Aileen Kraditor, *Means and Ends in American Abolitionism: Garrison and His Critics on Strategy and Tactics, 1834–1850* (New York: Pantheon, 1969); William S. McFeely, *Frederick Douglass* (New York: W. W. Norton, 1991); John R. McKivigan, *The War against Proslavery Religion: Abolitionism and the Northern Churches, 1830–1865* (Ithaca: Cornell University Press, 1984); Edward Magdol, *The Antislavery Rank and File: A Social Profile of the Abolitionists' Constituency* (New York: Greenwood Press, 1986); Waldo E. Martin, Jr., *The Mind of Frederick Douglass* (Chapel Hill: University of North Carolina Press, 1984); Earl Ofari, *"Let Your Motto Be Resistance": The Life and Thought of Henry Highland Garnet* (Boston: Beacon Press, 1972); Lewis Perry, *Radical Abolitionism: Anarchy and the Government of God in Antislavery Thought* (Ithaca: Cornell University Press, 1973); Richard H. Sewell, *Ballots for Freedom: Antislavery Politics in the United States, 1837–1860* (New York: Oxford University Press, 1976); James Brewer Stewart, *William Lloyd Garrison and the Challenge of Emancipation* (Arlington Heights, Ill.; Harlan-Davidson, 1992); John L. Thomas, *The Liberator: William Lloyd Garrison, a Biography* (Boston: Little, Brown, 1963); William M. Wiecek, *The Sources of Antislavery Constitutionalism in America, 1760–1848* (Ithaca: Cornell University Press, 1977); Bertram Wyatt-Brown, *Lewis Tappan and the Evangelical War against Slavery* (Cleveland: Case-Western Reserve University Press, 1969); Donald Yacovone, *Samuel Joseph May and the Dilemmas of the Liberal Persuasion, 1797–1871* (Philadelphia: Temple University Press, 1991); Jean Fagan Yellin, *Women & Sisters: The Antislavery Feminists in American Culture* (New Haven: Yale University Press, 1989).

Some of the most significant essays on abolition were found in the following anthologies: Christine Bolt and Seymour Drescher, eds., *Anti-Slavery, Religion, and Reform: Essays in Memory of Roger Anstey,* (Folkestone, Kent: Wm. Dawson & Sons, 1980); Martin Duberman, ed., *The Antislavery Vanguard: New Essays on the Abolitionists* (Princeton: Princeton University Press, 1965); Paul Finkelman, ed., *Articles on American Slavery*, vol. 14, *Antislavery* (New York, London: Garland Publishing, 1989); Alan M. Kraut, ed., *Crusaders and Compromisers: Essays on the Relationship of the Antislavery Struggle to the Antebellum Party System* (Westport, Conn.: Greenwood Press, 1983); Lewis Perry and Michael Fellman, eds., *Antislavery Reconsidered: New Perspectives on the Abolitionists* (Baton Rouge: Louisiana State University Press, 1979); Eric J. Sundquist, ed., *New Essays on Uncle Tom's Cabin* (Cambridge: Cambridge University Press, 1986).

REPUBLICANISM

For overviews of the literature on republicanism, see: Daniel T. Rodgers, "Republicanism: The Career of a Concept," *Journal of American History* 79 (June 1992): 11–38; Robert E. Shalhope, "Toward a Republican Synthesis: The Emergence of an Understanding of Republicanism in American Historiography," *William and Mary Quarterly*, third series, 29 (January 1972): 49–80, and "Republicanism and Early American Historiography," *William and Mary Quarterly*, third series, 39 (April 1982): 334–56.

On the European background of republicanism, see: H. Trevor Colbourn, *The Lamp of Experience: Whig History and the Intellectual Origins of the American Revolution* (Chapel Hill: University of North Carolina Press, 1965); Patrice Higonnet, *Sister Republics: The Origins of French and American Republicanism* (Cambridge: Harvard University Press, 1988); J. R. Jones, *Country and Court: England, 1658–1714* (Cambridge: Harvard University Press, 1978); Isaac Kramnick, *Bolingbroke and His Circle: The Politics of Nostalgia in the Age of Walpole* (Cambridge: Harvard University Press, 1968); J. G. A. Pocock, *The Machiavellian Moment: Florentine Political Thought and the Atlantic Republican Tradition* (Princeton: Princeton University Press, 1975), and "*The Machiavellian Moment* Revisited: A Study in History and Ideology," *Journal of Modern History* 53 (March 1981): 49–72; Caroline Robbins, *The Eighteenth-Century Commonwealthman: Studies in the Transmission, Development, and Circumstances of English Liberal Thought from the Restoration of Charles II until the War with the Thirteen Colonies* (Cambridge:

Harvard University Press, 1959); Perez Zagorin, *The Court and the Country: The Beginning of the English Revolution* (London: Routledge & K. Paul, 1969).

Key studies of American republican thought include: Bernard Bailyn, *The Ideological Origins of the American Revolution* (Cambridge: The Belknap Press of Harvard University Press, 1967); Gordon S. Wood, *The Creation of the American Republic, 1776–1787* (Chapel Hill: University of North Carolina Press, 1969), *The Radicalism of the American Revolution* (New York: Knopf, 1992); and special issue, "Republicanism in the History and Historiography of the United States," *American Quarterly* 37 (Fall 1985). See also: Lance Banning, *The Jeffersonian Persuasion: Evolution of a Party Ideology* (Ithaca: Cornell University Press, 1978); Lester H. Cohen, *The Revolutionary Histories: Contemporary Narratives of the American Revolution* (Ithaca: Cornell University Press, 1980); Pauline Maier, *From Resistance to Revolution: Colonial Radicals and the Development of American Opposition to Britain, 1765–1776* (New York: Knopf, 1972); Drew R. McCoy, *The Elusive Republic: Political Economy in Jeffersonian America* (Chapel Hill: University of North Carolina Press, 1980); John M. Murrin, "The Great Inversion, or Court Versus Country: A Comparison of the Revolution Settlements in England (1688–1721) and America (1776–1816)," in *Three British Revolutions: 1641, 1688, 1776*, ed. J. G. A. Pocock (Princeton: Princeton University Press, 1980); Gerald Stourzh, *Alexander Hamilton and the Idea of Republican Government* (Stanford: Stanford University Press, 1970).

On the relationship between republicanism and liberalism, see: Joyce Appleby, *Capitalism and a New Social Order: The Republican Vision of the 1790s* (New York: New York University Press, 1984) and *Liberalism and Republicanism in the Historical Imagination* (Cambridge: Harvard University Press, 1992); Lance Banning, "Jeffersonian Ideology Revisited: Liberal and Classical Ideas in the New American Republic," *William and Mary Quarterly*, third series, 43 (January 1986): 3–19; John Patrick Diggins, *The Lost Soul of American Politics: Virtue, Self-Interest, and the Foundations of Liberalism* (New York: Basic Books, 1984); James T. Kloppenberg, "The Virtues of Liberalism: Christianity, Republicanism, and Ethics in Early American Political Discourse," *Journal of American History* 74 (June

1987): 9–33; Isaac Kramnick, *Republicanism and Bourgeois Radical-ism: Political Ideology in Late Eighteenth-Century England and America* (Ithaca: Cornell University Press, 1990); Cathy D. Matson and Peter S. Onuf, *A Union of Interests: Political and Economic Thought in Revolutionary America* (Lawrence: University Press of Kansas, 1990); Dorothy Ross, "The Liberal Tradition Revisited and the Republican Tradition Addressed," in *New Directions in American Intellectual History,* ed. John Higham and Paul K. Conkin (Baltimore: Johns Hopkins University Press, 1979); Steven J. Ross, "The Transfor-mation of Republican Ideology," *Journal of the Early Republic* 10 (Fall 1990): 323–30. See also two useful book review essays: Doron S. Ben-Atar, "Republicanism, Liberalism, and Radicalism in the Ameri-can Founding," *Intellectual History Newsletter* 14 (1992): 47–59; and Gordon S. Wood, "The Virtues and the Interests," *The New Re-public* (11 February 1991): 32–35.

Other studies that explore republicanism's variant possibilities and conflicts in the eighteenth century include: James M. Banner, Jr., *To the Hartford Convention: The Federalists and the Origins of Party Politics in Massachusetts, 1789–1815* (New York: Knopf, 1969); Richard R. Beeman, "Deference, Republicanism, and the Emergence of Popular Politics in Eighteenth-Century America," *William and Mary Quarterly,* third series, 49 (July 1992): 401–30; Richard Buel, Jr., *Securing the Revolution: Ideology in American Politics, 1789–1815* (Ithaca: Cornell University Press, 1972); Eric Foner, *Tom Paine and Revolutionary America* (New York: Oxford University Press, 1976); H. James Henderson, "The Structure of Politics in the Conti-nental Congress," in *Essays on the American Revolution,* ed. Stephen G. Kurtz and James H. Hutson (Chapel Hill: University of North Car-olina Press, 1973), 157–96; Regina Ann Markell Morantz, "'Democ-racy' and 'Republic' in American Ideology, 1787–1840" (Ph.D. diss., Columbia University, 1971), ch. 7; Pocock, "Languages and Their Im-plications," 18; Shalhope, "Toward a Republican Synthesis," 49–80; and Stourzh, *Alexander Hamilton;* Shalhope, *John Taylor;* and Wood, *Creation of the American Republic,* pts. 4 and 5, the last three men-tioned above.

Numerous works demonstrate the varieties of republicanism in nineteenth-century political culture. For an overview, see William L.

Bibliographic Essay

Barney, *The Passage of the Republic: An Interdisciplinary History of Nineteenth-Century America* (Lexington, Mass.: D. C. Heath, 1987).

For nineteenth-century Southern readings of republicanism, see: William J. Cooper, Jr., *Liberty and Slavery: Southern Politics to 1860* (New York: Knopf, 1983); Richard Latner, "The Nullification Crisis and Republican Subversion," *Journal of Southern History* 43 (February 1977): 19–38; Stephanie McCurry, "The Two Faces of Republicanism: Gender and Proslavery Politics in Antebellum South Carolina," *Journal of American History* 78 (March 1992): 1245–64; Robert E. Shalhope, "Thomas Jefferson's Republicanism and Antebellum Southern Thought," *Journal of Southern History* 42 (November 1976): 529–56; and Larry E. Tise, *Proslavery: A History of the Defense of Slavery in America, 1701–1840* (Athens: University of Georgia Press, 1987).

For examples of nineteenth-century Northern readings, see: Jean H. Baker, *Affairs of Party: The Political Culture of Northern Democrats in the Mid-Nineteenth Century* (Ithaca: Cornell University Press, 1983); John L. Brooke, *The Heart of the Commonwealth: Society and Political Culture in Worcester County, Massachusetts, 1713–1861* (Cambridge: Cambridge University Press, 1989); Eric Foner, *Free Soil, Free Labor, Free Men: The Ideology of the Republican Party before the Civil War* (New York: Oxford University Press, 1980); Earl J. Hess, *Liberty, Virtue, and Progress: Northerners and Their War for the Union* (New York: New York University Press, 1988); John F. Kasson, *Civilizing the Machine: Technology and Republican Values in America, 1776–1900* (New York: Grossman Publishers, 1976); Donald K. Pickens, "The Republican Synthesis and Thaddeus Stevens," *Civil War History* 31 (March 1985): 57–73; and Sean Wilentz, *Chants Democratic: New York City & the Rise of the American Working Class, 1788–1850* (New York: Oxford University Press, 1984).

On republicanism in nineteenth-century national politics, see: Lloyd E. Ambrosius, ed., *A Crisis of Republicanism: American Politics in the Civil War Era* (Lincoln: University of Nebraska Press, 1990); Michael F. Holt, *The Political Crisis of the 1850s* (New York: John Wiley & Sons, 1978); Daniel Walker Howe, *The Political Culture of the American Whigs* (Chicago: University of Chicago Press, 1979); Michael A. Morrison, "Westward the Course of Empire: Texas Annexation and the American Whig Party," *Journal of the Early Re-*

public 10 (Summer 1990): 221–49; and Harry L. Watson, *Liberty and Power: The Politics of Jacksonian America* (New York: Hill and Wang, 1990).

On the relationship between republicanism and nineteenth-century reform, see: Douglas B. A. Ansdell, "William Lloyd Garrison's Ambivalent Approach to Labour Reform," *Journal of American Studies* 24 (December 1990): 402–7; Anne M. Boylan, *Sunday School: The Formation of an American Institution, 1790–1880* (New Haven: Yale University Press, 1988); Paul Goodman, *Towards a Christian Republic: Antimasonry and the Great Transition in New England, 1826–1836* (New York: Oxford University Press, 1988); Carl F. Kaestle, *Pillars of the Republic: Common Schools and American Society, 1780–1860* (New York: Hill and Wang, 1983); and David M. Streifford, "The American Colonization Society: An Application of Republican Ideology to Early Antebellum Reform," *Journal of Southern History* 45 (May 1979): 201–20.

On the relationship between republicanism and religion, see: William Gribbin, "Republicanism, Reform, and the Sense of Sin in Ante Bellum America," *Cithara* 14 (December 1974): 25–41; Nathan O. Hatch, *The Democratization of American Christianity* (New Haven: Yale University Press, 1989), and *The Sacred Cause of Liberty: Republican Thought and the Millennium in Revolutionary New England* (New Haven: Yale University Press, 1977); and Gordon S. Wood, "Evangelical America and Early Mormonism," *New York History* 61 (October 1980): 359–86.

INDEX

Abolition movement, 2; and American culture and identity, 127–47; British, 24–25; debates among abolitionists, 79–80, 93–106; defined by abolitionists, 55–56, 122–23, 151–52; history of, 9, 28, 48–50, 93–95; and language, 121, 128, 132–41; and literature, 141–47; Morris on, 103, 189 n.26; and religion, 59–78; strategies of, 93–95, 152–56. *See also* Republicanism and abolitionism

Abolitionists, definition of, 2; Fourth of July interpretation, 32, 90–91, 140; on Henry, 46, 90–91; identities of, 55–56, 151; on Israelites, 64, 73, 74, 75, 78; on Jefferson, 85–86, 108; on nature of society, 152–56; outlook of, 150–56; on race, 39–42, 152, 170 n.28; on reform, 149–50, 151–52. *See also* Agitation; Republicanism and abolitionism

Abolitionist party, 93–106; arguments against, 52, 94, 95–100; arguments for, 94–95, 100–105; history of, 9, 93–95

Adams, John Quincy, 50

Adams, John, 13–14

African Americans: Colored National Conventions, 8, 49, 61; history of, 145–46; on Saxonism and race, 39–42; on slavery's distinctive threats, 45–46

Agitation, 1, 90, 91, 100; and moral reform, 97–99; and political parties, 97–99, 103–4; and republican values, 88–93, 140

Allen, George: on language, 133; on self and society, 153; on slave-power aristocracy, 115

American and Foreign Anti-Slavery Reporter, 74–75

American and Foreign Anti-Slavery Society, 95; support of abolition party, 103

American Anti-Slavery Almanac, 92

American Anti-Slavery Society: on abolitionists' duty, 24, 53; and Adams, 50; on advancement of republicanism, 53; appeals to first principles, 50; *Declaration of Sentiments,* 53, 93–94; divisions within, 95; on nature of sin, 72; on power and governance, 79; on reform tactics, 93–94; on Roman slavery, 47

American Revolution: and agitation, 90–91, 99; and nonresistance, 70; parallels to abolition, 48–51, 99, 103; as perceived by abolitionists, 22, 28–29, 48–49, 76, 82, 87–88, 90, 91, 119–20, 151; in popular history, 28–36; and power and morality, 87; principles of, in abolition, 22, 23, 24, 53–55, 82, 101–2, 151–52; and religion, 62,

223

Index